SELF WITHIN MARRIAGE

SELF WITHIN MARRIAGE

THE FOUNDATION FOR LASTING RELATIONSHIPS

Richard M. Zeitner

Routledge
Taylor & Francis Group
New York London

Routledge
Taylor & Francis Group
270 Madison Avenue
New York, NY 10016

Routledge
Taylor & Francis Group
27 Church Road
Hove, East Sussex BN3 2FA

© 2012 by Taylor and Francis Group, LLC
Routledge is an imprint of Taylor & Francis Group, an Informa business

Printed in the United States of America on acid-free paper
10 9 8 7 6 5 4 3 2 1

International Standard Book Number: 978-0-415-99732-4 (Hardback)

Library of Congress Cataloging-in-Publication Data

Zeitner, Richard M.
  Self within marriage : the foundation for lasting relationships / Richard M. Zeitner.
    p. cm.
  Summary: "Self Within Marriage combines the theoretical orientations of object-relations theory, self psychology, and systems theory to illustrate and discuss a way of understanding and working with couples and individuals whose relationship and emotional difficulties have centered on the very common conundrum of balancing individuality and intimacy in romantic relationships. Based on detailed case examples and couples therapy techniques, Self Within Marriage provides individual and analytic therapists with a refreshing new framework for working with clients and for helping them understand who they are as individuals and as partners"-- Provided by publisher.
  Includes bibliographical references and index.
  ISBN 978-0-415-99732-4 (hardback)
  1. Marital psychotherapy. 2. Couples therapy. I. Title.

RC488.5.Z45 2011
616.89'1562--dc22   2010052733

Visit the Taylor & Francis Web site at
http://www.taylorandfrancis.com

and the Routledge Web site at
http://www.routledgementalhealth.com

For Jane

CONTENTS

FOREWORD

By way of foreword to Richard Zeitner's extremely interesting contribution to the psychology of couples and to couple therapy, I would like to begin with a bit of history. The field of psychoanalytic marital therapy has evolved considerably since its founding by Enid Balint and her colleagues at the Family Discussion Bureau of the Tavistock Institute in London in the late 1940s. They began with ideas of the function of the unconscious in marriage and, in working with individuals and couples, began to build a literature that first contributed to understanding couples in depth.

Henry Dicks's contribution, which came to fruition in his landmark book, *Marital Tensions,* in 1967, provided a significant landmark and became the starting place for many of us who sought to understand the unconscious organization of marriage, the role of the individual and shared unconscious in the formation of intimate partnerships, and the fate of these shared unconscious organizations in long-term marriages or partnerships. Dicks's "laboratory" consisted of a setting in which two individual therapists saw husband and wife and then met with a shared supervisor—often Henry Dicks—to put together a picture of each marriage and its unconscious organization.

Dicks used foundational ideas from Klein and Fairbairn as his model. From Fairbairn he took the idea of the organization of the mind as a system of subunits of object and ego, with the splitting off and repression of rejecting internal relationships and overly exciting or overly seductive ones, both of these repressed constellations in dynamic relationship with a more conscious and reasonable central ego.

From Klein, Dicks drew the notion of projective identification as the vehicle for unconscious communication. Klein had first described this process as a baby (but also a more mature individual) getting rid of dangerous parts of self by putting them into the mother defensively and then treating the mother (or other person) as though she were like that hidden part of the baby's self. By the time Dicks was writing about marriage, the idea of projective identification had broadened to be a normal process of unconscious communication, serving not only defensive purposes, but also basic, everyday functions of communication in depth— the search for understanding and being understood. Dicks realized that, in marriage, the processes of projective and introjective identification were mutual and continuous. In this process, each partner sought to find lost, repressed parts of the self and to cure aspects of the internal world that felt deficient or dangerous; these could be described best in terms of Fairbairn's formulation of mental organization.

Bion's work, which established mutual projective identification as the crucible in which the mind forms, was going on at the same time that Dicks was writing about marriage. It should be taken as a crucial and complementary development, which, however, requires some of what Dicks brought to understanding marriage to become also a more complete model. Dicks and his colleagues at the Tavistock Clinic, as well as those working in the Family Discussion Bureau (now called the Tavistock Centre for Couple Relationships), realized latterly that it was more efficient to see couples conjointly, and they changed their technique to reflect this realization. In the field of psychoanalytic marital and couple therapy, many of the richest findings have come from this group. My contributions investigating the role of sexuality in forming and maintaining relationships and in looking to explore the dynamics of couple therapy have also drawn most centrally from this fount.

While there are many studies of couple therapy and the psychology of marriage in the United States and Europe drawn from other clinical disciplines and from more social psychological approaches—the work of the late Neil Jacobson or of John Gottman or Susan Johnson currently, for example—psychoanalytic understanding has continued to evolve in ways that show unique depths of understanding and offer descriptions in depth that other schools lack. Furthermore, analytic understanding values the complexity of organization of these intimate relationships that surpasses other models. Not infrequently, one of the other schools will arrive at an understanding that has been fundamental to an analytic approach for a long time: the central role of affect or the use of transference and countertransference as organizing dynamics for couple therapy, for instance.

Self Within Marriage draws on the richness of the tradition I have been describing, but Dr. Zeitner adds new ideas from the evolving analytic world. His description of the "selfdyad" draws on contemporary investigations of the evolution of the self throughout the life cycle. Drawing on the contributions of Kohut and modern object relations writers, he sees the organization of couples as a complex structure that should grow throughout marriages or partnerships. In this process of continual maturation, the tension between the innate need for each person to be an individual and simultaneous need to be a full member of the couple can never be fully resolved. It is a struggle that is continually lived through the ebb and flow between the needs for autonomy and individuality, on the one hand, and the need to support the couple made of two people in continual interaction on the other.

This interaction is carried out both through daily "trivial" exchanges and through the unconscious exchanges that always accompany these interactions. Dicks told us that it is these unconscious exchanges that determine the quality of the long-term partnerships as two people together form a "joint marital personality." In this process, the needs and makeup of each individual constantly contribute to the couple's organization, and that couple organization, jointly constructed, contributes to each individual. Zeitner refers to this irreducible complexity in his discussion of "the link," a theoretical set of ideas that is only now being introduced to English-speaking professionals.

This idea—that there is an organization of the couple that is jointly constructed and that in turn contributes to each individual—is a relatively new, extremely helpful idea. But Zeitner's contribution of the self-dyad takes us a step further: He goes inside the individuals who form partnerships, to look at the way the tension between their individual development and their need to belong in the relationship is played out both in the autonomous interior of each individual and in their shared interactional daily lives. The developmental histories and personal qualities of each individual matter here, but what the individuals construct as partners has an organization that is new, or at least it should be. What happens in couple relationships should bring new life and creative organization to the individuals and new opportunities for growth and mutual validation. But for those couples that come to us suffering from any number of marital and partnership difficulties, the balance is not holding.

This book explores the way in which individual needs and relational needs so often come to be at war with each other. It gives a newly vivid description of the tension between the needs of the individual and of the couple, an investigation of many of the difficulties that result from a variety of imbalances, and a method for investigating and treating them. Indeed, it is the plethora of clinical examples that most informs Zeitner's investigation that lets us see the working of a master clinician dealing with some of life's most painful and intractable dilemmas.

Self Within Marriage tills new soil in investigating the "selfdyad." It lets us see the uniqueness of each couple's organization from which each individual also draws. In vividly describing the tension in and between partners who need to maintain two individual selves at the same time as belonging to a long-term couple relationship, Zeitner adds dimensionality to theories about marriage and to the possibilities for treatment. I think this book will enrich your understanding of marriage, as it has mine, and will enable you to carry a newly enlarged understanding into the consulting room as you work to improve the lives of the many couples who come to you for help.

David E. Scharff, MD

PREFACE

This book is about relationships. More specifically, it is about how intimate partnerships are formed and are then maintained. Although I am writing about the permanence of marriage, the principles I develop apply to all romantic intimate partnerships that endure, whether married, unmarried heterosexual, or unmarried homosexual. Although in many of my case studies the partners are married, I have attempted to include many examples of those who are not—those who are instead permanently partnered and who have chosen to remain together through an intimate connection. In a clear sense, the core theme throughout this book is the intimacy that has been established within the relationship, how and why it has been formed by the two partners, how and why it holds, and, importantly, how and why it falters and sometimes deteriorates.

This is not a self-help book, but neither is it a textbook. I have intended it first and foremost to be a virtual consultation room for my readers— one in which I have been able to shape and sharpen my ideas about the psychology of relationships, while drawing on my many years of study, teaching, and practice as a psychologist and psychoanalyst who has maintained an enduring and passionate interest in applying both psychoanalytic and systems theoretical ideas to my understanding of the couple and couples' struggles. I believe that the real value of this book is not the theoretical ideas that I have learned and studied or even those that I draw on and sometimes modify. Instead, its value is in the richness of my chosen case studies—those represented by my patients and couples whom I have had the privilege of knowing and working with over the years. It is in the consultation room, as we all know, that theory comes alive and reminds us once again that the science of psychology is alive and well.

In one sense, this book is a compendium of case studies that pertains to the central ideas that I have found to be important and fundamental in understanding and treating couples. It is my hope that it will allow those of you who read it to understand not just how theoretical ideas apply, but also how I personally think and work in couple therapy. Subscribing to projective identification as a fundamental form of human communication, I make liberal use of this concept in my work with couples.

The communication that flows from one person to another in all close encounters is only partly conscious. Throughout this book, I adhere to the underlying assumption that what is communicated between partners in the consulting room is also in part communicated to me and through me—that is, if I pay close attention. In each case study, I attempt to demonstrate how I observe and listen to what is said and unsaid between the partners and how it is experienced and incubated inside me and my internal world, while then subjecting my personal reactions and private musings to a higher level of cognitive processing that allows me to understand the unconscious nature of the couple's functioning and their difficulties in relating.

But what is it that I listen for? Within all psychotherapies, analytically informed or not, the psychotherapist has his or her ear cocked in a particular direction, looking for a set of clues that usually reside comfortably within the preferred theoretical framework of that clinician. It is here that I am no different. I, too, am listening for something of great importance that, when discovered, will enable me to intervene in ways to assist my couple to better understand the predicament they have brought to me. What I listen for is the self-functioning of both partners within the confines of their relationship.

Self Within Marriage: The Foundation for Lasting Relationships, first and foremost, refers to the importance of possessing an identity or a continuity of one's subjective experience that must both transcend the relationship and support it. When this does not happen, fails to develop or to continue, or somehow ends, intimacy will also end. This is the central struggle for lasting intimate partners: having and retaining a sense of self and identity, while simultaneously establishing a relationship that functions to support both selves.

Although the concept of the self, as described in psychology and psychoanalysis, is admittedly complex and occasionally daunting, in the first two chapters I provide an abbreviated understanding of the self as it applies to the thesis of this book, avoiding a laborious theoretical discussion of the many existing definitions and theoretical differences. What I add, however, and what is possibly unique to this book is the concept of the selfdyad, which I develop in Chapter 6. With this concept, I, as a therapist, am not only listening for the self-functioning of both partners, but also listening for the functions of their selfdyad, a term that I have developed to describe a variation of Henry Dicks's concept of the joint marital personality. I define the selfdyad as a conjoint structure or shared unconscious space of two individuals who have come together to project, metabolize, and contain various features of the self, including unconscious fears, wishes, needs, longings, and drive states—all recruited from early development.

Furthermore, this structure must also provide for both individuals support and affirmation, partly to repair and compensate for deficiencies experienced during early life. The importance of the selfdyad now is that, inevitably, for each and every couple coming for treatment, it has somehow gone awry. It is no longer in support of the self of one or both partners. Our task in therapy is then to find out how and why the original selfdyad of the couple no longer functions toward that end, with the goal of restoring it.

This book is intended for anyone who would like more than just a superficial glimpse into the unconscious nature of intimacy. It will appeal to mental health professionals of all kinds—perhaps especially those who are interested in and work with relationships, couples, and families. It is for you that reading this book will provide a road map, outlining how I work with couples by applying the concept of the selfdyad. But for the individual psychotherapist and psychoanalyst, too, an understanding of the complexity of partner formation will enrich his or her thinking and way of working, especially at those times when the patient's intimate relations come into analytic focus. Finally, this book will appeal to those laypersons who are highly curious about applying depth psychology—and especially object relations theories, systems theory, and self psychology—to their understanding of intimacy and loving partnerships.

I invite all my readers, then, to move forward to get a clearer and deeper sense about the intricacies of human intimacy. For both the professional and the layperson who read this book, it is my hope that you will gain some appreciation for the intersection between the inner workings of the mind and how it connects with the mind of another, while sometimes forming an intimacy and romance that becomes permanent, but that, unfortunately, at other times fails.

ACKNOWLEDGMENTS

I am deeply indebted to so many who have contributed to the writing of this book. First of all, I am greatly appreciative of my publisher at Routledge, Dr. George Zimmar, who gave me the opportunity and encouragement to put my ideas down on paper in a form that, I hope, will be useful to all who take the time to read this book. Second, I am grateful to Anna Moore, my editor, whose support and immediate responsiveness to my sometimes frivolous questions and pressing concerns helped move my writing forward, while giving me the security to complete it. Furthermore, her gentle prodding and frequent indulgences around time requirements allowed me to complete my project while simultaneously maintaining my busy life and practice. Then, I must thank Terri Kelly, who provided me her expertise in computer graphics to complete my pictorial diagram of the selfdyad depicted in Chapter 6. Similarly, I must express my gratitude to my assistant and office manager of nearly 15 years, Cheryl Bartshe, who persisted throughout writing and rewriting, while making astute suggestions, edits, and comments. Without her persistence I simply could not have completed this book.

I am grateful to all my teachers and mentors over the years, for it is because of them and through them that I have been able to absorb their knowledge and the wisdom that I otherwise might not have acquired. First, I am deeply indebted to and wish to thank Dr. Michael Harty, my longtime friend and psychoanalytic colleague, who endured through the reading of my manuscript, making keen observations and critiques that were always in the spirit of erudition. Then, there are my many supervisors, who over the years challenged me, sometimes argued with me, but always supported me. It was Dr. Don Shoulberg, in my post-doctoral training at the Menninger Foundation in marriage and family therapy, who introduced me to family systems theory. Don's willingness to tolerate my sometimes obsessional questioning as I worked to integrate that way of thinking into my preferred psychoanalytic framework has had an enduring and positive impact on my development as a clinician. When I announced to him that his superb teaching served as an inspiration for me to enter psychoanalytic training at the Topeka Institute for Psychoanalysis, he and I were able to laugh at this irony. Ascribing my decision to having achieved a "differentiation of self" is the mark of Don's empathy as a fine teacher and wise supervisor.

The high-powered intellectual climate of my next training stint, Topeka and the world of psychoanalysis, provided me intensive training and exposure to some of the finest psychological minds in the world as I worked to become a psychoanalyst. Upon graduating, and by this time having had such a combination of diverse mentoring, I would now proceed to develop my own way of thinking about couples and their struggles and how best to go about helping them. It is the combination of all these voices that has provided me the inspiration to write this book.

My association with Dr. David Scharff has been of inestimable importance and inspiration to me. Our collaboration in developing a now annually held discussion group on psychoanalytic family therapy at the meeting of the American Psychoanalytic Association has served to help me sharpen my ideas about couples and families. Furthermore, his encouragement for me to write this book, while supporting me as I negotiated in the world of publishing companies, will always be appreciated.

Finally, I am most indebted to and thankful for my loving wife, Jane, as well as my children, Nicolle and Aaron; my son-in-law, Kevin; and my grandchildren, Taylor and Sierra. They are, in every sense of the word, my family—a family that continues to provide a real live example of what it means to be connected. Jane's enduring support through the travails of my writing, while sacrificing time with me and even vacations, reinforces for me all that I have come to understand about the selfdyad—the essential quality of its functioning in support of the self. This is an example of love, devotion, and affirmation at its finest.

1

THAT VITAL BALANCE
Being and Intimacy

Martin, a 45-year-old corporate CEO, and his wife, Janet, a 42-year-old fifth-grade teacher, called for a consultation because of some recurrent strife that centered on Janet's recent career advancement. They had been married for 15 years and had been reasonably content in most aspects of their relationship. They had two children and had worked out a mutually acceptable balance between two careers while raising their busy and active children. In her spare time after getting home from school, Janet had recently authored some children's books, which over this past year had been published and had been receiving literary accolades.

Martin and Janet entered the consultation room with Martin taking the lead. He notably ignored any social proprieties, failing to allow Janet to enter first while seemingly unconcerned about where either Janet or I might sit. Martin did in fact sit in my chair, which is for almost everyone else easily recognized as the chair in which the therapist would sit. He sat down before Janet and I had entered the room, positioning himself comfortably in the chair as if on his throne. He seemed to perch himself expectantly as though he were awaiting his courtiers to take their proper places. I had a fleeting fantasy that he might have felt most comfortable with a scepter in his hand.

Martin was of medium build and well-dressed in a suit and white shirt with a tasteful conservative red-and-blue striped tie. Although he was polished in dress, his formality seemed an anachronism, as if he were being coached to be a senatorial candidate in the late 60s. He sat stiffly in his chair with nose slightly elevated as if he were sniffing a foul odor. He was serious in demeanor as he began speaking of his busy life and career. He emphasized his successful company, with the clear but unspoken implication that it was he who was responsible for its success. He mentioned that he grew up in impoverished circumstances and that he had been raised by an aunt and uncle after his parents had been killed in an automobile accident. He commented that his professional success had been hard won and that no one had supported him in his pursuit of higher education or while on the road to success. He added that it was his fighting spirit and ferocity that allowed him his ticket into the corporate world. Although at this point he had not said it directly, I privately filled in the blank. Martin seemed to be saying that, with all that he had achieved, he was not going to take a chance on losing it now. At this time I could not be sure, however, what "it" was that he was so afraid of losing.

As Martin spoke I was struck by his deep voice and measured diction. I found myself wondering about where he had taken his voice lessons. And without having heard more than a few words from Janet, I already found myself sympathizing with her, musing that she must sometimes feel overwhelmed and even bullied by Martin's barrage of words and pulpit-like eloquence. But then it was my next private reaction that provided me a most useful clinical clue. "How safe the world must seem when possessing such certainty," I thought.

Martin repetitiously went on to describe his busy career while emphasizing the importance of Janet's availability to him and the children. Their two teenaged boys had been doing quite well, but he feared that with Janet's frequent luncheon engagements, meetings with editors, and hours spent in various activities pertaining to her book, family life as he had known it might not be sustained. At this time, feeling a bit barraged myself, I reluctantly raised my left hand as a gesture that I often use when seeing couples and families—a signal that I want to speak or want another to have his turn. In retrospect I wondered if my gesture here was a symbolic expression of my wish to raise my own scepter as a way of countering Martin's regality. With palpable hesitancy Janet glanced uncomfortably at Martin. It was clear to me that my directive was not enough for her to speak comfortably. Her furtive glance from Martin to me and back again confirmed that she questioned who really had the power here. Most certainly, she doubted her own and probably mine as well. As she began speaking she cleared her throat. She first spoke softly, and then, as if reluctantly adjusting the volume control on her television, she turned toward me to tell her version of the problem, but now with more oomph.

As Janet began, I suddenly noted a rise of tension within the room. While just moments ago my room had seemed well lit and airy, with its many windows and considerable space, it now felt more like a closet that was too small for its contents. Although Martin was sitting back in his chair with arms crossed, he strangely had the appearance of a hawk that was ready to pounce on its prey. No wonder everything seemed small and crowded, I thought. Suddenly, I recovered from my reverie, realizing that I, like Janet, was waiting to be plucked and possibly overpowered in the next moment. In a somewhat calculated way I now sat forward in my chair and turned my right shoulder slightly toward Martin as if to simulate a body block while I protected the potential prey, Janet. At this moment Martin began to interrupt Janet, to which I responded, "Let Janet speak." Here my voice sounded even to me as if I were using a microphone with the volume turned up too high. During this pregnant moment, however, the power balance seemed to shift, while it previously had the potential to become one sided, with the CEO presiding over his boardroom.

As she finally spoke, I noted that Janet's voice and general demeanor were gentle and unassuming, if not mousy. When considering my fantasy of Martin as the king on his throne and the hawk about to pounce on his prey, with Janet as a courtier or diminutive mouse about to be plucked, it would be easy, but clinically incorrect, to view Martin as the sole problem. Here was a couple—and I emphasize a couple, not one individual more than another—who had developed their relationship along the dimension of dominance and subordination. Furthermore, it had worked for a number of years and, by their reports, had worked reasonably well. While Martin had apparently been the more dominant partner in the relationship, Janet had an equal stake in assuming a role of subordination.

Responding to my question about what it had been like to balance the roles of CEO wife, mother, and career woman, I was met with more hesitancy. Janet cleared her throat nervously as she reinstituted her furtive glances between Martin and me as if checking out the extent of safety in the field. Once again my own tension mounted as I experienced her discomfort. Having permission to speak, could she do so in a way that was forthright while she revealed aspects of herself that had likely been hidden during the years that she had maintained the status quo of marriage and family life? Or would there be resistance in one form or another?

Again Janet spoke, but this time I felt relief as she uttered her next words: "It's been very reward…no, *difficult*, I'd say." She now proceeded to describe the frenetic quality of their lives as a family, while her voice grew stronger and she spoke with more eloquence as she described the day-to-day activities of family life that included the activities of the children, driving pools, teaching and housekeeping responsibilities, as well as the various chores she took care of for Martin. I was struck by the detail she provided, as if she had rehearsed her oratory for weeks or even years. Here she did not retreat into denial or other defensive postures, but in fact was speaking with such candor that I began to worry what might erupt if Martin experienced her diatribe as an attack on his authority.

Once again my tension began to rise, but this time for different reasons. How would Martin, the CEO, experience an honesty that he rarely encountered? My invitation for Janet to speak about her feelings about balancing these multiple roles, while I intended to provide safety for a more candid exploration of their marital crisis, now allowed Janet the opportunity to reveal the underlying issues that threatened the relationship. These feelings simultaneously contained her wish to give expression to a more hidden but repudiated self—a self that had been submerged by a mutually created couple arrangement during the years of their marriage.

Already Martin's presentation suggested a picture of a man who had developed his identity around aggression and competence, with an accompanying sense of certainty and a strong tendency to control others within his sphere of influence. Notice that I use the word "presentation." He tells us at the outset that his battle for success has been hard won. He also hints that, without his world under these familiar controls, his empire might collapse like a house of cards. Janet's new success represented a threat, not simply to family life as he had known it or even to his career, but instead to his way of being—fundamentally his identity or his sense of self. A most revealing clue in coming to understand the problem at hand was Janet's initial hesitancy to speak. This tells us something important about her, but it also reveals something fundamental about the dynamics of their relationship.

Janet's inner push to be audible, along with Martin's formidable presentation of exaggerated dominance, suggested a marital interaction in which Martin had assumed the role of the competent and aggressive executive, while Janet had become the supplicant partner who had subordinated herself to this busy and competent professional. So far so good, as long as it worked for both individuals and for family life as well. But what happens when the dance steps change, either as a function of fortuitous circumstances of everyday life or when one partner makes a protest or a simple assertion to enhance, exercise, or in some other way initiate a change in the self? Now there might be trouble. And there was for Martin and Janet.

Janet had not been unfulfilled in her roles as teacher, wife, and mother. She had in fact felt reasonably content. She simply had been encouraged by her friends, because of her talent for writing and illustrating, to consider becoming an author of children's books. Deciding to give it a try, she soon discovered that expressing herself as an author represented a new voice and a sense of being that she had not previously known. Her initial throat clearing when I gestured for her to speak represented her conflict symbolically: "Should I or should I not use my voice?" Is it alright to *be*—to have or to establish a separate self and a sense of agency without threatening another—in this case, her husband?

Martin's presentation suggested that it might not. For Martin, his sense of being had been founded around a dominance and control that included a superiority over others. And yet Martin had not been the only one to determine whether Janet was able to achieve or enhance a self of her own. Janet, too, had been an active participant in this *couple field* in which two people had joined to create a duality—a dyad that would continue to execute the various functions and roles that would be in support of family life. In creating this entity Martin and Janet had embarked upon an ineluctable journey of togetherness in which mutual influence and continuous modification of the other would be inevitable. Sometimes this influence would be within their awareness, but mostly it would occur on an unconscious level.

This is a book about relationships, and it is also about treating relationships. It is also about the complications of maintaining and achieving a sense of self and individuality while having and maintaining an intimate partnership. I began this chapter with a segment of Martin and Janet's initial consultation as a way of introducing my ideas about what I have learned from my patients as they have struggled to attain this most vital balance—that is, a state of "being"—having a reasonably solid and coherent sense of self while simultaneously maintaining a fulfilling and intimate relationship.

In our culture the most common of committed relationships is that of marriage, although the psychological processes that I will discuss throughout this writing apply to all intimate partnerships of any enduring quality. Usually, I will be speaking about two people who, for whatever reasons, have defined themselves as a couple and who are beyond the courtship phase. They will have come to experience an emotional investment in one another, whether or not the relationship has become sexual. If for some period of time these two people have remained in a romantic relationship and if they have defined themselves as a couple, the partnership has likely become sexual. If not, there are likely to have been some moral or religious proscriptions precluding sexuality. Or its lack may represent an inhibition in the physical realm of the relationship. With or without actual sexuality or physical intimacy, a couple and even a marriage can exist. Some of the principles I will describe in this book may also apply to friendships, but the dynamics of friendship are also different from the kinds of relationships that will be described here—those that have become both intimate and committed.

Although there might be some variability in what readers consider to be an ideal couple, marriage, or romance, I will begin this writing with the assumption that there is at least some commonality in my readers' definitions of the "couple." And because many of my readers are currently married, have been married, or will be married, the state of marriage will sometimes be referred to, but that might not represent the actual state for any one reader. Furthermore, there are some partners, married or unmarried, who might live separately, but because of having at least some of the characteristics and dynamics outlined in this book, might still represent a couple. Throughout this book, then, I will refer to marriage, couple, partnership, and relationship, using these terms interchangeably.

Finally, the principles I address in this work are not reserved for heterosexual couples. The mechanisms and dynamics I address transcend gender and apply to gay and lesbian relationships, although we will discover that there are sometimes special considerations that apply to same-sex partnerships that must be addressed in the treatment process. The psychological processes by which couples form, attach, and develop relationship difficulties apply then to both gay and straight couples, married or unmarried, and those living together or apart.

The reader might still ask, "So what does the self have to do with the thesis of this writing? Furthermore, how does it relate to marriage and relationships?" In the next section I will define a few terms, while making a brief excursion into the theory that will provide a structure for answering these questions.

WHAT DOES IT MEAN TO HAVE A SELF?

Many definitions of "self" have been offered by writers, philosophers, and theoreticians, spanning the various schools of philosophy and psychology from existentialism to the more contemporary psychoanalytic theories of self psychology and interpersonal psychoanalysis. For our purposes, a subjective sense of self exists when one is able to experience a clarity and consistency of one's separateness and uniqueness, while also having the capacity to act in accordance with subjective experiences that include one's ideals, needs, wishes, and beliefs about the universe.

In the title of this book I refer to "self within marriage" to demonstrate the fundamental importance of the self maintaining its integration and agency while existing within marriage or within an alternative form of permanent partnership. To be a self while remaining intimate with a sense of fulfillment and contentment requires first of all that both persons in the relationship define themselves as a couple. In many cases this partnership will be marriage. To have a mutually fulfilling relationship both partners must also be capable of maintaining and embracing a sense of themselves as individuals.

But what does it mean to be an individual? This is about having an identity. To be and remain part of a reasonably fulfilled, contented, and intimate couple, either partnered or married, one must then also be able to maintain a reasonably consistent subjective sense of oneself. This is a most crucial and yet sometimes difficult achievement—how to have a relationship and also embrace one's sense of identity and agency.

Because of the intimacy of the partnering process, with two people living together while establishing some form of family life, influencing one another will continue for the duration of the relationship. As a result both partners will usually experience a modification in attitudes, beliefs, and other qualities of the self. This mutual influence and modification of each other extends far beyond how couples compromise and negotiate how the bathroom is shared, the toothpaste squeezed, and who will pick up the kids at daycare. In a later chapter I will describe how these psychological processes occur and how they ultimately influence and alter features of the self and the other, while demonstrating how both subtle and even dramatic modifications can occur as roles are established and the relationship takes form.

Maintaining one's identity is not the same as remaining rigid or stubborn in one's opinions, position, or ideologies. In fact, "being" or having a clear sense of self and identity presumes an optimal flexibility of personal style and character. The individual with a reasonably solid sense of self will consider the input and feedback from outside. But to maintain a subjective sense of self and identity presumes that the person is able to maintain his distinctness and personal agency, even in the face of others' influence, whether or not the other person's ideas have contributed to a modification in his position or attitude. A person possessing a self and agency might then on one occasion remain steadfast in his position, but on another permit himself to be influenced in attitude while allowing a compromise or shift in beliefs. What is critical here is less about what is manifested in the person's overt behavior and more about the individual's felt subjective experience and sense of identity when encountering the various influences and impingements from others, including an intimate partner.

The individual with a sense of self and agency, then, is not rigid, stubborn, or unyielding, but neither is he characteristically wishy-washy in relationships or his convictions. There are many who will appear resolute and even highly convincing about almost anything discussed. This person might exude qualities of certainty, integrity, and infallibility. But what appears as a solid sense of self can in some cases represent a defense against impingements from outside stimuli. Although it was too early in the consultation to know with certainty, I hypothesized that Martin was such a person—resolute and rigid on the surface, but internally fearful that Janet's changes and successes would erode his sense of being. Martin's demeanor of conviction and certainty likely then represented a defense to protect a fragile self-structure. To be anything other than certain represented a danger, for his being might then collapse if Janet's budding autonomy were given expression within the relationship.

THE VAGARIES OF NONBEING: THE CASE OF MARILYN

Struggles between selfhood and partnering can be represented in many ways. Individuals coming for treatment, not just couples, will frequently demonstrate these same kinds of difficulties. Many patients report in the first session that they are uncertain about the onset or the circumstances in which a depression or other symptom began. The patient might provide vague hints about difficulties in the relationship, but a focused complaint about the partner is not evident during the initial consultation. Even when asked directly about the marriage, the patient's response might be that she has been quite content and even happily married. Instead, the patient might describe a feeling of malaise and general dissatisfaction with herself and with her life and circumstances. There might be a focus on vaguely described physical symptoms, but without a diagnosed medical problem. Nonetheless, the patient feels pain, discomfort, and unhappiness.

Marilyn was such a patient—depressed and dissatisfied, but initially unable to speak directly about her relationship concerns. She called my office for an appointment, then cancelled, and after several weeks called back to reschedule. Her second call provided a most interesting gambit that contained important diagnostic clues about her situation. Marilyn had neglected to leave her phone number on my voicemail, while at the same time she expressed a strong sense of urgency that I reach her as quickly as possible. In her message she reminded me that she had set up an appointment with me a number of weeks ago, but because of her "illness, severe pain, and recent hospitalization" she had to cancel. Now, she said that her emotional situation had worsened and that she needed to see me as soon as possible. I searched through my appointment book to secure her phone number from her previously made appointment. I located the phone number and dialed it. Her phone had been disconnected. I then called directory assistance, but to no avail. There was nothing I could do at this point but to await a second call. I mused that because of the situation surrounding the missing phone number, along with the previously cancelled appointment, Marilyn quite likely had apprehensions about seeking a consultation.

Apprehensions about treatment are expressed in a myriad of ways. A situation might be set up in which the person expresses a desire for help. The patient might even make an appointment, but something then transpires to sabotage the consultation. Here the seasoned psychotherapist always incubates the possibility that the patient is ambivalent about seeking psychological help or embarking upon the change process itself. Alongside the patient's desire for assistance and the possibilities for psychological change and growth is also the reluctance to change. To do so one must be prepared to look inside the self and to consider one's contributions to those difficulties, whether these problems are expressed in the form of overt emotional symptoms or interpersonal or couple struggles. To look at the self is, then, almost always painful, while sometimes even threatening to one's interpersonal network, family system, or intimate partnership. Because of this potential threat, difficulties with the intimate partnership are sometimes expressed through physical symptoms, which protect the person and the partnership from becoming aware and having to deal directly with the couple's problem areas. The price paid for this compromise, however, is often huge.

To project one's emotional difficulties into one's body or onto the intimate partner can then represent a symptom for the individual and for the couple, while at the same time functioning as a resistance to facing one's own internal strife and personal responsibility. While one may suffer internally, one may simultaneously resist treatment—either through misgivings about therapy, as with Marilyn, or with more subtlety, as with Martin and Janet while they struggled with issues around autonomy.

After 2 days Marilyn called back. This time she left a working cell phone number and had less urgency in her voice. In her message she once again commented that she had been ill. She expressed the concern that while she was bedridden with a headache, I might have called back and if so she had missed my call. It was here that I found her message interesting in light of today's telephone technology and etiquette. With answering devices almost routine, would she not think that I would have left a message had I returned her call? I wondered then if, on some level, Marilyn had been aware that I was unable to reach her, while she unconsciously arranged a predicament in which she and I were unable to make contact. Quite likely, Marilyn's desire for a consultation and the accompanying desire for help were at this moment outweighing her apprehension about pursuing it.

When I returned Marilyn's call, a soft-spoken woman answered the telephone. After I had identified myself, she thanked me for returning her call, saying that she was sorry that she was difficult to reach. I found myself marveling that, on some level, she knew that she had been difficult to reach, while she apologized for contributing to the difficulty. She had no way of knowing that I had tried to return her call, but she likely knew on some level of awareness that she had failed to provide me with the information that would have allowed me to make contact with her.

Marilyn proceeded to inform me that she would like to make an appointment to see me, but she had concerns that, with her many medical appointments over the next several weeks, she could fit it in. Here again, she seemed to be giving herself an "out," while simultaneously requesting an appointment. She quickly added that she was seeing a doctor at the pain center, and he had recommended that she make an appointment to see me. Her headaches had become worse over the past year, and the injections she was receiving on a routine basis were not helping. She went on to say that her physician suggested that psychological treatment was frequently useful for a variety of pain disorders and that a psychologist was the specialist that she should contact.

Suddenly, Marilyn blurted out that she had lots of available time to come in to see me, but that she expected that I was very busy, so she would be grateful for any appointment that I could give her. I immediately noted the contradiction in our less than 2-minute conversation. Marilyn had just told me that she had doubts about whether she had the time to see me, while also expressing her willingness to accept any appointment time I could give her. Without yet knowing her, I could not be certain about the specific nature of her fears and anxieties, but I was already gathering some impressions about this woman and how she negotiated her world and her relationships. I found myself wondering about the role that her headaches played in her life and the immense price she was likely paying for maintaining her pain disorder.

Marilyn and I were able to set up an appointment for the following week. The pain treatment center was only 15 minutes away, and she thought that after getting her injection that morning she would be able to make the short drive, although she thought that she might be several minutes late. Marilyn arrived at my office notably 25 minutes in advance of her appointment time. Instead of being late as she had feared, she was conspicuously early.

I ushered Marilyn into my consultation area as she looked nervously around the room. Because of her apparent apprehension, perhaps more quickly than usual I made a motion with my hand to show her where she might sit. She seemed relieved, already suggesting to me that this was a woman who might become emotionally paralyzed at times when she was confronted with new and uncertain situations.

Marilyn was somewhat like a pixie in appearance. A woman in her mid-40s, whose attire and underweight physique suggested a woman much younger, sat uncomfortably while she waited for me to take charge of the consultation. I had a momentary flash that her childlike appearance, coupled with her unassuming manner, might make it difficult for her to be "heard" and taken seriously by people to whom she was close. As I invited her to tell me about what brought her to see me I was prepared to hear less about her emotional life, but instead a description of her medical problems. My expectation was based on our initial phone contact and my knowledge about how she was referred, but also my considerable experience with patients having physical problems as the reason for referral. But I was surprised.

As Marilyn began speaking, her diffidence seemed to fade. She suddenly became more audible. Her presentation seemed to shift as I now observed what appeared to be a precision and elegance in her choice of words as she described her experiences. I privately noted the striking disparity between her presentation on the phone and her discordant, verbal-linguistic opening. Notably, she did not mention her medical history or her headaches. She instead commented that for several years she had been depressed and had sometimes felt so hopeless that she had actually considered suicide. She went on to tell me that she had chosen to retire from her career in nursing in order to care for her mother, who was in the late stages of Alzheimer's dementia. She described the difficulty she had been having in responding appropriately to her mother's fluctuating mental state, with her sometimes rapid shifts between withdrawal and aggression along with verbal abuse.

Marilyn went on to say that both of her children were away at college and that her husband was supportive of her plight, but that he was very busy with his career as a trial lawyer. She commented that interrupting her successful nursing career had been very difficult for her. Just before resigning she had been promoted to a position of considerable prestige of director of her department and the next-in-line administrator to the president of a university medical school department of nursing.

Marilyn's husband, John, had strongly encouraged her to quit her job because he felt that she was unable to handle her mother's affairs adequately while she was working. The mother's affairs included the management of a substantial amount of money, which in the future would become theirs because Marilyn was the only heir to the mother's considerable fortune. It was here that I asked Marilyn if her resignation was something that she wanted. She paused for what seemed to be an inordinately long time and then seemed to break out of her otherwise lucid presentation, proceeding with a long and convoluted reply, which struck me as vague and elusive. It occurred to me that I had no idea whether she had replied affirmatively or negatively.

Once again, Marilyn had shifted into a state of uncertainty that appeared confusing even to me. More importantly, I thought it was indicative of her difficulty in attaining clarity about her position on this matter. Here was what on the surface appeared to be a very simple question about whether John's desire that she quit her job was also what she wanted for herself. I wondered whether, without her husband's persuasion, she would have made this important life-changing move on her own. Was this *her* choice? I wanted to know. She responded *as if* to answer my question, but with a vagueness leading me to hypothesize that quite likely her volition and personal agency had been bypassed in favor of her husband's and possibly her mother's needs.

With only a few minutes into the initial interview, I was already getting a glimpse of what I have come to regard as a most critical achievement, while also a potential conflict for those who marry or who are otherwise coupled. Although Marilyn was not yet consciously aware of her struggle, there were already hints to suggest that her depression and her headaches were manifestations of a conflict between adhering to her convictions and her sense of self versus abiding by the preferences of those in her intimate circle. These pressures appeared to be imposed by her husband and her ailing mother. Notice that I said "appeared."

THE ILLUSION OF CULPABILITY

On the surface Marilyn did not appear to blame John or her mother for her decision to quit her job. Many patients will hint or directly state that it is the husband, wife, or mother, for example, who creates the pressure or the conditions compelling the patient to behave in ways that she might not otherwise have chosen were it not for those influences. Not uncommonly, a patient might focus entire sessions on blaming the other person for the patient's choice or unacceptable predicament. These hours might even constitute the brunt of the therapy while becoming its focus over weeks or months, as if therapy were a forum for building the case against the spouse, parent, boss, or other significant person in the patient's life.

In my teaching and supervision of therapists and psychoanalysts in training, I have noted that, when treatment unfolds in this manner, sometimes bypassing self-exploration or insight into oneself and one's contributions to the presenting difficulty, there is increased risk that the patient might make life-altering decisions that can have disastrous consequences. Many precipitous divorces and destructive extramarital affairs have occurred under conditions that, had the patient or couple worked in a therapeutic self-exploratory way to understand their difficulties, might then have been avoided.

The therapist, too, can potentially and unwittingly contribute to the patient's belief or assertion that it is the partner who is really at fault and who is the reason that the patient is in the current predicament. Sometimes the patient's complaints can be presented with such conviction that the therapist, in the name of empathy and understanding, can inadvertently collude with the patient by agreeing, even if not explicitly, that it is indeed the partner who is ultimately responsible for the patient's plight. It is not uncommon for the therapist to listen to countless hours of a patient's complaints about a significant other who is portrayed as the source of the problem. To the extent that the therapist maintains this sympathetic focus, unaccompanied by an essential skepticism and an inherent belief in the intersubjectivity of relationships, there is a heightened risk that the treatment process will remain predominantly supportive while never completely addressing the patient's role in the relationship difficulty.

This is not said as a criticism or as a way to underemphasize the importance of the supportive features of treatment. All psychological treatments must be essentially supportive from the beginning to the end, for without support the patient cannot grow. However, blaming the other in the absence of honest self-scrutiny frequently represents a defensive cover in order to escape the more painful realization that the patient's symptoms and dissatisfaction are fundamentally determined by the patient. Indeed, the patient's marital partner or significant other plays a role. Obscured by blame and externalizing defenses is the patient's awareness that there are options to respond and to behave in alternative ways. To the extent that the therapist colludes or openly agrees with the patient that the partner is responsible for the difficulties, the therapy is more likely to falter. It is this kind of clinical presentation that I have termed the "illusion of culpability."

Marilyn did not at first openly assign blame to either her husband or her mother. She could not easily respond to my question regarding whether she would have ended her career on her own had it not been for John's influence. It was here that I thought something was up—quite likely something of which Marilyn was not aware. I invited Marilyn to tell me more about her relationship with both her husband and her mother. I wanted to understand more about how and why *she* made the decision to end her career—a decision that I would later come to understand was one of many in her life that was motivated by her excessive need for approval, beginning with her mother and continuing into her marriage. Importantly, Marilyn and I together would need to better understand how it was that her sense of self and personal agency could so easily be jettisoned at times when she feared that she might lose the approval of those within her intimate circle.

Marilyn had grown up as an only child. Because of the family's wealth, she had led a somewhat privileged life. Her father had acquired a considerable fortune that was partially inherited. With the inheritance he subsequently founded his own company, multiplying his original inheritance considerably. Both of Marilyn's parents worked long hours in the company. Marilyn was born 10 years after her parents' marriage. It was no secret in the family that her parents regarded her birth to be an "accident." Neither parent had wanted children. Marilyn proceeded to tell me that a prevailing feeling during her childhood was that of loneliness. She recalled that her mother would return home at the end of a long day at her office after Marilyn had already been home from school for a number of hours. She recalled her mother's almost constant irritability and how she would look for ways to be helpful to and considerate of her mother while remaining quiet and unassuming so that she would not be a bother to this already burdened woman.

As Marilyn informed me about how she had come to adapt to her mother with her solicitous demeanor, I privately thought about her hesitant presentation on the phone while scheduling her appointment. I flashed to the previous hour in which I had a first impression of her as a waif-like pixie who, on the one hand, seemed to want to hide from me and yet, on the other, presented with an eloquence and style that commanded my attention. So far she had not even mentioned her headaches except in passing, only briefly making reference to the pain clinic from which she had just come. Now I was hypothesizing that her pain problem was likely a manifestation of an impoverished sense of self. If she maintained passivity and failed to exercise her own agency, she could then feel assured that she was not a bother to me, her mother, or her husband.

Suddenly, Marilyn dropped her eyes. She was quiet for several minutes as tears rolled down her cheeks. I noted her pained and contorted facial expression, suggesting that she might be struggling with whether to address her feelings openly. Now with a vehemence that contradicted her tentativeness, she suddenly blurted out in a tone of anger that it was her husband who wanted her to quit her job to care for her mother. John had been convinced that if she did not assume the care of her mother, the mother's fortune might be shunted into the various charitable endowments about which Marilyn's mother had talked in recent years.

John undoubtedly held an opinion that his future and fortune might be better served if Marilyn were to care for her aging mother. Yet, this was merely John's opinion and desire, not a mandate. It was Marilyn who ultimately made the choice about leaving her career to take care of her mother. While convinced that it was her husband who had created this predicament, Marilyn had been able to avoid looking at her role in exercising this option—one that had altered her life considerably. Here Marilyn was engaged in the illusion of culpability.

What was it then about Marilyn that had caused her to give up her rewarding career while blaming her husband for her decision? It was here that I wondered about John, whether he might actually be forceful, persuasive, threatening, or possibly none of the above. Could it be that Marilyn made unfounded assumptions about the consequences that she might incur if she were to disagree with him? And to complicate matters more, I additionally wondered whether blaming John for her decision might represent a projection of her own wish, making it his requirement, rather than owning this action herself. And finally what was it about Marilyn's early and more current relationship with her mother that had set the stage for the struggle around whether she should end her career to care for her mother? These questions represented only a sampling of the hypotheses that passed through my mind as Marilyn's story unfolded.

Again, here, in a nutshell, is the ubiquitous struggle of adult marital and couple life: how to be engaged in an intimate and enduring relationship with the partner while being a self—an individual who is able to maintain autonomy without proneness to relinquishing personal agency by either acquiescing or psychologically merging with the partner. By inviting you into the treatment settings and lives of Martin and Janet, Marilyn, and others of my patients, I will demonstrate how this basic struggle for selfhood and separateness functions along a continuum from intimacy, closeness, and intermittent merger to autonomy—in ways that are especially pertinent for marriage and other forms of committed partnering. This dialectic between being a self and being a couple exists throughout the life of the couple. When well regulated within marriage, it provides the maximum of human fulfillment while serving to enrich the selves of both partners, the couple's intimate life, and the life of the wider family, including the children and the generations to follow.

2

THE INCOMPLETE SELF

The behavioral sciences have traditionally taught us that the mind and the self are closed systems. The central thesis here is that every human is born with genetic material to parents by whom the child will be influenced for approximately 20 years, give or take a few, after which will emerge the finished product—the adult. This traditional paradigm has posited that the young adult now has a mind of his own, for better or worse; is essentially complete; and will not significantly change unless intensive psychological treatment ensues or he experiences a major life or catastrophic event to affect his being.

With the proliferation of contemporary theories of psychology and psychoanalysis, including the research in neuroscience and human development, we now know that the mind is not a finished product when childhood comes to its end. Object relations theories, self psychology, intersubjectivity theories, and family systems theories (all extensions of psychoanalysis) inform us that the inborn temperament and predispositions to behave, feel, think, and experience the world, although shaped during childhood, remain plastic throughout the entire life span and are able to be modified by various environmental and relationship influences. Furthermore, current research in neuroscience has also corroborated that the brain is able to make structural changes throughout the development. Although at the end of adolescence and at the onset of early adulthood the individual has indeed developed some form of self, it remains malleable and is capable of change and revision throughout the life span (Kandel, 2005; Siegel, 1999; Solms & Turnbull, 2002).

Not only are we humans capable of change, but we also actually seek it. We look for the novel as we explore the world. We are fascinated by the advertisements that we see on television, as well as opportunities that are implied in the magazines and the books that we read. We embrace new technology and are busy in anticipation of our next vacation, often to places we have not been before. We look forward to remodeling an existing house, we buy new cars, and we change our hairstyles and wardrobes. We go on to higher education to learn new skills and, having attained a degree, will even proceed to advanced degrees or learn new trades. Our consumer habits suggest that what we purchase or wish to have for ourselves is almost always in some attempt to change or improve what we have, what we are, and how we experience ourselves.

Searching for and developing relationships works in a similar manner. We indeed seek friendships, companions, lovers, and spouses to counter aloneness and for purposes of attachment, sexuality, and procreation. A vast literature on the psychology of these processes approaches these topics from a number of different perspectives (Collins, Guichard, Ford, & Feeney, 2006; Hazan, Campa, & Gur-Yaish, 2006; Mikulincer, 2006). But how and why we choose one partner over another is the subject of this chapter. Here we are dealing with attachment phenomena—more specifically, the essence of attraction as a way of understanding the psychological processes involved in establishing permanent partnerships.

Attraction as a psychological concept is complex and multifaceted. It can refer to physical appeal and its many components, including how any one individual experiences another's physique, hair, eyes, mouth, and symmetry of facial characteristics. It includes how the other carries himself, his ways of speaking, tonality, olfactory features, conformity to his gender, and many other characteristics as well. In understanding the psychology of partnering, however, we must go beyond physical attraction because each individual may encounter any number of potential partners with physically attractive features, but perhaps only one or two will be experienced by this person as having the qualities of a potential partner.

How an individual determines what is interpersonally attractive is based largely on how the qualities of the partner are experienced vis-a-vis the self. It is as if, in the encounter with this other person, the individual is asking, "How does she fit with who I am, how I want to be, or how I want to be experienced by another?" Much of this perceptual processing occurs on a subliminal or unconscious level. It is this interpersonal and unconscious realm of attraction that becomes fundamental in understanding how relationships become romantic, ultimately intimate, and finally permanent. The point at which physical attraction and interpersonal attraction then converge might ultimately represent that crucial juncture and the phenomenon that we have come to know as falling in love.

THE DESIRE TO BE TRANSFORMED

Partner selection cannot be reduced to one or even two psychological constructs. To establish an intimate partnership a couple must have romance, some kind of physical compatibility, friendship, and mutuality along a number of dimensions. Here we will elaborate on these elusive concepts of compatibility and mutuality. When establishing an intimate partnership that potentially leads to marriage or another form of permanent partnership, there must first be a series of interpersonal encounters during which both individuals experience the self vis-a-vis various qualities of the self of the other. Simply put, this involves getting to know this person in more than just a perfunctory way.

Although some of this occurs consciously, there is simultaneously an ongoing unconscious appraisal process in which both individuals continue to monitor and experience the extent to which aspects of the self will mesh and fit with aspects of the other. This is a process in which the self tunes in to another while perceiving but also appraising qualities, traits, strengths, deficits, and so forth that either complement or fail to complement various features and traits of the self. The thesis here is that this searching, scanning, and appraisal process precedes the decision to unite, during which the stage is becoming set for establishing an intimate and eventually a permanent arrangement. While this relationship is being established, there is frequently just enough experienced sameness in the other to feel the safety of familiarity and enough perceived difference to be intrigued and stimulated.

Through continuous relating and the increasing closeness and sometimes permanency that follow, both partners now have the opportunity to experience a revision of the self in various ways—all as a function of a change in the intersubjective context of the relationship: the self vis-a-vis the self of the other. Intrigued and stimulated by the other's differentness, there will emerge an accompanying desire and even a longing to experience that change continuously; through continuous intimate involvement, this provides a subjective sense of now having been transformed. The desire to experience this revision continuously, now represented as a feeling of completeness, will function as a propellant to maintain this closeness and intimacy with the partner. Ultimately, this process forms the basis of adult attachment.

It is during this process of uniting and continuously throughout the relationship that both persons will transform—sometimes gradually, ineffably, and imperceptibly and at other times more apparently—even to others who observe the couple from afar. It is not unusual, for example, for college male chums to remark when observing their buddy Joe College that he seems to have changed since marrying Susie Sorority. Often these observations and comments are made with teasing jocularity that belies an understanding and envy of the transformative quality of a loving and intimate partnership. The revision of the self then becomes a basic feature and fundamental purpose of marriage and even other forms of permanent partnerships, notwithstanding evolutionary motives including sexuality, procreation, and formation of the family.

THE SEARCH FOR THE SELF IN THE OTHER

The cognitive-affective scanning and monitoring process of the other during the courtship stage of the relationship is motivated in part by the awareness within the self of what one is, including one's strengths, limitations, and deficiencies. The sense of self includes inner templates of experiences with others that have emerged throughout development and are now structured into a personality with its nuances of traits, characteristic defensive strategies, affective regulation, and attachment style. Further motivated by inherent needs for affiliation, there is then a search for another person with qualities that will complement or supply one with what is experienced by the self as missing, needed, and desired.

To experience one's insufficiencies does not presume having conscious insight into the self or possessing a capacity for introspection. It would in fact be rare in the courtship process for one consciously to experience attraction to another from the standpoint of one's inner deficiencies or needs for complementarity. The individual does not say to himself, for example, "I sometimes feel socially awkward and because of this I long to experience and have her for her gregariousness" or "I've been admired my entire life for my beauty only, but this person values me for my intelligence."

Instead, one perceives in the other a quality that is admired or features to which one is particularly drawn. There might be a sense of intrigue about the other person simply because she is especially comfortable to be with or is different from the self in a way that seems interesting. But, nearly always, there is the subjective experience that this other person is unique from other previously encountered partners.

The search for the self in the other might represent an evolutionary phenomenon, much like the sexual drive that is prerequisite for procreation or attachment phenomena that John Bowlby has demonstrated to be inborn and hardwired, serving the function of relationship formation and survival of the species (Bowlby, 1980, 1982). Furthermore, it is fundamentally a cognitive-emotional process that, because of our relatively more complex neurological structures, is more influential for the human species than for lower animals. While lower animals select their partners based on hormonal and biological factors that drive sexual receptivity and reproduction, humans, because of the complexity of our brains and our capacity for thought, rely significantly on cognitive-affective factors in determining the selection of a permanent partner; reproduction and drive satisfaction are of lesser importance.

THE FIT OR FAILURE TO FIT

Experiencing the self in the other begins and continues through the courtship, as well as throughout the relationship. Both individuals will continuously appraise features, traits, and qualities of the other while unconsciously assessing how these features match or fit with aspects of the self. The well-known adage that "opposites attract"—that one selects partners with opposite qualities—has at least some merit, although it is actually an oversimplification of how two persons relate and make actual determinations regarding a fit or a failure to fit. Henry Dicks first offered an elegant description of how the unconscious processes of two individuals intersect in an effort to find or reclaim a lost part of the self. Although his studies were based mostly on troubled marriages treated at the Tavistock Clinic and are now dated, his work has had wide applicability in understanding the dynamics of interpersonal attraction and the breakdown of the marital system (Dicks, 1993).

A more contemporary understanding of this process that extends Dicks's work is that each person searches for an aspect of the self within the self of the other that offers a possibility or provides a hope for compensation for some self-perceived insufficiency. This thesis in no way presumes that the search for complementarity is based on psychopathology per se, but instead that the person desires a wholeness that is more likely to be achieved while partnered with this person.

Insufficiencies are inevitable for us all, no matter how seemingly confident, competent, or emotionally healthy an individual might appear to be or feel on a conscious level. The scanning process might then take the form of locating in the partner a quality that is needed or desired—a quality that compensates for some deficiency of self. Furthermore, the desired feature may not be entirely absent in the partner desiring it; instead, it might represent a part of the self that has been repressed for any number of reasons. Now, through the intimate connection with the partner, there is the possibility for its liberation.

Through introjective and projective identification—the modes of communication through which we humans and especially intimate partners come to experience each other's mental states on an unconscious level, qualities of the self are then exchanged, felt, and ideally contained by the partner. It is the mutual containment of what is projected by the partner that accounts for the experience of having been transformed and is fundamental to establishing and maintaining the permanent partnership or marriage. While Dicks emphasized the importance of locating the lost part of the self in the other, I emphasize the partner's willingness and capacity to contain the projected part of the self while simultaneously providing the essential affirmation for this now revised self of the partner.

While some might find the repressed part of the self in a partner who offers the possibility for its compensation, others might search for a partner to provide a mirroring, idealizing, or twinship function to shore up a fragile or narcissistically vulnerable part of the self (Kohut, 1971, 1977; Shaddock, 2000; these terms will be described in Chapter 7 as they apply to the couple relationship). Conceptualizing from the framework of self psychology, we are considering the individual whose grandiose self has been repressed, and who searches for an affirming other to encourage its expression and enhance its stability.

Here fulfilling the selfobject function serves as a condition to establishing the permanent partnership and frequently underlies the idealization that accompanies the loving experience. With some couples, one might then observe not apparently opposite features, but instead two individuals who appear similar to one another and have similar characteristics. Or the partners might have similar background experiences or family of origin structures that are alike in many ways, including shared traumatic histories. It is as if these commonalities provide a security for both partners, without which both feel less integrated and whole. Here the partnership offers both individuals the hope for mastering the shared trauma.

In summary, there is a lost part of the self—one that is repressed or possibly experienced as deficient, needed, or longed for—that is unconsciously found in the self of a potential partner. It is experienced as not only desirable and enhancing of the self, but also attainable by establishing an intimate partnership through which the hope for experiencing a more complete and coherent revision of the self might occur. When a comfortable mutuality of this process is achieved between two people, there is an increased likelihood that the partnership will be maintained. To the extent that the partners are unable to maintain this balanced reciprocity, the relationship will likely experience difficulty or will simply come to an end.

Martin and Janet

On the day of their graduation from a large Midwestern university, Martin and Janet met for the first time while assembling for their graduation procession. Both Martin and Janet were moving toward the head of the line, where those students graduating with honors were asked to gather. Struggling to find their places, they literally stumbled into one another, asking each other where to enter the line. Laughing at each other's ignorance of the protocol, which had already been explained to the graduating class, they agreed to meet after the ceremony. Because neither Martin nor Janet had family attending their graduation festivities, there was a mutual eagerness to meet at a coffee house just outside the university campus where many of the graduates would go to celebrate. Upon meeting later in the day, they quickly learned from each other why neither had family members attending the graduation. Having this in common seemed then to jump start their relationship.

Martin told Janet that he had been raised by an aunt and uncle as an only child after his parents were killed in a tragic auto accident when he was 3 years of age. His uncle had been ill recently, preventing both his uncle and aunt from attending the graduation ceremonies. Janet was the second born of two children, having an older brother. Janet's brother and sister-in-law had just had their first child, and her parents were torn between flying to Hawaii to see their grandchild or attending Janet's graduation. To relieve her mother's conflict over making this decision, Janet graciously reassured her parents that she wanted them to make the trip to Hawaii. Furthermore, to assuage her mother's guilt, she told her parents that she would undoubtedly pursue an advanced degree in the future, so they would have the opportunity to see her walk across a university stage on a later occasion. During the initial interview, Janet repeated several times that she was fine with her parents' decision and, in fact, would have felt very uncomfortable had her parents chosen otherwise.

In this first session with Martin and Janet I was impressed with this piece of historical information regarding how they first met. It is useful in the initial or second interview with a couple to ask about their first meeting and what especially struck or impressed each of them about the other one. The circumstances of the couple's first encounters and especially the memories of their initial impressions of each other are almost always revealing from a diagnostic standpoint. It is less useful to ask the couple what attracted each to the other. The word "attracted" is leading; in fact, it is not unusual for the partners to respond that initially there was no attraction or simply to list appealing physical features or other superficial qualities. A more neutral opening asking about the details of their initial encounters, their impressions of each other, and how they decided to get together will usually provide more clues about the unconscious search for the self within the other. This method of intervening allows the clinician to make more cogent inferences about both individuals' self-perceived insufficiencies and how they might relate to the qualities in the other that were initially admired, desired, and even needed.

Momentarily, Martin smiled as he recalled that bright sunny day in late May on which he first met Janet. For the first time I had a fleeting impression of him as a man who likely struggles to permit himself any variability in his affective life. It was as if my question about their first meeting allowed Martin to enter a world he had left behind. During these brief moments his nose no longer appeared so elevated. His demeanor of superiority and contempt seemed to have melted while he briefly allowed himself a bit more room for a previously hidden wistful sensitivity as he described his first encounters with Janet.

"What I really remember was that she seemed so giving," he said. He then added:

> That stood out to me more than anything else. I hadn't dated much through high school or college, so I didn't have a lot of other girls to compare her to, but I do remember how impressed I was when she seemed so concerned about her mother's struggle with the decision about coming to graduation. I remember thinking that, when she told her parents that they should go to Hawaii and not worry about her graduation and that she would walk across a university stage again, it seemed almost...sacrificial.

Although for the next several minutes Martin proceeded to describe what he remembered about Janet's physical features at the time of their first meeting, his word "sacrificial" seemed to stick in my mind—so much so that I was briefly distracted from Martin's otherwise prosaic physical description of Janet. He could have used any number of synonyms to describe Janet's "giving" qualities, but he said "sacrificial"—a word that brought to my mind vague images pertaining to religious rites, biblical parables, pagan temples, and the Mayan altars I had seen while traveling in Central America and Mexico. "Also," he said, "when we started to see each other, she would leave me cards and even cleaned my apartment from time to time." Clearly, Martin seemed to be saying that not only had he felt cared for by Janet, but also, even in the beginning of their relationship, he had perceived in her a quality of nurturance that was highly important to him. But with his use of the word "sacrificial," I wondered if it was also important to him that Janet give in a manner that conveys a relinquishment of something that is important to *her*. And if that were the case, how did it relate to the difficulties for which they had come to see me? I would wait to see.

With the same hesitancy that characterized her opening remarks, Janet once again stumbled into the conversation, emphasizing that her mother had never taken a vacation during the many years that she was caring for Janet's now deceased grandmother, so Janet wanted to be certain that her mother had an opportunity to do so. Janet's clarification at this moment about a trivial matter about her mother seemed to convey a sense of discomfort, as if she felt a need to mitigate Martin's laudatory remarks about her. But I had the impression that, by doing so, she was paradoxically confirming this self-sacrificing quality, as she now seemed to be attempting to diminish herself in my eyes. Furthermore, upon hearing that Janet's mother had taken care of her own mother while never taking a vacation, I now speculated that there might exist a tendency for women in this family to renounce their needs, possibly represented in Janet as a masochistic introject of her mother—a relationship paradigm in which one gives to another while relinquishing personal needs and painfully sacrificing oneself.

In the technique of couple therapy, the therapist must track the patterns of interaction between himself and each partner while also monitoring the interaction of the couple. Also, the therapist must be mindful that his presence with the couple exerts a powerful contextual modification in the couple's relationship that may significantly affect their more usual ways of communicating with each other. Considering the multiplicity of variables, the therapist is constantly making choices about which partner to address with a comment, question, or interpretation or whether the couple dyad should instead be addressed. Although at this moment I was tempted to turn to Martin to ask more about his background as a way to clarify why Janet's sacrificial qualities were important to him, I chose to proceed with Janet. Her diffidence with Martin and with me as well evoked my desire to encourage her voice beyond her more usual hesitancy.

I now turned to Janet and asked, "And what was it, Janet, about Martin in your first encounters that you noticed and have remembered over the years?" This time, without hesitation, Janet replied:

I remember first of all how sad I was when he commented that his parents had been killed and that he had been raised by his aunt and uncle. He didn't say *he* was sad, but somehow I sensed that he really was. But somehow...well, maybe not right at the beginning...but after we started seeing each other...well, I always felt as though I should do something for him. I mean...I really wanted to, but there was something about his independence that made me feel sorry for him...like maybe underneath he really needed something. His aunt and uncle never visited him and he never went home.

Here I interjected, "Possibly you felt that you might fill in something for him that was missing." Janet did not directly reply to my interpretation, but proceeded to recall other early encounters with Martin. "My family had always been so close. So it seemed very odd to me...not that I couldn't understand it...but it all seemed sad to me," she added. Here I replied:

So you would make it a point to clean his room and leave him cards and notes. This was your way of giving him support and maybe demonstrating your care for him, especially since you wondered if he felt cared about, or whether his independence was really as it appeared. Perhaps you felt a desire to make up for something you felt he didn't have.

At this juncture it seemed especially important to clarify Janet's motivation for her actions as it related to her sympathy for Martin, while conveying my understanding of Martin's vulnerability and Janet's experience of him. Here I was beginning to acquire some understanding about the caretaking role that Janet had assumed in the relationship and its significance in the dynamics of their interactions. "Yeah, he always seemed appreciative when I would do these little things for him...that is...unless he was busy. Then, he didn't notice," she replied.

Within a span of just a few minutes Janet had revealed a most critical aspect of those first encounters with Martin that would ultimately become important in their attraction to each other. On the one hand, Janet admired Martin's independence; on the other, she also wondered if this quality defended against a fundamental insufficiency or dependent core. From the very beginning of their relationship, Janet felt a desire to go to extra lengths to provide nurturance for Martin as a way of making up for what she felt he had missed during his formative years. She commented on how he had unconsciously communicated this to her and how she then felt compelled to respond to this need.

Yet I also wondered what it was within Janet that might additionally contribute to her need to respond to Martin's underlying dependency and inner sadness. In other words, the couple therapist is always assessing what it is within each person, as well as what is unconsciously communicated between the partners, that motivates them to respond to, be drawn to, or repelled by the other along the various dimensions that emerge during the consultation. I had by this time learned that Janet perceived Martin's underlying neediness. But beyond this, why was Janet drawn to his repressed dependency in a way that compelled her to take care of him? Could it be that *her* neediness, possibly repressed or denied, was projected onto Martin?

Now I turned to Martin, asking him how it was that he sensed that Janet's giving qualities were sacrificial. He had already commented on her encouragement of her parents to take their trip to Hawaii. But was there more? He responded:

> I remember that after she washed my car once she became ill. It had been very hot that summer. It was 102° that day and very muggy. I was working hard at my summer job and my car needed a good cleaning. I remarked to her that I had been so busy that I didn't even have time to get it washed. I called her after I got home from work, and she was in bed. She said that she had fainted after washing my car and that her roommate had taken her to the emergency room. They told her that she had suffered a heat stroke.

At this moment Janet interrupted the dialogue between Martin and me, protesting that she was not at all convinced it was a heat stroke, but instead that because she had been ill several days before, it was more likely that she had not yet fully recovered. "I made a very poor decision to wash your car when there actually were heat advisories on the news," Janet said. Here it seemed to me as though Janet once again felt compelled to subtract a quality of goodness from the car-washing incident. By her ascribing her fainting spell to a "poor decision" rather than to any inherent quality of helpfulness or goodness, I was now even more convinced that sacrificing for others, and notably Martin, was an essential ingredient in their relationship architecture.

I chose to respond to Janet at this juncture. By now aware of her penchant for self-effacement, I said, "You seem so very humble about these giving qualities that Martin speaks about." To illustrate my point I reminded her that she had encouraged her parents to take the trip to Hawaii and that she seemed dismissive of the significance of the heat stroke that she had suffered while washing Martin's car. Somewhat less defensively Janet responded:

My mother always taught me that giving to others was much more important that putting yourself first. I grew up in a small town where everybody knew everyone else. My mother was always baking pies for others in town, taking them to their homes when they were sick or when someone's family member had died. I remember a time when she got so busy getting food ready to take to the Johnsons across town that she missed my school concert. I was performing a solo on my flute, so I really wanted her there to hear me. It was a solo that got me into the state music contest. Well, I've never been sure why taking the food to the Johnsons kept her from my concert. She told me that she had to make the delivery before seven o'clock and that she might be late. Well, she never arrived. My dad showed, but she didn't. I was okay with it though…well, I said I was. My mother had a habit of being late for everything. So when I first noticed that she wasn't in the audience I assumed that she would finally get there before I performed. Well, she didn't.

It was here that I observed an almost imperceptible tearing in Janet's eyes, along with an ever so slight grimace that momentarily cracked her usually poised smile. Picking up on this discrepancy between her affect and her statement about her mother's virtuous qualities, I commented, "It must have been quite hurtful that your mother was not present at this important event, especially when you suspected that she was typically running late or was fulfilling another commitment to someone in the community." Here I couched my observation as affectively neutral as possible because it was not yet clear how Janet experienced her mother's obligations. Did she perceive them as virtuous or as irresponsible and neglectful? Furthermore, I wondered if she had identified with her mother's nurturing qualities or whether her sacrificing features were a defense against a denied or repressed anger toward a nurturing person who had repeatedly hurt her.

In any case it was by this time becoming clear that Janet's nurturing qualities were an important ingredient in Martin's initial attraction to her. Furthermore, I was now hypothesizing that these features might represent something more than just a considerate attitude that was a function of her identification with her giving mother. Early in their relationship Martin would openly express his gratitude and appreciation while Janet in turn would feel valued for the attention he would then give her—that is, "unless he was busy…then he didn't notice." Janet's words stood out to me. Her statement about Martin's failure to notice her kind gestures at times of busyness seemed to represent not just a conscious recollection of their early relationship, but also an unconscious reference to her busy mother, who did not have time for her. It was likely then that Janet's loving ministrations and self-sacrifice were in part motivated by a desire to evoke Martin's attention, appreciation, and love, which Janet perhaps experienced as conditional—a pattern of connection that was reminiscent of her relationship with her mother.

This vignette of the opening phase of my work with Martin and Janet demonstrates several important features pertaining to working with couples. I have shown how the therapist's careful exploration of the couple's earliest encounters with one another reveals highly useful information pertaining to the unconscious search for the self in the other. Inquiring about their beginning circumstances assists the therapist in developing an understanding of those qualities in the partners that were especially appealing, desired, and even needed. Addressing the couple's initial attraction to one another from this standpoint provides the rudiments of understanding the incomplete self of both partners, which by forming an intimate connection provides an opportunity for achieving or building a whole or more complete self. By understanding the couple's original connection to each other the therapist is then positioned to come to understand how the original bond has broken down or become outmoded and dysfunctional.

In the following vignette featuring Marilyn, the woman referred by her physician for depression and accompanying psychosomatic symptoms, we will expand on how the therapist was able to address her symptoms by tracking the incomplete self and its implications for her marriage. Although in this book I focus mainly on working with marriages and other intimate partnerships, psychological difficulties stemming from the loss of the self within the intimate partnership are frequently encountered in patients who come for individual therapy. Whether or not couple therapy is considered, the therapist's understanding of these dynamics will greatly assist in working with individuals appearing for consultation, regardless of the presenting symptoms.

Marilyn

Marilyn began the second hour by saying that she had given considerable thought to our discussion about her husband, John, and that she now realized how controlling he had been in their marriage. My initial enthusiasm about the introspection Marilyn had demonstrated during the first hour regarding the way she had allowed herself to acquiesce to her husband and her mother was now deflated. It seemed that Marilyn had reconstituted her externalizing defenses since the first session, returning to the illusion of culpability, while she was now assuring me that John's controlling qualities were really at the root of her problem.

She proceeded to tell me that in spite of realizing that John was selfish in many ways, she wanted to remain married to him. I was surprised by her remark about remaining married because she had so far not even directly addressed a marital conflict, much less divorce as a solution. Given this comment, I now thought that she had likely experienced more dissatisfaction and conscious conflict about her marriage than had actually surfaced in the opening hour. Here I responded, "Marilyn, I think that you are telling me that you have been aware of some intensely angry feelings toward John, but perhaps in ways that you've not even let yourself know about over time." With my comment I wanted to clarify her feelings and, moreover, to underscore the manner in which she had suppressed her angry feelings toward her husband.

Marilyn proceeded to describe John as a "brilliant attorney," whose primary focus during the years of their marriage had been on his strivings for power and professional recognition. Furthermore, she felt that his concerns that she not shirk her responsibilities to her aged mother were actually motivated by his fear of losing what would be a substantial inheritance if it was redirected into the charities her mother had earmarked. "My mother is a very controlling woman, and she has always made it known that her charities were more important than anything else in her life," Marilyn said emphatically. "More important than you?" I asked with undisguised surprise in my voice. Although my question seemed especially abrupt, even to me, I felt quite certain that Marilyn had already asked herself that question many times before. Yet she momentarily appeared stunned, quite likely because I had dared to speak what she had difficulty addressing. Marilyn paused for nearly a minute. She sighed, and then responded:

> That is very hard to say. If I were to ask her, she would be very hurt and maybe even angry that I would ask such a thing. My father has been gone for a long time, so I have really been all that she has had. I've often wondered whether, if she had other children, or even anyone else in her life, I'd have any importance to her at all. So in a way I feel dishonest.

Marilyn paused again, accompanied by a sigh. At this moment she seemed especially burdened. Her brow was furrowed, and a look of consternation and despair seemed to overcome her. "You said 'dishonest.' Why?" I asked. "Because I don't have any desire to care for her. Much of the time I don't even like her. I do it out of some kind of duty I think.

I don't think that she cares about me…not really. She has some kind of control over me," Marilyn said.

I once again noticed the word "control." Just moments ago she had described her husband John as "controlling" and had previously used the same root word in referring to her mother. I momentarily reflected on Marilyn's initial phone presentation, her initial diffidence and hesitancy, which seemed to melt away during the first session. I recalled how surprised and impressed I was upon learning of her professional standing in the college of nursing. Knowing what I do about college administration and what kinds of people are selected for promotions into these positions, I wondered how this competent professional woman, who most certainly was adept at taking charge and asserting herself in a professional venue, was now in a position of being controlled by these two important people in her life.

I had already learned in the previous hour that during childhood Marilyn had been especially concerned about wanting to please her preoccupied and burdened mother, who Marilyn felt was unavailable as a consistently supportive and nurturing figure. During those years she had made it a point to assist her mother while making few demands as her way of earning her mother's love. There was now an emerging picture for me of Marilyn as a woman who was highly talented and competent as a professional, but who had acquiesced to her husband's desire to terminate her career in order to care for her ailing mother. It was likely, then, that her capitulation to his wishes repeated a pattern of pleasing a mother who she feared would not love or care for her if she enacted her own autonomy.

Marilyn suddenly shifted topics as she reflected on her rewarding career as a doctoral-level nurse who had worked on a busy surgical unit in a prestigious university hospital. Early in her career she had been promoted into various high-level supervisory positions. She met John shortly after he had graduated from law school while he was working on a case that involved her hospital. He had interviewed her in conjunction with the case. When leaving the hospital at the end of the day, Marilyn and John met at the elevator, after which they lingered in the lobby to speak for a few moments. It was at that time that John asked her if she would like to go for coffee. Although she had other plans to attend a movie that evening with a friend, she agreed, and canceled her other plans. Marilyn remarked:

> He was so very interesting. I was kind of quiet and shy and never felt that I had a lot to contribute in conversations. He was very spontaneous and so excited as he spoke about his work. But he didn't just talk about himself. He was very forward and charming—maybe

even a little aggressive. And even though it seemed as though he was interviewing me, he seemed really interested in me—you know, my work, my family background, and where I was from.

It was here that I noted an increase in Marilyn's animation as she spoke about her earliest encounters with John. Because I was now aware of her early history with a controlling but distant and uninvolved mother and how she also felt controlled and possibly neglected by her husband, I responded, "Although he was quite forward and aggressive, his manner might have also conveyed the genuine interest in you that you had always longed for." Marilyn was quick to respond to my comment:

I think I actually needed it. He seemed to really listen to me when I spoke. If I got quiet or was somewhat vague about something, he would ask me to clarify what I meant. I really felt different with him—I mean different than I had felt with other men—like maybe I was actually interesting to him. In those days he didn't seem at all interested in the wealth of my family, even though I think that he was a bit intrigued by the history of the family fortune. And when he met my parents, he wasn't intimidated by them.

I began to see how Marilyn's early relationship with John and the ingredients of her early attraction to him connected to important developmental issues with her mother. Marilyn's relationship with her mother had never been overtly conflictual. Instead, she had grown up in a family in which she questioned her mother's love for her. It was my impression that her relationship with her mother represented a form of insecure attachment that was now repeated in her marriage (Clulow, 2001). Marilyn's unassertive and cautious presentation, which had been especially evident in our initial telephone interactions, appeared as a manifestation of a devitalized self—a function of developing with a mother who was burdened herself and who demonstrated little interest in her daughter.

John's far more spirited and assertive style, initially displayed with Marilyn as an aggressive interest in her, provided an affirming attention that she had needed from her mother. This provided the critical but heretofore missing function of mirroring, the selfobject function that Kohut (1971, 1977) and others have described as a fundamental ingredient in the development of the self. Over time, however, John's career ambitions seemed to overshadow his interest in Marilyn, thereby repeating the relational paradigm with her mother. Furthermore, John's concern about being cut out of the mother's inheritance had been experienced by Marilyn as a profound disappointment, diminishing her idealization of him. His suggestion that she quit her job in order to take care of her mother now raised the question for Marilyn about whether she was truly loved and valued by her husband or whether he was interested in the money she would later inherit.

For many years Marilyn had been sustained by her successful career and the affirmation she received from colleagues. This had served to stabilize and enhance her shaky self-structure. However, her retirement, encouraged by John, now removed this crucial source of affirmation and self-esteem while it simultaneously returned her to a situation that approximated her early relationship with her mother. Having to care for this difficult and controlling woman, Marilyn was once again immersed in a relationship that was devoid of affection and love.

DISCUSSION

These two somewhat lengthy vignettes—one of a couple and another of a woman who came for a consultation with a mixed clinical picture of depression and somatization—are illustrative of a most important and fundamental struggle for those who marry or form another kind of permanent partnership. A critical achievement for those who become and remain a couple is the preservation of crucial features of the self while simultaneously developing a satisfying and intimate relationship. With the requirement that partners both give and take, linked with the need to compromise while sometimes renouncing certain wishes, desires, and preferences, remaining a self while engaging intimately with another is a most ambitious and complicated undertaking.

To summarize, all individuals entering the domain of dating, courtship, and partnership formation have a self-structure that is incomplete in some way. The lack of wholeness is not in most circumstances experienced as consciously troubling to the individual, but instead represents the nuances of personality existing throughout the human species. As the therapist works to understand and clarify the earliest encounters in the relationship of the couple—either by actively questioning or as information emerges spontaneously—the therapist is able to make inferences pertaining to the insufficient selves of both partners. These inferences will in most instances be pertinent in coming to understand the struggles for which the couple now seeks treatment.

Developing the story line of the couple's emerging love relationship in conjunction with coming to understand both partners' individual developmental histories, the therapist is then equipped to assist the couple in working out those developmental issues and insufficiencies of self that have cried out for repair and compensation by the partner. Having identified these dynamics, the therapist is positioned to help the couple to understand the ways in which the relationship is no longer providing the enrichment that once existed. The therapeutic work will now rest on the therapist's ability to work with the couple in restoring these original compensations or, alternatively, to move to new levels of growth within the relationship.

3

YOU COMPLETE ME

Attachment as the Antidote

Having established that partner formation is a process in which a needed or repressed part of the self is found in the other, we will now address why we humans strive for this connection in the first place. This brings us to a discussion of attachment phenomena and their implications for adult partner formation. *Jerry Maguire* (Crowe, 1996), a romantic comedy of the 1990s, illustrates many of the principles of partner formation and attachment that will be addressed in this chapter. The film features a man who recently has fallen on hard times while working for a sports agency. The plot highlights the emerging romance between Jerry and Dorothy, which we are led to understand launches a revision of Jerry's character, enhancing his capacity to love others while enriching his personal and professional life.

Jerry, the leading figure in the film, is portrayed as a superficial, narcissistic, and yet idealistic young man who finds Dorothy, a coworker, to be an adoring and faithful woman whose main interest becomes Jerry himself. She believes in his new vision and his ideals for a kinder and gentler corporate world of professional sports representation, the industry that had employed them both. She listens and understands him without judgment, modeling the essence of compassion and empathy while coming to love him unconditionally. Dorothy is the antithesis of the ruthless and disingenuous world in which Jerry has been living and working.

In the film we are given the impression that Dorothy's charming little boy, Ray, with whom Jerry becomes enamored, is experienced by Jerry as the little boy within himself who longs for a loving father. Jerry's coming to love both Dorothy and Ray represents a transformation of Jerry's narcissism as he evolves into a person who is more capable of genuinely caring for others. As he becomes aware of his metamorphosis, Jerry turns to his new love, Dorothy, and professes, "You complete me." It is at this moment of Jerry's soliloquy, where he extols his love for Dorothy, that this crucial quality of adult partner formation is highlighted and where this otherwise insipid story portrays some of the features of adult partner formation that are addressed throughout this book.

The completion Jerry speaks about, a feature that is frequently referred to in modern-day marital vows, was first explored in the psychological literature by Henry Dicks at the Tavistock Clinic in London in the 1960s. Dicks, a psychiatrist who was interested in marital dysfunction and its treatment, conducted detailed qualitative research on couples presenting to his clinic for treatment of marital and sexual dysfunction. Applying object relations theories—especially Ronald Fairbairn's endopsychic model of psychological functioning—to his work with couples, Dicks developed a theoretical structure for understanding the psychology of the couple, with implications for understanding how couples come to form their bonds and ultimately remain in a permanent partnership (Dicks, 1993; Fairbairn, 1944). His work has greatly influenced my understanding about the unconscious basis of attraction and its implications for the ideas that I have developed throughout this book, especially in coming to understand that a fundamental purpose of the couple relationship is to be in support of the selves of the two partners comprising the relationship.

First, a quality is encountered in another person that is experienced by the individual as particularly intriguing or interesting. This feature, or constellation of features, is usually not immediately conscious to the individual, but is instead a component of a subliminal or unconsciously activated perceptual experience embedded within a total nexus of an interpersonal encounter or, more often, a series of encounters with that partner. This intriguing feature represents a fundamental ingredient in the initial attraction, although it might not be immediately evident even to the therapist when it is first asked about in the consultation. Instead, it must often be inferred from the history of the couple's first encounters and emerging courtship, in conjunction with each partner's developmental history.

This quality is usually something other than mere physical appeal, although many couples, when first asked what drew them to one another, will initially comment on those more easily recognized physical or other superficial qualities that are closer to consciousness. The person might respond, for example, "Well, I really liked her smile" or "He seemed so considerate when I compared him to the other guys I dated." Although these more easily perceived appealing qualities will not be especially informative for the therapist, with an attuned ear and skillful interviewing, the unconsciously experienced feature that at one time resonated between the partners will usually be revealed in the therapeutic encounter. The history of the couple's relationship then ultimately provides the therapist the essential clues in coming to understand the unconscious psychological fit of the partnership, including what both partners needed or desired, which for some period of time was likely provided.

For one individual this feature might represent a part of the self that has been largely repressed. For another it might represent an undeveloped part of the self that, during formative years, was experienced as needed and even consciously desired. These needed or longed for qualities are frequently found to have originated in early experiences with parental figures or surrogates, who at one time either frustrated the need or longing by failing to provide it or rebuffed the developing child while the child in turn concluded that the parent's rejection was specifically because of that need.

Subsequently, the needed quality or constellation of features is found in a partner who seems to provide it or offers the hope or possibility of compensating for this need in some way. The process is reciprocal while both monitor the other, unconsciously searching for and discovering qualities of fit and misfit. An equilibrium is eventually established in which both partners unconsciously experience a liberation or a hope for liberation of those parts of self that previously were unexpressed, now providing the unconscious basis for loving intimacy and the experience of psychological completeness.

Perkel refers to this process as fusion, a phenomenon where two individuals coming together will pair with each other while unconsciously experiencing a quality in the other that will yield a more complete entity, ultimately enriching both partners beyond what each is individually. This pairing phenomenon is enabled by a relatively diffuse emotional boundary formed between the two selves, permitting a mutual exchange of mental contents. Through projective identification the couple will then continuously place into and take from the other partner those needed, longed for, or repressed qualities of the self (Perkel, 2001, 2007).

Although the psychoanalytic literature has provided many nuanced explanations and versions of projective identification, because of its simplicity and clarity, I have preferred John Zinner's definition. Zinner has described the partnering process as a "mutually gratifying collusive system" (1976, pp. 8–9) to which each partner contributes parts of the self and parts of the object through a communication process that is largely unconscious. According to Zinner, in projective identification the individual finds or perceives the object, or the relationship paradigm from early life, as if it were inside the partner rather than inside the self. This is tantamount to *projecting* a part of the self into the partner. This projection in turn affects a response in the partner that is potentially adaptive if the receiving partner's response is empathic and if the first partner happens to project a quality that is needed, desired, or otherwise fits. Some authors have referred to this "fit" as *valency* (Scharff & Scharff, 1991).

On the other hand, if the projected feature is experienced as incongruent with aspects of the receiving partner's self, that partner's response may become pathological. In this case the projecting partner's behavior might function as a mode for externalizing a toxic object relationship rather than giving and receiving needed qualities that affirm and support the partner. Alternatively, if the quality or the intensity of the partner's projection is such that the receiving partner attempts to contain it while, however, experiencing it as incongruent with the self, a situation may erupt in which the receiving partner now experiences the self as having been evacuated. This was the situation with both Janet and Marilyn in previous chapters. In such situations the partnership fails to enhance the self; instead, crucial features of the self are suppressed or otherwise disavowed. The eventual outcome is emotional disequilibrium, symptoms in one or both partners, or couple dysfunction.

In the film *Jerry Maguire* we come to understand that the protagonist, Jerry, had at one time been a sports agent employed by a company that had disregarded human values while showing little empathy and concern for its clients. During a crisis of conscience Jerry becomes aware of his participation in this corporate exploitation by remaining employed by a company that had supported his arrogance and shallowness. Jerry's narcissism eventually becomes evident as he discovers the emptiness of his existence. Bravely but naively, he speaks out about his dissatisfaction and then he is fired. Because of his courage and idealism, Dorothy remains steadfast in her admiration of him through the entire ordeal, and she then chooses to leave the firm to accompany him on his next professional endeavor. As Dorothy continues to respect and support him for his emerging ideals, Jerry begins to transform both professionally and personally while he simultaneously comes to love her and her young son. As their relationship deepens, the completion Jerry speaks about refers to his emerging awareness that something about his self-experience has changed as a function of his developing intimacy with Dorothy.

For one engaged in emerging intimacy, the feelings for the partner are generally experienced as highly positive, exciting, passionate, and sometimes euphoric. The partner is typically idealized while simultaneously one feels enhanced by the relationship, without which one feels incomplete. The feelings of enhancement and elevation are specifically due to the idealized features of the partner now being felt as part of the self. The experience of having been transformed, in conjunction with the idealization, passion, and intense friendship, defines what we have come to know as falling and being in love.

Although in the film we learn little about Jerry's developmental history, by following the story line the discerning viewer is able to infer qualities pointing to Jerry's psychological vulnerabilities. While Dorothy continues to admire him for his vision and emerging idealism, she provides him the necessary affirmation and mirroring that Kohut and the contemporary self psychologists have emphasized as essential in the transformation of narcissism (Kohut, 1977). Jerry eventually finds within Dorothy a lost or undeveloped aspect of himself, a kinder and gentler revision of a self—a person who is now more capable of loving and genuinely caring for others in an empathic way. As Jerry experiences these changes in his relationship with Dorothy, his professional and personal relationships simultaneously evolve.

THE SELFDYAD

As with Martin and Janet and Marilyn and John in previous chapters, *Jerry Maguire* illustrates a crucial quality of relationship formation that will be developed throughout this book: the search for a part of the self in the self of a partner who is able to provide a needed quality that is potentially transformative. For the loving experience to be mutual, the provision of these needed qualities must be reciprocal—that is, *both* persons must contribute an essential feature for the other that is experienced as meaningful for the partner in the ways described. In doing so, an interlocking fit of two personalities will eventually be formed, creating a dynamic system that is different from the sum of its parts (e.g., those individual traits and personalities comprising the dyad).

This couple dynamic system I have called the *selfdyad,* a term I use to describe this now revised whole couple relationship system—an extension of two individual personalities who have now evolved into an amalgam of revised parts of two selves. In agreement with Perkel and Dicks, there will continue to be an exchange of inner mental contents of two individuals, who during the process of relating intimately will unconsciously project parts of the self while simultaneously incorporating projected parts of the other (Dicks, 1993; Perkel, 2001, 2007).

COMPARING THE ANALYTIC THIRD, SELFOBJECT, AND SELFDYAD

The selfdyad is unique to any one couple and cannot be replicated, even with a different partner. For example, if a partner were to establish a different relationship or to remarry, an entirely new selfdyad would then be established, as the selfdyad is an original and unconscious construction of any two individuals developing a romantic and permanent partnership. In its formation and structure it is akin to Ogden's concept of the analytic third, while in dynamic action it functions similarly to Kohut's selfobject (Kohut, 1977; Ogden, 1994). The concept of the analytic third refers to the intersubjectivity of the analyst and patient—an analytic pair with two subjective realities functioning together as a dynamic whole while establishing meaning and unconscious understanding for the patient; the selfdyad refers to the unique intersubjective relationship of the permanent partnership or marriage. Like the analytic third, which cannot be replicated by another analytic pair, the selfdyad cannot be replicated by another romantic couple or permanent partnership.

With respect to its function, the reader has by this time noted that the term "selfdyad" shares with Kohut's selfobject the feature of "unhyphenation." By constructing the term in this way, I have intended to emphasize that the selfdyad functions similarly to the selfobject in the ways Kohut discussed throughout his writings. The selfdyad, then, is a hypothetical construction of two selves who, through a continuous process of exchanging mental contents and mutual shaping through projective identification, form a conjoint couple or marital system that is a modification from its individual components.

In *my* conceptualization of the selfdyad, I emphasize that for the couple to remain intimate and stable, this now revised entity must continue to provide essential affirmation for both partners for the qualities that at one time were fundamental in the construction of the relationship. Although Kohut's selfobject functions of mirroring, idealization, and twinship have usually described essential features of the mother–infant and analyst–patient pairs, these same selfobject functions are necessary for providing the affirmation required for continued closeness and intimacy. Commonly, couple and/or sexual dysfunction occurs at the time of breakdown in these essential selfobject functions—when the selfdyad no longer supports the self of one or both partners.

FROM LIBIDO TO ATTACHMENT

Although in Freud's original writings he did not discuss human attachment per se, he did address the sexual drive or the libido as a fundamental feature of human motivation. Many psychologists and psychoanalysts today believe that his construct of the libido represented his rudimentary attempt to understand attachment phenomena but that, conceptualized within his theoretical structure, there was a better fit with the accepted science of the times (Eagle, 1984; Greenberg & Mitchell, 1983). Although Freud's now outdated energic infrastructure has been discussed, critiqued, and unfortunately sometimes devalued as outmoded, a more credulous reading of his work suggests that the qualitative aspects of relationships—what psychoanalysts describe as "object relations"—were always fundamental to his thinking and in his theorizing. His theoretical constructs, however, were predicated on a structure that was aligned with the pre-Einsteinian physics extant within the scientific community at the time of Freud's career.

Scientific theories and discoveries infrequently occur by momentous leaps and bounds. More typically, scientific theories emerge gradually while theory building utilizes the tools, including the already existing theories and discoveries, preceding the investigator (Kuhn, 1962). At the time of Freud, little was known about the brain, and there was only a rudimentary psychiatry that went little beyond a primitive classification of mental disorders and gross diseases of the brain. Neurotransmitters had not yet been discovered, and most certainly there was no science of human relationships or knowledge that a connection to others was a psychobiological phenomenon that would later develop into its own science. Freud's concept of the oral stage and its implications for the infant's survival presaged what the British object relations theorists would later expand into a richer understanding of the mother–infant matrix (Klein, 1952; Winnicott, 1958).

It was not until John Bowlby, a psychoanalyst in Great Britain, came on the scene that the psychology of attachment was conceived (Bowlby, 1958, 1969). From a biological–ethological perspective Bowlby demonstrated how humans and animals attach, while providing a foundation for object relations theories and shifting the existing psychoanalytic paradigm of the times. Later, Mary Ainsworth and Mary Main, followed by others, corroborated and expanded Bowlby's writings and provided attachment theory an important niche in the history of psychology, psychoanalysis, and human development (Ainsworth, Blehan, Waters, & Wall, 1978; Main, Kaplan, & Cassidy, 1985). Finally, attachment theory, now linked with our richly textured psychoanalytic theories, including Henry Dicks's extrapolations to the psychology of interaction, has allowed us to develop a more complete perspective of Freud's seminal ideas pertaining to human connectedness.

A SYNERGY OF BOTH

In Freud's classic cases he repeatedly demonstrated that the libido having gone awry was the primary etiological factor in neurotic conditions and other forms of mental disorder. Because the science of psychoanalysis was in its infancy as Freud strove to develop a legitimate science of mind that would eventually become accepted and integrated into other fields of study, including medicine, it is not surprising that he would not develop a psychology of attachment, much less a theory of partner formation. Instead, his emphasis would be on a psychobiological concept that he called libido.

For Freud the libido described a psychic energy derived from basic and primitive urges within the body that was governed by biological influences (Freud, 1898, 1905). Although at the time of his writing there was little known about the biochemistry of hormones, specific brain functions, and their influence on sexual functioning, the libido seemed to represent a motivational construct that simultaneously implied a biological basis to its existence. Even today, in the fields of psychology, psychotherapy, and medicine, the term "libido" continues to be used in describing qualities pertaining to sexuality when referring to the strength of the sexual drive, as well as the role played by sexuality in a patient's unconscious mental life. There is no denying the importance of the libido and its biological substrates for a more comprehensive understanding of sexual functioning and its significance for partner formation. Were it not for these psychoendocrinological influences propelling the sexual drive, partner formation and ultimately the animal kingdom would cease to exist.

The psychology of attachment has demonstrated that not just the libido drives the species toward propagation; the need for contact and closeness to another has equal importance. Attachment plays an essential role in partner formation, as well as ensuring the survival of the infant and ultimately the species. Libido and attachment then function synergistically, both making contributions to the development and maintenance of interpersonal bond formation.

ATTACHMENT AND THE COUPLE

Attachment theory has its roots in the work of John Bowlby (1958, 1969). Although Bowlby's original observations were not quickly embraced by academic psychology and psychoanalysis, when their applicability across the animal kingdom was eventually discovered, a new paradigm in the behavioral sciences was spawned. In addition to Bowlby's original studies, Mary Ainsworth and her now famous "strange situation" have had important implications in helping us come to understand the nature of bonding between parent and child, as well as human connection in general (Ainsworth et al., 1978). More recently, psychotherapists, including couple therapists, have applied attachment theory in understanding human intimacy, helping us to better understand how couples form their bonds.

It is useful to review briefly the essence of the laboratory paradigm that came to be known as the "strange situation." Ainsworth and her coworkers conducted a study in which 12- to 18-month-old infants were allowed to play with toys with their mothers in a laboratory environment. A stranger was then introduced into the room who later interacted with the child when the mother left the room. Sometime later, the stranger left and the mother returned; the entire process was observed by the researchers. The experimenters determined that how the various infants responded to the mother's reentry into the room differentiated the quality of attachment to the mother.

"Securely attached" infants interacted freely with the stranger and continued to explore the environment freely while in the mother's presence. Although the child would get upset upon the mother's departure, these children would quickly and easily calm upon her return. Two kinds of "insecurely attached" infants were observed. The "anxious resistant" infants were those who appeared to cling to the mother and were distressed upon her departure. Upon the mother's return, these children were not easily calmed and often resisted her when she returned. "Anxious avoidant" infants demonstrated questionable attachment. They did not show overt signs of distress when the mother left and did not pursue contact upon her return to the room. Later, Mary Main and her research group (1985) added a fourth group that has come to be known as "disorganized." These children would respond with a disorganized form of behavior, sometimes approaching the mother at the time of the reunion and then changing strategy by pulling away or dropping to the floor.

Perhaps one of the most important elaborations of this research paradigm has been the work on adult attachment. Main and Goldwyn (unpublished manuscript, 1994) later developed the adult attachment interview (AAI) as a way to identify representational models of attachment in adulthood. Briefly, on the AAI adults were asked to provide adjectives describing their relationship with their parents. They were then to provide memories and other information to support the choice of the adjectives. Verbal transcripts were then rated on a number of dimensions, including quality, coherence, and consistency of the narrative. Significantly, four categories of adult attachment styles were observed, paralleling the findings of Ainsworth's original findings: secure, dismissing, preoccupied, and unresolved/disorganized.

Finally, and perhaps most importantly for our purposes, investigators have more recently considered the implications of attachment styles for the quality of intimate relationships developed in adulthood. Out of this work has emerged the concept of *complex attachment,* which refers to the partners' bidirectional attachment system in which both partners depend and are depended upon. Although the data from this line of research are now just emerging, the hypothesis is that the couple's complex attachment system is influenced by both partners' internal working models of attachment deriving from early life (Fisher & Crandell, 2001). Because a couple's complex attachment has implications for both affect regulation and communication, it might also be implicated in the couple's ability to form a stable selfdyad organization.

By now, then, the field of attachment as an academic discipline has an impressive history. Recent developments have enabled psychologists to understand and treat a wider variety of emotional conditions more comprehensively—especially those involving anomalies of closeness in forming relationships, as well as various difficulties in achieving separation, autonomy, and identity. The psychology of attachment has made a significant contribution in understanding the intricacies of transference and countertransference, as well as enhancing our understanding of psychotic disorders and borderline and narcissistic conditions.

A place for attachment within the more general fields of human and animal behavior has also been established. Its link to the biological sciences, as well as its heuristic value in understanding the nature of connections in general and even the psychobiological basis of the psychotherapies, is now being considered by psychologists, psychoanalysts, and neuroscientists (Kandel, 2005; Siegel, 1999; Solms & Turnbull, 2002). Attachment theory has also provided additional explanatory power and strengthened our convictions about the more purely psychoanalytic theories of human behavior, including object relations theory, self psychology, and its derivatives of relational and intersubjectivity theory.

Furthermore, attachment theory has rendered some corrective and clarifying influences on our more classical psychoanalytic paradigms by helping us better understand what Freud might have been addressing in his drive and ego psychologies, while allowing us to investigate human relationships through all developmental stages from infancy through old age. Finally, attachment theory has now more recently enabled us to study intimate relationships, including marriage and the family system, while deepening our understanding about how and why relationship systems become disrupted (Clulow, 2001; Mikulincer, 2006).

A DISRUPTION OF ATTACHMENT: SARA AND WILLIAM

Sara called for an appointment, saying on the telephone that her attorney suggested that she seek a psychological consultation because she had been unable to come to a decision about divorce. She had made her first legal appointment nearly 1 year ago and had filed for divorce soon after. However, on each occasion that she was given a court date she would ask her lawyer to file an extension with the court. Sara expressed considerable urgency in coming in to see me, saying that her attorney had admonished her that unless she pressed on with her divorce she would have to refile with the court while incurring additional expenses.

Sara commented further that she likely would be coming without her husband, as he had been opposed to any kind of therapy. She quickly added, however, that she would attempt to persuade him because she was usually able to convince him after he first opposed her. Here I noted that Sara's remarks about her husband contained a slight tone of mockery, while also reflecting some aggression in her style of relating. Not surprisingly, Sara arrived at the session accompanied by her husband, William.

Whether the individual or the couple presents for the initial appointment is almost always significant. The question about who would show up for the appointment certainly reflected the uncertainty of the marriage, and I also noted in Sara's brief introduction a conviction that, in spite of William's reluctance, she would likely persuade him to come to the session. Here I found myself not as much interested in who might ultimately come to the appointment as I was intrigued with what appeared to be Sara's forcefulness and its implications for their relationship.

Sara's phone introduction, with her staccato-like diction and well-articulated presentation, conveyed an intensity that gave rise to my own desire to respond to her out of obedience, rather than my more usual desire to help. Noting my acquiescence to her, I already wondered about her need to control, and to what extent my initial reaction to her might forecast some understanding of the actual problem for which Sara was coming to see me. Her remarks and her style certainly reflected her assertion, but perhaps also a penchant for getting her own way, with a thinly veiled sense of aggression that appeared officious.

Sara was a 44-year-old woman who had married her husband right out of high school. William, just 2 years older, had always worked in a successful family business that, by this time, had afforded them a comfortable lifestyle. Their four children were nearly grown and were doing quite well. Sara explained that she had been unhappy in her relationship for nearly the entirety of their marriage. She went on to say that her discontent centered on William's "unwillingness to talk." "He just doesn't talk," she repeated, to be certain that I clearly understood her complaint and that William did also. She proceeded to describe his eagerness to be on the golf course and his easy and affable nature with acquaintances, friends, and extended family, while she reaped none of these benefits. William provided her little conversation, and he was seldom of help around the house or with their children.

Sara proceeded to say that she had grown up in a family in which there was almost constant bickering, fighting, and turbulence between her parents, often in the context of her father's excessive drinking. There was no affection between her parents and little bestowed on her or her older brother, who today was an alcoholic. She dated William during the last 2 years of high school and recalled that what attracted her to William were his calm demeanor and the warm relationship she developed with William's parents, siblings, and large extended family. Sara offered the hypothesis that the calm atmosphere provided by William and his family, with their loving and welcoming environment, provided her a sense of security and safety that she had never known while living in her own home. She recalled that she much preferred being with William and his family than being in her home with her parents.

Noting Sara's spontaneous excursion into the early relationship with William, described as comfortable because it was "calm," I interrupted her by asking, "In those early days, did he talk more?" "Not really," Sara replied with no hesitation, "but I enjoyed being around him anyway because he listened to me, especially when I complained about my father. When I was with him and his family, it showed me how families should really be." "Quiet and loving, and without conflict and tension, you mean," I clarified. "Yes," Sara replied.

Within these first few minutes with Sara and William, while not yet having heard a single word from William, I was beginning to develop some hypotheses about the architecture of this couple's relationship, along with some impressions about their respective contributions to their selfdyad. This would become better understood, I thought, when I was able to hear from William.

Having had a substance-abusing parent, Sara had grown up in a family characterized by turbulence and conflict. Already she had described what appeared to be a highly conflictual family background in which she had likely developed a form of insecure attachment to one and possibly both parents (Ainsworth et al., 1978; Crowell & Treboux, 2001). She recalled the tumult in her family, as well as the lack of affection from both parents. She then met William, who at one time listened to her as she discussed her family problems, while providing an atmosphere of tranquility in which Sara could feel more comfortably and securely attached. The closeness to William and his family, with their loving and welcoming qualities, provided Sara a place of protection where she could safely complete her adolescence and finally enter into adulthood by marrying William.

Sara sought to find in William a part of herself that she experienced as incomplete. At one time William adequately provided her those needed qualities of calm and affirmation, while his family served as a refuge from her more troubled and chaotic family life. By providing a warm and affectionate presence and a listening ear, although always more taciturn, William originally provided Sara a relationship and a surrogate family environment in which she could feel safely comforted and more securely attached.

The adult intimate partnership serves as a place of refuge where both partners can feel safe and in some instances even provides a space for the partners to rework developmental difficulties, wounds, and traumas. In the couple relationship both partners are able to depend on each other, much like the infant or toddler who is able to be comforted when turning to the parent at times of distress. Similarly to this original paradigm of the mother who presents herself as an available and reliable person who soothes and reassures the young child at times of distress, the adult intimate partnership functions in a bidirectional manner, where both partners provide for the other the experience of being supported, reassured, and comforted at times of difficulty or distress.

Fisher and Crandell (2001) have applied Bowlby's original attachment concept to their work with couples. Somewhat different from Bowlby's original paradigm of the immature offspring and a mother functioning as a pair, the concept of complex attachment instead describes a unique feature of the adult intimate partnership where both partners move flexibly between the roles of depending *on* the partner and being depended on *by* the partner. Crowell and Treboux (2001) have referred to this characteristic of the adult intimate partnership as the "secure base" in which each person is able to depend and be depended on, to soothe and be soothed, to reassure and be reassured, while flexibly exchanging these roles and positions.

Although Sara appeared to have a great deal more to say, I was aware that William had spoken only a few words since arriving for the appointment. He sat quietly during Sara's opening, while shifting about in his chair with an apparent sense of discomfort. I had the impression of an adolescent in church who was required by his parents to be present out of obligation and was eager to get this over with. I now turned to William to invite his reactions to Sara's remarks. It was here that he surprised me with a question that he directed to me. Boldly, he asked, "Are you a golfer?" Puzzled about what at the very least seemed to be a non sequitur, I responded predictably, "Why do you ask?" I was quite certain that his reasons for asking what seemed to be an outlandish question in a first consultation would ultimately shed some light on understanding this couple and William's contribution to the difficulties that had brought them here.

William subsequently responded to my question, quite likely aware that it was irrelevant whether I was a golfer and probably something he was not especially interested in knowing anyway. "When you step onto that course, knowing that you'll be there for 3 or 4 hours, that you don't have to talk to anyone if you don't want to, there is a sense of peace and tranquility that comes over you that you can't get in very many places," he said. At this point, I hypothesized that the peace that he was craving was a reaction to the turbulence that existed in his relationship with Sara. I also thought about Sara's description of William's taciturn style and the peace and harmony of his family of origin, all of which she had found highly salutary in her teenage years, but which now left her feeling lonely, abandoned, and without the support of the secure base that Crowell and Treboux described.

William proceeded to emphasize how important it was for him to have his quiet time. He commented that his work was frequently stressful and that discussions with Sara were frequently unpleasant, especially at those times when he arrived home late in the afternoon and she bombarded him with her demands and requests for one thing or another. Because I had already heard something about William's family of origin, here I chose to ask him about his memories of their early relationship. He recalled that he enjoyed being with Sara because she "talked so much." Cracking a somewhat tentative smile, he proceeded to describe how Sara was able to talk continuously while he mostly listened, merely asking a question here and there. He said:

I guess I always sensed that she wanted me to listen to her and that I was easily able to do. I was always kind of shy and had a lot of trouble talking to people. She could talk to anybody, so when we would go out to parties or school activities, I somehow felt that it was much easier when I was with Sara. Then I felt included by the other kids, and I didn't have to worry about whether people wanted me around.

With some additional encouragement, William proceeded to shed additional light on his shyness, which more accurately could be described as his anxiety in social relationships. He went on to say that he was the third child in a family of four children. The two eldest children were twins, 2 years older than William. Both were developmentally delayed with cerebral palsy because they had been born prematurely. The children required a great deal of care by both his mother and father. As William described the complications and time spent by his parents in dealing with two impaired siblings, it was becoming clear to me that William had likely experienced some neglect of his own developmental needs, a function of having a burdened mother who had to care for two special-needs children. Now I thought that William too had experienced a form of insecure attachment, which likely had important implications for his social anxiety, as well as his difficulties in relating to Sara.

William went on to describe in some detail the frequent visits that his parents and his brothers would make to the pediatricians and neurologists in nearby cities, while he remained behind in the care of relatives. The family's focus on the medical care of his brothers would continue for a number of years until their medical problems had stabilized and they were eventually placed into permanent custodial care outside the home.

William's description of this highly relevant background information struck me as both enlightening and sad. In his presentation I was struck by the somewhat flat and affectively detached way by which he related his history. His style of communicating was discursive, with many detours and a lack of clarity requiring me to clarify many details and the chronology of events. I began to consider that, while growing up in a family in which there was considerable focus on impaired children, William had likely developed a dismissing form of insecure attachment and had come to experience a hopelessness in getting dependency needs met (Main et al., 1985). Down-regulating and disavowing painful emotions in his relationship with his parents likely became a characteristic way of relating to others in close relationships. Shyness and social anxiety became symptomatic outcomes as functions of a desire to depend while simultaneously fearing it.

The attachment subsequently formed with Sara during their courtship, in part because of her loquacity and vivacious style, provided William a conduit into social groups that would embrace him. The selfdyad with Sara had been highly important in shoring up a fragile self that might otherwise have collapsed, albeit a self that emerged as shy and socially anxious. Early in the relationship with Sara he could experience himself as more relaxed and open, while having avenues into social groups and peers who would accept him.

William had now provided the other half of highly relevant developmental data, allowing me a more complete understanding of the selfdyad that he and Sara had constructed. Both Sara and William had family backgrounds with circumstances setting the stage for developing insecure attachments with one or both parents. Their selfdyad had at one time functioned as a secure base in which they were able to form a complex attachment permitting them both to function better together than individually. William's calm and quiet demeanor, in part a product of his shyness and low self-esteem, provided Sara an accepting and welcoming atmosphere in which she could express herself without fear. Sara's more gregarious qualities provided William a pathway into social groups and also a means of more open expression, which he was unable to accomplish on his own. Their selfdyad functioned for them in the beginning of their relationship as a medium for psychological stability, providing them a secure base where both had the opportunity to rework and repair their respective developmental difficulties and traumas.

THE SELFDYAD BREACH

The couple therapist, as with the individual therapist, must always address the breaking point of the relationship after which one or both partners no longer feel sustained and enhanced by the partnership. The point at which couple dissatisfaction appears is an essential diagnostic feature that should always be assessed by the therapist.

Why, after 26 years, had Sara and William just now come to their breaking point? There had been no previous couple or individual therapy for either, and their couple relationship and family life had evolved in such a way that they were able to raise their children and prosper financially. Although Sara emphasized that she had been unhappy for nearly the entire time of their marriage, I had the impression that the relationship between her and William had been able to survive, maybe even comfortably, because of the emotional support provided by William's extended family.

Because the selfdyad is co-constructed, with contributions by two partners who function in their roles to sustain and enhance each other in a synergistic way, it is inherently fragile. And because maintaining a role in family life is partially a function of environmental circumstances, the selfdyad can easily become disrupted as a function of changing life circumstances and changes in relationship patterns occurring within the nuclear and extended families. These environmental influences and changes include traumas, losses, deaths, health crises, job changes, the addition of family members, relocations, children departing the home or entering school, and other environmental alterations that can affect the nuclear family, one or both partners, the children, and even extended family members. When either partner is affected in a way that alters the ability to function in the role—sometimes the very role that was instrumental in forming the original partnership—the selfdyad can become disorganized by the emotional disruptions occurring within the extended family system.

These altered relationships have the capacity to influence attachment patterns of the partners, while disrupting the selfdyad. The breach might then be expressed as couple dissatisfaction or dysfunction, emotional symptoms in a partner, or even symptoms in a child. The therapist must then be highly attuned to the intricacies and significance of the relationship subsystems existing within the extended family and their impact on the couple and the nuclear family (Bowen, 1978; Kerr & Bowen, 1988).

Sara had functioned quite well for many years in the traditional role as a wife and mother living in the suburbs, driving children to and from their activities, while serving on various boards in a variety of community organizations. She had a small group of friends and was active in her church, all while she, William, and the children dutifully attended the obligatory family gatherings of William's large extended family of parents, aunts, uncles, and cousins. Sara had not worked outside the home and had no formal education beyond high school. Although her lack of a higher education had posed no apparent difficulty for her during the years that her children were young, she now entertained fantasies of getting a job and attending college. She attributed these new interests to her loneliness, William's unavailability, and especially his uncommunicative style.

I privately mused that William had been quiet and uncommunicative for the entirety of their relationship. Why, now, was Sara more apparently bored and depressed? Because two of the children were still at home while keeping her quite busy, I wondered about the possibility of other changes within the social surround that might additionally contribute to her dissatisfaction. It was here that I asked, "Is there anything else, either in your relationship as a couple or in the family, that might have changed within the last several years?" Following a long pause and an immediate tearing in William's eyes, he responded softly that his mother had died suddenly last year. He said that both he and Sara had been close to her and that Sara would visit her sometimes two or three times weekly for lunch or coffee. Sara quickly added that she deeply missed talking with her mother-in-law in the way she had not been able to do with her own mother.

I came more fully to understand how it was that Sara and William's selfdyad was no longer sustaining them as it had over the years. Although the death of William's mother represented a painful loss of a significant attachment figure for both, for Sara especially her mother-in-law's death resurrected the pain of her traumatic family background, which had been partially compensated by her attachment to William's mother. The loss of this attachment figure activated an unconscious link with her unavailable mother, now liberating a preoccupied/insecure state of mind. While their selfdyad had been reasonably stable for a number of years, its previous functionality and constancy had been partially attributable to Sara's relationship with a mother-in law who had functioned as a surrogate for her mother.

Following the loss of William's mother, Sara began looking to William to provide the attachment security that was no longer fulfilled. Her intensified need for the secure base of the couple relationship and her anger at William for failing to provide it now resulted in relationship upheaval in a way that William was unable to tolerate. His withdrawal, which now included more retreats to the golf course and even less emotional availability, represented an exacerbation of his dismissive attachment style—a reaction to Sara's increased needs for more support. Furthermore, William's unmet needs for support from the unavailable mother of his youth were now revived as a function of his mother's death, while Sara's barrage of angry demands further disrupted their relationship. Now the secure base of their marriage was at a virtual low ebb.

In considering combined attachment styles of marital partners and their implications for treatment, Fisher and Crandell have provided an overview of common and expected clinical patterns of couples presenting for treatment. In their descriptions of the dismissing/dismissing, preoccupied/preoccupied, and the dismissing/preoccupied patterns, they found the latter to be most frequently represented in the clinical setting. Here the preoccupied partner frequently complains of emotional abandonment as the dismissing partner pulls away to avoid further involvement while rejecting that partner's dependency. From an object relations perspective, each partner's insecurely attached part object is projected onto the other, while both partners play out one side of the shared unconscious problem with dependency (Fisher & Crandell, 2001; Scharff & Scharff, 1991). The dismissing/preoccupied attachment pattern aptly described Sara and William's shared conflict, which contributed to their inability to sustain the secure base of their marriage.

In this chapter we have elaborated our understanding of the psychology of the couple by addressing how and why couples develop their bonds. By deepening our understanding of attachment phenomena we are better equipped to understand the unconscious dynamics occurring between two individuals—that is, why an individual is unconsciously motivated to find a partner who is able to contain those parts of the self requiring repair or compensation.

By considering the film *Jerry Maguire* and looking into the lives of Sara and William, we have hopefully come to better understand how and why the selfdyad is formed—an entity offering both partners an opportunity to contain and heal those emotional lesions and deficiencies of self that are inevitable for us all. In this chapter I have emphasized that the need for attachment continues throughout the entire life span. For the adult person, marriage, as well as other forms of permanent partnerships, is a state in which the individual has the potential to modify, adapt, and work through the vicissitudes of conflicts as well as developmental wounds and traumas. In the following chapter, by drawing from other fields of study, we will address some of the additional variables pertaining to partner formation as a way of more comprehensively understanding the intricacies of maintaining an enriching partnership that is simultaneously in support of the self.

4

MARRIAGE AND OTHER LOVING PARTNERSHIPS
An Interface of Psychology, Biology, and Sociology

The institution of marriage has existed throughout history. Depending upon the person or the discipline describing it, however, the definition and parameters vary considerably. The 10th edition of *Merriam–Webster's Collegiate Dictionary* (1993) defines marriage as "the institution whereby men and women are joined in a special kind of social and legal dependence for the purpose of founding and maintaining a family." Although at first blush Mr. Webster's definition appears to be quite comprehensive, our contemporary world might now view it as outmoded, unenlightened, or even homophobic. While the disciplines of sociology, law, theology, and psychology define and describe their unique parameters of marriage, there also exist more nuanced versions, depending upon personal ideologies and one's unique developmental history. All these variables affect one's definition of and attitudes about traditional marriage, gay marriage, and other alternative forms of civil union as ways to provide equivalent social and legal advantages for those who are permanently partnered.

In this chapter we will consider the institution of marriage by looking through the lens of other disciplines. Although a psychological model of the partnering process prevails as a way of understanding the dynamics of the intimate couple, whether married or unmarried, to address how other disciplines have contributed to understanding marriage permits us a richer understanding of the commonalities shared by marriage and cohabitation, as well as the differences between them.

LEGAL DEFINITION

In early times marriage was considered to be a business arrangement in which the woman was regarded as a piece of property that was given to a man or his family, purchased, or even bartered. This kind of arrangement presumed the subservience of the woman to the man and frequently her subjugation by him as well. The arrangement was considered permanent and could only be altered by the death of the spouse. Marriage during these times may or may not have included the sanctioning by clergy or a religious ceremony. Although the arranged marriage is now infrequent in the Western world, it is still practiced in other parts of the globe.

The legal definition of marriage emphasizes a contractual union of a man and a woman that is sanctioned by the state and by law. It cannot be terminated except through legal means. From the legal perspective there is an assumption that the arrangement entails a merger of two lives, which includes the co-ownership of income, possessions, and any children born of that union. Contemporary Western marriages are generally consensual today, while in other parts of the world arranged marriages still exist. Because in Western culture there is usually equality between the man and the woman in making the decision to marry, it is less likely that the marital state will necessarily remain permanent. Accordingly, in the Western world there is an increase in the use of divorce as the legal means to terminate the relationship when one or both parties no longer wish to remain in their contract.

RELIGIOUS DEFINITION

From a religious standpoint marriage entails and becomes finalized through a ceremony conducted by a clergyman whose function is to make explicit the couple's vows to each other, emphasizing their rights and obligations to each other throughout the life cycle. The religious ceremony emphasizes the spiritual component of promises that must be made to each other that include sexual fidelity, loyalty, and kindness. The couple's promises to each other include a covenant with God as an additionally binding feature of the sacred contract.

SOCIOLOGICAL DEFINITION

Sociologically, the institution of marriage emphasizes the couple as the foundation of a potentially larger family unit with a structure composed of a father, mother, and the children born into that family. The family unit provides a medium for care, shelter, and nurturance, as well as the guidance and learning that are necessary for children. In addition to its implications for raising the children, the sociological perspective of marriage emphasizes that the family unit and its members all function according to roles and expectations. Although the modern world has effected significant revisions in the traditional roles for men and women—reflected, for example, in the sharp increase in women working outside the home and the concomitant rise in two-income families—there still remains a fundamental expectation within most cultures that women will assume the primary role of nurturing and protecting the children, while men fulfill the role of the breadwinner who protects his wife and children.

A subset of the sociological definition is the anthropological. From this perspective, marriage and the family unit have existed throughout civilization. Their survival through time might be explained as examples of Carl Jung's concept of collective unconscious. Unlike the personal unconscious, Jung regarded the collective unconscious to be an aspect of the mind that is not unique to any one individual, but is instead shared among all mankind. It is passed down through the ages specifically because it is required for the survival of the species (Jung, 1968). As the family unit expands with the birth of children, the man and the woman will often further divide, distribute, and enact their roles as caretakers, providers, and teachers of their children, ultimately ensuring the survival, well-being, and growth of the children.

The sociological–anthropological perspective of marriage presumes that the partnership between a man and a woman is the foundation of a potentially larger family unit as children are born of that union. Furthermore, it is connected to a wider extended family unit of grandparents, uncles, aunts, and cousins. The extended family potentially provides additional structure and support for the couple as well as for the children born into the nuclear family. The family unit in its entirety, according to the sociological formulation, is provided its foundation, form, various functions, and role designations by virtue of the marriage as the legally regulated and sometimes religiously prescribed institution that confers it as a cultural entity and an adult stage of life.

PSYCHOLOGICAL DEFINITION

A psychological perspective of marriage, the subject of this book, entails a more extensive set of constructs and functions. The psychological viewpoint does not preclude the preceding perspectives. Instead, it assumes that marriage, in contrast to other forms of permanent partnering, is given its structure and form in part because of the theological, sociological, and legal aspects previously described, all playing crucial and mutually supporting roles in conferring its status. The legal contract of marriage, for example, provides for the individual's expectation of permanence to the relationship, without which relationship difficulties and the inevitable hardships of life might otherwise undermine. The ceremonial and religious rites of marriage, including vows taken before friends and relatives emphasizing promises to each other and to a deity, further reinforce the expectation that marriage is to be both a permanent and a durable partnership.

Finally, contained within most marital vows and religious rituals are statements pertaining to commitments and promises of fidelity that must be honored throughout the couple's life, emphasizing the importance of mutual caretaking and support through sickness and in health as the couple encounters the vicissitudes of life. Without these sociological, legal, and in some cases religious aspects of marriage to support the foundation of the family unit, family life would have less structure and durability, reducing the sense of permanence and safety that would otherwise support and encourage the guidance, health, and welfare of the children.

Although we have described marriage from the legal, sociological, and religious standpoints and considered their implications for a psychological model of marriage, it must be emphasized that understanding how and why couples actually form and maintain their bonds, the central theme of this book, is not limited to married couples only. The psychological model applies to all couples who have defined themselves as a permanent and intimate partnership, regardless of a marital contract or a religious ceremony to sanction its status. Although it might be that the unmarried couple lacks the contractually imposed permanence of the married couple, the psychological dynamics and unconscious processes involved in establishing intimacy, developing emotional bonds, and maintaining attachment occur with or without marriage, whether homosexual or heterosexual. For purposes of our discussion, then, we are less interested in whether a couple is legally married than in whether the two individuals have defined themselves as an intimate, exclusive, and permanent partnership.

MARRIAGE VERSUS COMMITTED COHABITATION

We have established that marriage has acquired its status as a cultural institution through a network of mutually supporting bodies of thought, all of which have contributed to imprinting it into culture, society, and the minds of mankind. Today, however, as a function of an evolving society with its increased sexual freedom and alternative forms of its expression, marriage is down in popularity. Young people are waiting longer to marry; some choose to fulfill attachment needs and sexual intimacy through an alternative form of committed cohabitation that provides at least some structure to the relationship with its accompanying role expectations for the partners.

Although developing according to the same psychological principles as those for married partners, these forms of committed unmarried partnerships, lacking the legal and religious sanctions to support and make explicit the boundaries, rights, requirements, and moral obligations, also have some differences. Unmarried partnerships, although sometimes enduring for long periods of time, in general lack the infrastructure of permanence, the quality of resilience, and, of course, the feature of common ownership inherent to marriage. As an example, it is quite typical for couples of committed cohabitation to retain private ownership of personal property while separating financial matters, although any one couple might choose to own a home or another piece of property jointly as an exception. With the exception of a handful of states, no laws provide tax or other legal advantages for unmarried partners. The birth of a child as a progressive step in the life of the family is less likely or expected, although more gay and lesbian couples are today adopting a child.

Because there is no universal governance of unmarried partnerships and generally few ceremonial rites of passage to install them, these partnerships lack the expectation and the criterion of permanence that the marital state otherwise bestows. And because the institution of marriage, with its parameters defined by culture, law, and religion, provides a format and a set of expectations prescribing the eventual expansion of the family, couple conflict is more likely when unmarried partners' goals diverge from one another. Tricia and David were such a couple.

Tricia and David

Tricia and David, a couple in their early 30s, arrived a few minutes late for their first appointment. When ushering them into my consultation room I could easily discern Tricia's icy demeanor and anger toward David. David cast me a glance of discomfort as he walked behind Tricia. He began speaking by apologizing for their lateness, saying that he had to make a stop on his way home before picking up Tricia for the appointment. He quickly added that he had to pick up his Corvette before the dealership closed for the afternoon. In doing so he was late in meeting Tricia, who had cancelled her afternoon work schedule to come for the appointment. He knew that she was angry with him because she felt that his lateness represented his lack of commitment to their relationship and his objection to making this appointment.

Tricia and David were unmarried partners who had been living together for nearly 2 years. Tricia was a stockbroker for a large investment firm, and David worked as a pharmaceutical salesperson. David went on to say that for the past several months they had been discussing the possibility of marriage, but that recently he had been questioning whether it was necessary to get married when their lives together were working quite well. He went on to say that he and Tricia both made excellent salaries that permitted them to travel and to enjoy the many luxuries provided by two incomes.

Tricia interrupted David at this moment, saying emphatically that her years of fertility were waning and that she had been feeling some urgency to establish themselves as a family so that they could have a baby. Now David interrupted, adding that marriage entailed only "a piece of paper" and that today enlightened couples could have the same advantages without the contract or the ring. He proceeded to offer slightly different versions of the same argument, each time sounding more naïve and unconvincing, making the point that they could have a baby anyway because many children today have both a father and mother who live together but without the "trappings of marriage."

The use of the word "trappings" captured my attention. I wondered how it was that David had come to view marriage as a trap while Tricia considered marriage to be a step in the progression of a relationship. As a caveat, prior to marriage and often during the engagement period itself, most couples will discuss and openly dream about their future together, sometimes even planning the progression of their relationship. During the engagement period, the couple's goals, aspirations, and divergent expectations and disagreements usually become explicit, clarified, and then often resolved, permitting the couple to move forward into marriage with a sense of mutuality.

Because there had been no engagement period or previous discussions about marriage before moving in together, Tricia and David had accomplished none of the preparatory psychological work that typically occurs with couples entering marriage. As they continued cohabitating, their relationship deepened, with their individual goals and aspirations becoming more explicit but also divergent. Finally, they had developed an impasse with open conflict over whether they would get married, threatening the continuation of their relationship.

David went on to say that he had grown up in a divorced home with his mother and two older sisters. He spent time with his father on occasional weekend visits. When invited to tell me about his relationships with his family members, David commented that he had always gotten along well with his sisters, but that his mother was quite dependent and often difficult to deal with. He added that when he was growing up his sisters doted on him and met his every need. As he grew older and after his sisters had left home, his mother expected him to be the "man of the house," requiring him to make household repairs, pay bills, and do other errands that he now felt were unreasonable for a boy his age. He recalled that he frequently listened to his mother's laments about his errant and irresponsible father, while she implored David to become a "better man."

In his younger years David enjoyed taking care of his mother, flattered by her laudatory remarks about his capabilities. When later she actively objected to his going away to attend college, he came to realize that she had been controlling him through her dependency. He added that since he had left home he had come to think that his mother's demands and her dependency were likely reasons that his father eventually left her.

I now felt that I could identify a fundamental ingredient in their relationship impasse. I commented to them that I thought it was very likely that David feared that, if he and Tricia were to solidify their relationship through marriage, he might once again experience himself as trapped—no longer with a controlling mother, but instead within the confines of marriage and a wife who unconsciously represented the mother who drove his father away. I further added that Tricia might also feel that, unless she maintained the pressure on David to marry, he could possibly leave her as David's father left him and his mother. David fell silent, while Tricia quickly protested that she was not like David's mother in any way, but was instead a very "independent woman" who was quite capable of taking charge of her life, managing their finances, and assuming all household responsibilities without making any demands on David. "Furthermore," she said with thinly veiled hostility and a raised eyebrow, "who is really the responsible one here—the one who takes care of our personal life while you're off driving your sports car and taking your golf trips?"

Tricia proceeded to explain that she had grown up in a hard-working, conservative Catholic home. She had always worked hard and took considerable pride in her career and what she had achieved on her own. She added that it would be unacceptable to her and to her family for her to remain with David and have a baby without getting married and establishing a family life first. Although her parents did not openly object to their cohabitation, she knew that it was very much in opposition to their sense of morality.

With ongoing couple therapy David and Tricia were able to resolve their conflict about getting married while eventually establishing a more balanced partnership. As David was able to work through his fears of becoming ensnared by a woman, Tricia in turn was able to reduce the pressure on him to get married. As Tricia's urgency and her fears that David would leave her subsided, David in turn became more comfortable with closeness while he began to assume greater responsibility in the relationship. He reduced the frequency of his golf trips, sold his sports car, and began to share in the excitement as they made plans for their marriage.

The case of David and Tricia illustrates how marriage itself serves to initiate, sanction, and legitimize the life of the family as the two individuals become unified as a couple. Their situation further demonstrates how a couple's disagreement on whether they will marry can be symptomatic of more significant underlying conflict, ultimately affecting the survival of the relationship. As the pressure mounted for David and Tricia to marry, their unconscious conflicts and developmental issues surfaced. Couple therapy was instrumental in helping them both to elucidate and work through the crucial determinants of their life histories that were affecting their ability to move forward in the adult life cycle.

IMPLICATIONS OF FORMAL SANCTIONING

Although marriage is the most prevalent form of permanent adult partnership and is fully supported and structured by law, sociology, culture, and theology, other enduring partnerships have existed throughout time. Although these relationships lack the same cultural status as marriage, unmarried heterosexual couples, as well as gay and lesbian partnerships, have recently gained in social acceptance and even have achieved legal grounding in certain states and countries throughout the world.

Although less prevalent in the United States, permanent partnerships between a married man and his mistress are not uncommon in other parts of the world. Although these relationships certainly have some unique features, including secrecy and the intermittence of contact between the partners, they also develop and function according to the same psychological principles described for marriage and other permanent partnerships.

It is important here to emphasize that throughout history the rules and regulations for the adult permanent partnership have been made explicit by the formal structure of marriage in a way that does not exist for other adult intimate partnerships. These "rules" function in an unconscious way by encouraging both individuals to assume their roles, thereby guiding and supporting the couple and ultimately the wider family as it positions itself into society. For the unmarried couple, gay or straight, without the social norms of marriage, treatment must then often entail assisting the partners to make the parameters and guiding rules of their relationship explicit. Although marriage most generally spells these out, there are some married couples whose presenting conflicts also require the therapist's assistance in clarifying expectations, goals, and boundaries for the relationship.

In summary, unmarried heterosexual, gay/lesbian, and man/mistress relationships have unique characteristics differentiating them from married couples, although the psychodynamics and the attachment principles governing these relationships tend to be of a similar quality. It is important for the therapist to bear these in mind because they potentially affect the durability and the permanence of the partnership. The following vignette of Jake and Carl illustrates many of these features.

Jake and Carl

Jake and Carl, a couple in their late 50s, presented for a consultation by describing a conflict that had been escalating ever since Carl had retired. They had lived together for nearly 25 years, having met and worked in the same company during this period of time. Jake had retired several years earlier and since that time had developed a computer software business that required him to store his merchandise in the penthouse they owned together. Although this had always been an inconvenience for Carl, his heavy travel schedule and time away from home had previously permitted him to tolerate the congestion. Now spending much of his time at home in their apartment pursuing his hobbies and training his new dog, Carl found it intolerable. He implored Jake to locate a storage area elsewhere, but Jake responded that he needed the merchandise to be readily available to him. As their arguments escalated Jake became less tolerant of Carl's complaints, until finally in a heated argument and in exasperation he struck Carl with his fist.

Carl explained that in recent years he had been generally content in his relationship with Jake, although now, spending more time in his home, he had been feeling more resentful for having to renounce his preferences for orderliness. Born approximately 5 months after his father's death and having grown up as an only child, Carl recalled a painfully lonely youth while living with his depressed and insecure mother and grandmother. He explained that he had been a chronically ill child with severe asthma that was not easily controlled with medications. As a consequence, he became quite dependent on his mother and grandmother. When away from them, he would become anxious, often precipitating an asthmatic attack.

Jake described a chaotic family background. He grew up in a home with his mother and his three younger sisters. Like Carl, there was no father in the home. Family life consisted of considerable turmoil with a great deal of verbal conflict among family members. Jake recalled that he had no responsibilities and was permitted to do much as he pleased. If things did not go his way, he would become angry, and on one occasion during a family argument he actually struck his sister, blackening her eye. When I asked Jake how he felt that his family circumstances had impacted him, he responded thoughtfully that his self-centeredness as a child might now make it more difficult for him to compromise with others.

Jake and Carl launched their relationship after meeting at a sales convention hosted by the company that employed them both. Within a few months they began seeing each other regularly. Jake and Carl agreed that, during the early years of their relationship, there had been considerable turmoil between them, especially around issues pertaining to Jake's pursuit of other men. Carl's usual response to this was to tolerate Jake's behavior passively while painfully waiting on the sidelines for each liaison to come to an end. On two occasions Carl developed serious depressions that required hospitalization. Both times Jake returned to the relationship, after which they made the decision to move in together. They jointly purchased their condominium and evenly divided other expenses, including food, household furnishings, and other assets.

Jake's infidelity was never discussed again, although it seemed to me that it continued to be a lingering toxic issue that was still affecting their relationship. Observing how gingerly they approached this piece of history, I found myself wondering if their relationship had the resilience for it to be brought clearly into the open. I came to learn that over the years Carl had felt highly controlled by Jake. At one point in the session, he remarked angrily, "You've always held all the cards, Jake, and even now I still put up with all your shit." Carl's statement indirectly introduced the latent problem in their relationship. Although Carl and Jake had been together nearly 25 years, ostensibly agreeing that their relationship would be exclusive, Jake had for many years persisted in his affairs while Carl resentfully waited for him. Jake had considered their relationship to be merely cohabitating, but Carl viewed it as a commitment to each other that would exclude all others.

It was now becoming clear that this couple's difficulties were partially a function of having quite disparate internal rules and values for their partnership in a way that had confused the boundaries of their relationship. Obviously, there had been no marital, legal, or religious contract to confer their relationship status. And, like many cohabitating couples, Jake and Carl had not specifically defined the boundaries of their relationship in a verbal way. As a consequence, they were left with only vague expectations and parameters to guide them in maintaining it. Without these mutually agreed upon guiding features in a permanent partnership, there is an increased probability that unresolved interpersonal, developmental, and intrapsychic issues will interfere with the relationship.

Although Jake's infidelity and the murky boundaries of their partnership were certainly problematic, I was equally struck by Carl's passive but resentful tolerance of Jake's behavior. I asked at this juncture, "So, Carl, how is it that you *have* been able to put up with Jake's shit for as long as you have?" In response Carl began to elaborate on his enduring fears of abandonment that had developed while living with a depressed and pathologically dependent mother whom he could not count on. "When I met Jake," Carl said, "I felt that I had found someone strong and reliable." Here I responded with an interpretation:

> Possibly someone who you felt would better protect you than your mother had. But I also think, Carl, that you have sacrificed a part of yourself over the years with the illusion that if you simply tolerate Jake's behavior, permitting him to hold all the cards, he then won't leave you. But the price that you've paid is to harbor your deep resentment while keeping your feelings within you. Now having retired after a rewarding career, you might feel that you want to exercise your own voice. But if you make this shift, I think it will represent a significant change for both of you and will likely take some time for you to come to some new equilibrium.

In my intervention I chose to emphasize the imbalance in their partnership by indirectly addressing Jake's breach of trust, while simultaneously speaking to Carl's difficulty with assertion as a function of his abandonment fears.

This vignette illustrates several important features pertaining to the healing functions of the adult permanent partnership. Carl and Jake's relationship structure had thus far permitted them to move through their adult lives with at least a modicum of contentment, albeit with Carl sacrificing selfhood. Their selfdyad had been constructed on the basis of Carl projecting his dependency needs, but in a manner that Jake was unable to contain. Because Carl's insecure attachment to a depressed mother had left him riddled with anxiety around independent functioning, the way was paved for an adult partnership that could either encourage or sustain his existing autonomy or worsen it. The latter seemed to be the case. While Carl had projected his unrequited dependency onto Jake, Jake in turn projected onto Carl a representation of his sisters and a mother who were held hostage by his narcissism.

For years into their relationship, Jake had continued to indulge in promiscuous sexuality as Carl stood by waiting in resentful acquiescence. At least partially sustained by his active career, Carl had been able to function with a modicum of independence while earning his living. Now that they had retired, Jake and Carl were faced with more togetherness, which would require them to remodel their relationship for this next chapter of their lives. The task would in part require the repair of old injuries, including Carl's feelings of anger about Jake's betrayals and multiple breaches of trust.

To the extent that Carl and Jake could work through these issues, a new equilibrium for their selfdyad could emerge. Couple therapy would be essential in assisting them to establish more equality in their partnership, by coming to better contain each other's needs. For now it would remain an open question as to whether Carl might also benefit from individual psychotherapy as an adjunct to the couple treatment they would now undertake.

The case of Carl and Jake illustrates how each developmental transition encountered throughout the life cycle ushers in a new phase and brings with it a brand new or an exaggerated challenge that must be negotiated by the couple. Couple therapy frequently can help to address these transitions by assisting both individuals to work through long-standing developmental issues contributing to the relationship impasse. This vignette further illustrates how the absence of marriage or other contractual union can contribute to the uncertainty of boundaries, which often includes a lack of clarity of roles, responsibilities, and expectations for the partners. Although Carl and Jake had cohabitated for nearly the entire duration of their relationship and had ostensibly agreed on an exclusive partnership, the absence of a marital contract, religious vows, and the cultural conditions accompanying these formalities had contributed to a diffusion of emotional intimacy.

THE PERTINENCE OF BIOLOGY

Having addressed the sociological, legal, and theological implications of marriage, one might wonder why a book on the psychology of couple interaction would consider biological variables as pertinent to couple formation. Although some psychologists and other behavioral scientists resist reductionistic explanations of behavioral concepts, I take the position that it is useful to consider psychological and behavioral events from multiple perspectives, including those outside mainstream science, such as law and theology, so long as the scientific purpose is served.

To address couple formation from a biological perspective serves the purpose of amplifying our understanding of how the brain and its derivative functions contribute to understanding partnering and intimacy. It is not intended to reduce or simplify the richness of this complicated process of partnering. Although it might be appropriate to discuss the breeding habits of giraffes or hyenas from the standpoint of pheromone physiology and its implications for mate finding, for humans, with the complexity of our cognitive, behavioral, and affective repertoires and our capacity for unconscious emotional processing, there exists a far more complicated investigative task that should never be reduced to brain anatomy, hormones, or neurotransmission.

NEUROBIOLOGICAL CORRELATES OF LOVE AND PERMANENT PARTNERSHIPS

Romantic Attraction: The First Ingredient

Neuroscientists have recently contributed to our understanding of various aspects of coupling and partner formation. One might argue that these findings have less practical utility in the actual work with couples in a clinical setting than do findings from a behavioral perspective. However, clinicians with an understanding of the biological underpinnings of partner formation, including the biological basis of sexual desire, attraction, and the influences of hormones and neurotransmitters, can achieve a deeper understanding of how couples relate to one another.

When considering the biological components of sexuality and romantic love, it becomes evident that no one finding fully explains the loving experience. The libido, for example, is a hypothetical construct that contributes to the phenomenon we know as attraction. And yet sexual excitement, driven by the libido and presumably its biological underpinnings, is not synonymous with attraction, romance, or attachment. Instead, all of these factors appear as ingredients in partnership formation, with no single factor individually explaining how couples come together or fail to remain in a loving partnership.

Helen Fisher, an anthropologist and highly regarded researcher in the area of romantic behavior, has devoted her career to investigating the neurobiological underpinnings of sexuality and attraction, differentiating these states and their subtle variations with the use of brain-imaging technology (Fisher, 2004; Fisher, Aron, & Brown, 2005). In a series of studies, she and her collaborators explored the neural mechanisms involved in the loving and romantic experience. Her prototypical paradigm involved the use of functional magnetic resonance imaging (fMRI) to study the role of activation in various parts of the brain when subjects were exposed to various stimuli pertaining to their romantic partners.

In one study Fisher and her group examined early intense romantic love. Her criteria for this included intrusive obsessive thinking about the loved one, empathy toward that person, a craving for emotional union, and a desire for sexual contact with that person. Using fMRI technology, the subject was exposed to a photograph of the beloved, and brain scanning was conducted to assess which areas of the brain were activated by the stimulus photograph. It was found that activation occurred primarily in the subcortex, especially the right ventral tegmental and right caudate nucleus areas. The caudate nucleus is an area of the reptilian brain associated with attention and motivation to acquire rewards. It is also the area of the brain involved in the discrimination between stimuli, preferences, and expectations. It was also found that the more passionate the subject was about the beloved who was pictured, as determined by other pretest measures, the greater the activity in the caudate nucleus was.

Fisher and her group also found that the ventral tegmental area (VTA), an area of the brain rich in dopamine receptors, was activated when subjects were exposed to stimulus photos of their respective partners. With its widespread distribution of dopamine to various regions of the brain, the VTA has been shown to be instrumental in feelings of expansiveness, elation, and excitatory states, with its vast neural network providing communication to other areas of the brain, including the caudate nucleus. From the findings the researchers concluded that this rich communicative network likely comprises the motivational system that biologically defines the core experience of romantic love. They also remind us that this physiological arousal pattern is similar to brain activation patterns of subjects experiencing an addiction and is also distinct from the libido or sex drive and sexual arousal (Fisher et al., 2005).

When Bartels and Zeki, researchers in London, looked at these same phenomena, again using the fMRI research protocol, they also found that neural activity occurred in the caudate nucleus. But unlike Fisher, they found activation in the insular cortex and the anterior cingulate cortex. A fascinating difference was revealed when comparing the two sets of studies. While Fisher's subjects had been in love for an average of

7 months, those in Bartels and Zeki's study reported a loving relationship for an average of 2–3 years (Bartels & Zeki, 2000). Here was a study that validated Fisher's data, while discovering fortuitously that more enduring love relationships activated other brain regions as well.

Replicating her study, but now changing the length of the love relationship of her subjects, Fisher corroborated the findings from the British study. Could it be then that the two research groups had discovered a neural analog for what occurs in the brain as love emerges, grows, and endures? On the basis of these findings Fisher suggested that, because the anterior cingulum is a region of the brain in which emotion, attention, and memory converge and, additionally, where mentalization—the ability to assess others' states of mind accurately—occurs, it might be that the brain, through a convergence of memory, attention, and emotion, is establishing neural templates of enduring love that are qualitatively distinct from the more purely affectively driven experience of new love.

Lust: The Second Ingredient

Although the biological basis of attraction is one feature of the loving experience, it is doubtful that the reader has forgotten that lust is also of fundamental importance. Lust here is simply defined as the desire on the part of the individual for sexual gratification. Although it is physiologically associated with an increase in circulating testosterone, it is dependent on other factors as well (Edwards & Booth, 1994). When humans are administered androgen supplementation to enhance the libido, there is no greater tendency to feel attraction or to fall in love (Nyborg, 1994). Furthermore, it has been shown that the drive for sex or the ease with which an individual is sexually aroused is dependent on a number of factors that include the balance of androgens and estrogens, other interacting biological systems, and developmental experiences including attitudes about the self, feelings about the body, and sexuality, as well as a host of environmental cues and social factors (Fisher, 2004; Fisher, Aron, & Brown, 2006).

From all the studies, Fisher and her associates concluded that although there is an interaction between the sex drive and romantic attraction, the brain systems show distinct differences. When considering the biological data together with behavioral reports, she summarized these distinctions in the following way (Fisher et al., 2006, p. 2177):

- The sex drive is focused on a specific goal, sexual union with another, and romantic love is focused on a different goal, emotional union with another.

- The sex drive is often expressed toward a range of individuals, and romantic love is focused on a particular individual.
- The sex drive is often temporarily quelled when satisfied, and romantic love does not decrease with coitus and often persists unabated for months, even years.

Although brain systems and their correlates appear to differentiate lust from attraction, subjectively they are not necessarily so distinguishable. When one is romantically attracted to one's partner, for example, a lustful response is often more easily evoked. Here Fisher offers us a biochemical explanation by reminding us that the increases in dopamine of romantic attraction can cause a rise in circulating testosterone, the hormone of sexual desire in both genders. Norepinephrine, another neurotransmitter, may also play a role in romantic love because it also increases the production of testosterone, increasing the libido as it simultaneously lowers circulating serotonin, the neurotransmitter that, at low ebb, is implicated in obsessional thinking. Because norepinephrine increases while lowering serotonin, we might now have a neurochemical analog for the obsessive thinking that is so often characteristic of romantic love.

Fisher speculates that, for those taking antidepressant medications in the category of selective serotonin reuptake inhibitors, the same chemistry causing the diminished libido that is frequently reported by those taking these drugs may also be responsible for the dampening of affect that occurs when the excitement and obsessive thinking about the partner diminish (Fisher, 2004). It has been observed that, in patients who take SSRIs, supplemental medications that enhance both dopamine and norepinephrine will sometimes effect an elevation in sexual desire (Fisher et al., 2006). Once again, we note a complex interaction among the emotional states of the loving experience, their underlying brain structures, and their associated neurochemical events.

Finally, although we have made distinctions between lust and romantic attraction, emphasizing their complex interactions, researchers are also investigating the more specific mechanisms involved in penile erection, vaginal relaxation and lubrication, and clitoral engorgement. Although the nitric oxide-cyclic guanosine monophosphate neurohumoral pathway appears to be implicated in the essential increased blood flow for sexual readiness for both men and women and can be enhanced with supplemental androgen therapy, the subjective experience of sexual arousal, when compared to actual clitoral engorgement, has shown a generally poor correspondence (Pfaus & Scepkowski, 2005).

These findings may explain why, even with quite aggressive medical treatments for sexual dysfunctions, which often include androgen supplementation, hormone replacement in women, and medications to enhance the nitric oxide pathway, the positive effects described on the television ads do not necessarily hold up in the bedroom. These findings once again emphasize the complexity of the interactions of subjective mental states and biology. To treat sexual dysfunctions only with medications does not then necessarily yield the positive results that the purveyors of these drugs have led us to believe. Instead, it is essential for the psychotherapist to consider the intricacies of the patient's or couple's relationship issues, including each patient's unconscious and developmental experiences, while addressing the exigencies of sexuality within the context of the relationship with the partner.

Attachment: The Third Ingredient

We know that the obsessive thinking with its intense and immediate longing of new love diminishes over time as the relationship continues and grows. As the partnership with its accompanying intimacy deepens, there is a gradual emergence of security and safety, with the desire for companionship supplanting the urgency and ecstasy of new love. Attachment, a phenomenon addressed in a previous chapter, is the third component of the loving experience, and it exists as the sine qua non for relationships that become permanent. For these continuing romantic partnerships, complex attachment processes now ensue that, from a biological perspective, have distinguishing neural correlates. But here, again, we find that attachment has overlapping components with lust and attraction. In a previous chapter we addressed the binding features of the couple relationship; here we will examine the biological correlates of attachment while clarifying the differences from lust and attraction.

In attempting to biologically investigate the distinguishing features of enduring human relationships, a group of researchers considered animal species that had been noted to be monogamous. By studying pair-bonding behavior, the animal counterpart of attachment in humans, these researchers discovered some of the biological mechanisms involved in attachment.

Oxytocin and vasopressin, hormones produced in the hypothalamic structures of the brain and in the sex organs, have been implicated in attachment behavior. Once again, Helen Fisher reported the work of a group of scientists who had injected vasopressin into the brains of male prairie voles, a rodent species known to be predominantly monogamous throughout its life cycle. With increased circulating vasopressin, the male animals began to show a possessiveness of the females, while protecting the space around the females from other males. When vasopressin was suppressed in these animals, however, they abandoned the female and searched indiscriminately for opportunities to mate with other females. The scientists also found, however, that copulation itself caused a rise in vasopressin, also increasing observable pair-bonding behavior.

These findings once again reaffirm a complex interaction between sexual behavior and pair bonding even in animals, while giving rise to more questions. For example, is it only vasopressin that contributes to monogamy, pair bonding, and attachment? After all, copulation occurs throughout the animal kingdom, while only some species remain monogamous. Nonetheless, Fisher speculates that vasopressin is a hormone that at the very least makes a contribution to the monogamy and paternal behavior seen in certain species and may also have implications for human attachment (Fisher, 2004).

Oxytocin, a hormone produced in the hypothalamus, ovaries, and testicles, has also been associated with attachment phenomena. It is also the hormone associated with maternal behavior, including the intensely loving and protective feelings that mothers have about their infants. During orgasm and sexual foreplay that includes tactile stimulation of the nipples and genitals, women demonstrate a rise in oxytocin, while men show a rise in vasopressin. Again, in reviewing this line of research, Fisher informs us that these neurochemical alterations likely contribute to the feeling of closeness that is especially apparent during and after coitus and that this is similar to the experience of closeness and fusion that mothers experience with their infants during nursing (Fisher, 2004).

When summarizing the literature investigating the neurobiological substrates of lust, attraction, and attachment, we find that there are distinct brain structures and biochemical events that accompany these components of the loving experience. There is, however, a complex interplay in which the various emotional states and neurobiological events affect each other while also interacting with environmental circumstances, biological events within the body, relationships with others, feelings about the self, and the self within the partnership—the construct I have called the selfdyad.

CLINICAL IMPLICATIONS OF
NEUROBIOLOGICAL STUDIES

When considering the preceding variables and their complex interactions, it is reaffirmed that the brain is an integrated circuit whose sum is far more complicated than its individual parts. Furthermore, having knowledge about this circuitry contributes to our understanding of the entire realm of the behavioral sciences, the action of the psychotherapies, and a psychology of interaction. One's awareness of the biological distinctions of sexual arousal, desire, attraction, and attachment enhances one's clinical acumen and sophistication when encountering the multiplicity and complexity of relationship problems found in the consulting room.

Susan and Leo

Susan and Leo called for a consultation after they were referred by their pastor, who felt that their difficulties required therapy that was beyond the services that he could provide. Susan had recently discovered that Leo had been visiting Internet pornographic sites. Although she did not feel especially judgmental about this from a moral or spiritual standpoint, it had grave implications when considering the difficulties they had been having in their sexual relationship. Susan stated that their sexual relationship had been poor for a number of years, both in its frequency and its quality. Leo had difficulty achieving and sustaining an erection. When she discovered his frequent visits to pornographic sites, she inquired of Leo whether he was able to get an erection upon looking at this material. Leo's affirmative response prompted Susan's immediate outrage, followed by a call to their pastor who at that time referred them.

Susan was furious with Leo, emphasizing the betrayal she felt. She alternated between tears and a well-articulated argument that she had been rejected by Leo because he had been choosing "big-breasted porn stars" over her. She emphasized that it felt as though she had lost the competition to women that Leo did not even know.

Leo sat quietly during Susan's diatribe, looking at the floor. He reminded me of a school-aged child being scolded by a parent for a shameful transgression while simultaneously feeling resentful. When inquiring about their backgrounds I was able to discern a great deal more about the chronic problems in their relationship. Susan had been angry at Leo for a number of years about what she felt was his ineptitude in "romantic capabilities." She commented that he was clumsy in lovemaking and took little time for her to become aroused before attempting intercourse. It was at this point that Leo broke out of his petulant silence, saying that whenever he touched her she objected to whatever he did. "No matter where I touch her, it's either the wrong place, too rough, too timid, or the wrong timing—I can't win," Leo said in an exasperated tone. Susan sat quietly, looking shocked during Leo's oration.

I silently wondered if Leo had ever previously verbalized *his* complaints about Susan. In observing his passivity during Susan's introduction, I felt quite certain that he had not. Susan now remained quiet, transfixed by Leo's forthrightness. Suddenly Leo paused, as if just noticing that he had the floor and that others were listening. Concerned that he might again freeze up, I said encouragingly, "Leo, please go on. I have the impression that you have more to say." Leo proceeded, saying that he had always adored Susan. He remarked that he was especially proud of having such a beautiful wife who was so competent in her career and in so many other ways as well. He added that he had often wondered why she ever married him, that she did not really need him, in light of the fact that she made a much higher salary and that she could undoubtedly attract men who were better looking.

Susan broke in, still amazed by what she was hearing. Her demeanor now had grown more compassionate. "Leo," she said, "before we were married you seemed so much more certain of yourself, even in our lovemaking. I don't know what has happened to you over the years." I noted that, for reasons that were not yet clear, Leo and Susan had likely established a selfdyad with Susan as the more competent partner, while Leo had become less capable. This represented a shift in their relationship that had gradually developed over the years they had been together. Leo had been unable to maintain a sense of himself as both capable and masculine, while Susan flourished in the partnership and she became more openly disappointed in Leo. Although continuing to express her upset and disappointment in Leo, all under the guise of encouragement, Susan had instead established a pattern of denigrating him, as Leo's self-esteem plummeted.

Although Susan and Leo's enduring struggles would continue to be addressed, it seemed that the crisis around the pornography now threatened the continuation of their marriage. Once this was better understood, we would resume our focus on the more chronic difficulties created by a selfdyad in which Susan had become the more competent partner, but at the expense of Leo's potency and self-esteem. But first it was essential that I address Susan's intransigent belief that Leo's indulgence in pornography was a betrayal of her and their relationship. If dealt with successfully, the crisis might be ameliorated and the way paved for couple therapy that could then address the dynamics of their selfdyad and its impact on Leo's faltering sense of self.

Recalling the neurobiological distinctions between sexual arousal and romantic attraction, I turned to Susan and said in a tone of conviction:

Susan, I think that it is important for you to tune into something that Leo has been telling you, but which I'm not certain that you have been hearing. First of all, I am very struck by both Leo's admiration of you as well as his attraction to you. It is also clear how much he has wanted to please you, though feeling that he doesn't do a very good job. I think that it is important to take notice of the fact that there is a significant disparity between his respect, admiration, and attraction to you and the arousal that can easily be achieved with the use of pornographic stimulation. They are not one and the same and should not be considered as such. Now, all that said, Leo, I also think that although you admire Susan greatly, somehow you have lost a sense of yourself in this relationship as a capable and masculine person. As a result, you have split apart arousal and its need for discharge from the attraction, admiration, and love that you have had for Susan, thus turning to pornography. As we continue to understand these issues, including how it is that you have lost your sense of self in your relationship with Susan, hopefully we can work together to put these all back together again.

By providing this somewhat lengthy verbatim intervention that addressed the most urgent crisis of this couple, I am attempting to illustrate how knowledge of the neural underpinnings of the various components of partnering can inform psychological interventions for couples in treatment. In considering Leo's use of erotic stimuli from a neurobiological standpoint, I was able to assist Susan and Leo in ameliorating their anger and shame, while showing them how Leo's arousal over pornographic material had become conflated with the overall quality of their marital relationship. For Susan, this had become tantamount to a betrayal of her. My intervention also introduced the more enduring problem of their selfdyad, which included Leo's difficulties in maintaining a sense of self within his relationship with Susan. Exploring the mutual projection process between them would most likely be the next step in the course of treatment.

FINAL THOUGHTS

In this chapter we have considered the importance of therapists having a broad view of the couple, including a multifaceted understanding of the various bodies of thought pertaining to partnerships and marriage, including the biological, legal, spiritual–religious, and sociological as well as the psychological principles pertaining to relationships.

Understanding these principles in a comprehensive way provides clinicians a richer understanding of intimate partnerships by increasing the therapist's armamentarium of techniques and interventions when working with couples.

Finally, when considering the biological components of the loving experience, including attachment, lust, attraction, and arousal, we are wise to remember that troubled individuals, couples, and families who come to us for treatment are real live examples of the circuitry of the human brain becoming disintegrated. It is the work of our psychological therapies, as we help our patients establish and deepen cognitive-affective insight, that assists them toward a reintegration of brain circuitry—the human mind in relationship with others.

5

FUNCTIONS OF SEXUALITY IN
THE ADULT PARTNERSHIP

For both children and adults, the topic of sexuality is undeniably one of universal fascination. Even when that interest is repudiated by the vicissitudes of defenses, sexuality continues to exert a profound influence on the person and his or her relationships—sometimes because of the very denial or repression that attempts to remove it. Although young children are without the cognitive maturity to embrace its significance fully, we can witness the shadow of sexuality in their behavior and in their conversations with peers and siblings. When the child enters school, we are able to observe changes in what interests him and even what he speaks about as he becomes exposed to the fascinating social world existing outside the family, including the unconscious sexuality of each and every person that he will now encounter. Beginning in infancy and then evolving and maturing through childhood into old age, sexuality will continue to exert its impact. Even as it changes in the strength of its drive with the passage of years or when interrupted during times that preclude its more usual aim, channel, or capacity for discharge, its visage is always present as it continues to exert its ineluctable influence on human motivation.

By considering some of the important theoretical contributions of Ogden, Kernberg, Chasseguet-Smirgel, and others, we will explore sexuality—primarily its subjective meaning, place, and importance for the couple. We will discuss the ways in which sexuality is able to enhance the partnership, while simultaneously having the potential to undermine and even destroy it. We will expand on how the sexual partnership is unconsciously constructed by the couple, developing as a selfdyad function. And finally, with case studies I will demonstrate how having an understanding of the unconscious meaning of the couple's sexuality can provide guidelines for the therapist as he works with the couple to make changes that might be essential to the selfdyad and ultimately to the survival of the relationship.

The couple's sexuality is an unconscious composite of both partners' individual sexuality, including their psychological histories, character structure, inner objects, defensive organization, and Oedipal configurations. Within the partners' unconscious minds also lie the parents' and grandparents' sexuality, as well as the remote developmental antecedents lingering from their multigenerational lineage (Bowen, 1978; Kerr & Bowen, 1988). The sexuality of the couple is then a most complex entity whose intricacy far exceeds the hormonal and other biological variables discussed in the previous chapter.

With the proliferation of public interest in human sexuality, perhaps beginning with Sigmund Freud's brilliant studies over a century ago and followed many years later by Alfred Kinsey's and Masters and Johnson's work, the Western world has been caught up in a sexual revolution (Freud, 1905; Kinsey, 1948, 1953; Masters & Johnson, 1966). Browsing any bookstore or library, one cannot fail to notice the vast number of books and sex manuals filling the shelves of the medicine and health, psychology, and self-help sections. The misinformed thesis contained within many of these works is that proper sexual techniques, including creative sexual gymnastics, in conjunction with a fine wine and the proper array of alluring lingerie and aromatic candles will yield sexual and relationship bliss. Clinical evidence, however, demonstrates otherwise.

In this chapter I will emphasize how mutually satisfying sexuality of the couple functions like a relationship glue in which the private and exclusive physical-somatic component of the relationship bridges the gap of the mind and the body to form what psychoanalysts have called the psychosomatic partnership (Scharff & Scharff, 1991). I will show how the couple's psychological functioning affects the sexual relationship, while, conversely, the quality of the couple's sexual functioning affects the couple's interpersonal and psychological functioning, by demonstrating how that vital balance of being a self and being a couple is what governs relationship satisfaction.

SEXUALITY IN PERSPECTIVE

In the previous chapter we studied the individual features of the love relationship by differentiating the neural correlates of romantic attraction, lust, arousal, and attachment. In this chapter we will consider the sexuality of the couple as a gestalt of subjective experience, replete with unconscious meaning for the partners individually and for the couple as an integrated system. A focus on the subjectivity of the couple constitutes the work of the psychotherapist by teasing out the personal meaning of the component parts of the couple's sexuality. While one patient or couple might present with an inhibition of sexual arousal and orgasm based primarily on unresolved Oedipal difficulties with the opposite-sexed parent, another might present with a similar symptom as a defense against closeness, to maintain a safe distance from the partner who is unconsciously identified as a parent who failed to permit a healthy separation. In the latter case inhibition protects against the terror of psychological fusion.

In this chapter we will enlarge our understanding of sexuality by considering its unconscious meaning for the couple and how it supports or fails to enhance the partnership while it simultaneously remains tuned in to the overall relationship like a biopsychological computer monitoring the couple's psychological health. Through clinical vignettes I will illustrate how various couples have structured their selfdyads. Some integrate sexuality with greater ease and comfort, while others remain on the slippery slope of discontent with a foreboding that is capable of destroying passion, commitment, and permanence.

Although it is commonly assumed by laypersons and sometimes therapists too that sexuality is normally pleasurable simply because it involves the erogenous areas of the body, there is no assurance that any one aspect of sexual behavior or tactile stimulation will be predictably comfortable or erotic for every person or couple coming for treatment. Sometimes these assumptions of universal pleasure have led to recommendations and treatments for sexual difficulties using behavioral techniques that are isolated from the couple's relationship difficulties, their unconscious meanings, and their implications for the couple's sexual functioning. Here the outcome of treatment is often disappointing or at least short lived. Instead, an understanding of the unconscious aspects of the couple's sexuality, its component parts, and primitive meanings—rather than an isolated focus on the sensory qualities and arousal patterns—must become the working area for the clinician treating couples and their sexual issues.

Tom and Judy

Tom and Judy, physicians in their late 30s, had been married for 2 years; both had been married previously. They had a 4-year-old daughter from Judy's previous marriage. Their difficulties centered on Judy's desire to have another child as soon as possible. Their urgency stemmed from the awareness that Judy's years of safe fertility were waning. Furthermore, they wanted another child so that their daughter could have a sibling to grow up with; Tom and Judy were only children who both recalled their desire to have a sibling when growing up.

Although Tom shared in Judy's desire to have a child, he had been unable to maintain an erection, which over time had resulted in Judy's withdrawal to avoid feeling rejected by him. Successful and pleasurable sexual encounters had by this time become so infrequent that both feared they would be unable to conceive. Tom had consulted a series of urologists for his problem, while Judy had seen a gynecologist, an endocrinologist, and, most recently, a psychiatrist who prescribed an SSRI medication because he felt that she was depressed. Most recently, they had consulted a sex therapist who had worked with them by prescribing a series of "sexual techniques," but all to no avail. Now they were discouraged and frustrated with each other and with the professionals they had consulted.

Tom and Judy were articulate and intelligent people who spoke about the details of their families and their histories notably in affectless and sterile terms, using clinical terminology to describe their problems in a manner that obscured their feelings. They did not look at each other during the session, and when they spoke there were few references to their actual relationship. They instead spoke about their physiological functioning and their genitals as if describing them in a medical dictation. I considered that their use of medical terminology and jargon might be intended to impress me with their knowledge, while keeping me at bay, just as they were quite likely keeping each other at a distance.

Although their descriptions were at first fascinating, I soon experienced a tendency to distract from their verbose and obsessively presented details about their sexual functioning. There were vivid elaborations about Judy's vaginal dryness and the various hormonal and topical measures she had used to remedy her problem, while Tom spoke in laborious detail about his "penile detumescence upon intromission" and the various side effects he had experienced with the use of sildenafil. Their descriptions of their attempts to help themselves sounded like a medical textbook, while emotion in their relationship and passion in their sexuality appeared severely lacking. I had the impression that both Tom and Judy were relating more to their genitals and biological functions than to each other in a truly affective and loving way. My distraction from their laborious accounts seemed to represent a projection onto me of their lifelessness as a couple, as well as an emotional severing of their genitals from their emotional lives.

When I finally commented that they had been talking mostly about their physical functions and their experiences with professionals and previous treatments, but little about their relationship and feelings toward each other, they both looked at me as if stunned—speechless for the first time since I had met them. Suddenly bristling and unmistakably caustic, Judy responded, "Well, what do feelings have to do with it?"

Now I was stunned. Here were two intelligent and well-trained physicians, who seemed to believe that their sexuality was independent of their psychological functioning. Although I did not yet understand enough about their emotional lives to comprehend their dynamic functioning as a couple, it was becoming clear that here were two people who had developed the sexual dimension of their selfdyad around an unconsciously agreed upon solution that emotional involvement was out of the question and that their genitals would eventually respond if they could only find the right physiological intervention. Having ejected emotion from their selfdyad, it was no wonder that Tom had difficulty attaining an erection and that vaginal lubrication for Judy was also problematic.

Encountering Judy's defensiveness, I suddenly experienced some apprehension about how to proceed in working with this emotionally sterile couple. I expected additional denial at the very least and possibly more of Judy's barely disguised hostility. Going out on a limb I asserted emphatically, "Everything actually! Everything! Sex is about feelings and much less about the genitals. The genitals are merely parts of the anatomy through which people express tenderness and their passionate feelings for each other." My response to them felt strangely elementary for two educated physicians, and yet it seemed essential that I make a bold intervention that spoke to how they had eliminated emotion from their relationship.

Fortunately, it was Tom who now responded, saying that he had just recently spoken to one of his physician friends who also suggested that "impotence has an emotional basis." Still recovering from my surprise at Judy's remark about the irrelevance of feelings in sexuality, I was again amazed—this time because Tom actually seemed to find his friend's remark to be a new and enlightening idea. Perhaps then, with his friend as my ally, we could now make some progress, I thought.

Somewhat tentatively, Tom eventually went on to describe a family background in which he had experienced extensive physical abuse at the hands of two alcoholic parents. On one occasion he had been sent to a foster home until his parents were able to demonstrate to the court that they were rehabilitated and that they could again care for him. It was here that Judy added that from middle childhood into her teenage years she had been sexually abused by her stepfather. It was not until she entered college that the abuse finally stopped.

Tom and Judy both felt that their first marriages had perpetuated their traumas. Tom described himself as verbally abused by his first wife, while Judy felt that she had been enslaved by a husband who forced her to have sex against her will. Becoming acquainted at church and then gradually moving into a dating relationship, Tom and Judy agreed to provide each other considerable space to ensure that neither of them would ever again experience a trauma in their relationship. Their agreed upon solution for freedom and space, although well meaning in its intent, had affected a near shutdown of closeness and intimacy by minimizing any chance that aggression might erupt in their relationship. Eliminating this possibility carried with it the side effect of deadening their selfdyad and killing off all passion.

After 4 years of conjoint treatment that was primarily focused on resolving their mutual fears of aggression while simultaneously assisting them in desensitizing to various aspects of mutual touching, erotic caressing, and finally intercourse, Tom and Judy were gradually able to develop a sexual life that was mutually satisfying. Two years after treatment was terminated I received a note from them that Judy had given birth to a baby girl.

SEX, LOVE, AND IDEALIZATION

Sexuality, although biologically rooted and having definite neurological and neurohormonal correlates, is simultaneously a psychological phenomenon that lies at the foundation of the intimate partnership. To understand sexuality and how it functions for the couple requires a discussion of its interpersonal and intrapsychic dimensions. Even for couples who, without apparent disagreement, have eliminated sexuality from their relationship, its absence reflects significant limitations in closeness and frequently negative feelings about the self and about the physical body. Unconscious conflicts in one and usually both partners often abound, even when the ejection of sexuality from the relationship has become an unconsciously agreed upon solution to attenuate intimacy and sometimes anxiety in the relationship.

Otto Kernberg (1995) has defined mature sexual love as the expansion of erotic desire or lust into a relationship with a specific person. Kernberg is in agreement with my central thesis that this person is selected according to unconscious relationship scripts in conjunction with conscious expectations and goals for the future, which together form a joint ego ideal. Kernberg's concept of the joint ego ideal of the two partners as a combined entity in which each commits to the other and to the couple's future together emphasizes the mutuality of conscious decision making as these two people define themselves as a permanent relationship.

Instead, I view this joint ego ideal, which includes a commitment to the partner and the couple's future together, as a function of the selfdyad, the conjoint entity into which both persons unconsciously project but also consciously convey core ambitions and values for the future. These values and goals typically include the couple's plans about having children while together they construct their family as a place of safety, trust, and mutual dependency. These features ultimately determine the quality of attachment attained in the marriage or the committed partnership.

David Scharff (1998) has emphasized the developmental changes that both persons must undertake in making the transition from single adulthood and casual dating to the exclusivity of a permanent partnership that becomes sexual. Making this shift involves an intrapsychic transition for both partners in which attraction, erotic desire, and attachment combine with mutual idealization. For Scharff, this idealization involves a shared projection of the "antilibidinal qualities" of the partnership to the outside of the relationship.

Subscribing to Fairbairn's endopsychic model of psychological functioning, Scharff defines the antilibidinal features as internal object relationships tinged with aggression or rejection that are unconsciously linked to the partners' relationships with formative figures from the past. Both persons then deny and repress negative impressions of the other, including aggression and unconscious hatred, by projecting them outside of the relationship dyad; the good and loving qualities, the libidinal features of the partnership, are tightly contained within the dyad.

As the antilibidinal features of the self, other, and the selfdyad, under the sway of preexisting hierarchically organized negative affect states, are eliminated from the relationship, the libidinal features deriving from preexisting positive affective states take ascendancy. The partners experience each other as ideal, without faults or blemishes and perfect in nearly every way. To be in close proximity to the other is to feel safe, complete, and perfect in oneself, while both individuals continue to serve as mirrors reflecting the goodness and the ideal qualities of the other.

DE-IDEALIZING IDEALIZATION

To remain in love requires that the couple be able to maintain a predominance of libidinal qualities while the antilibidinal features are held at safe distance through the use of splitting, denial, and repression.

Operationally, this is exemplified by the partners' capacity and willingness to overlook the inevitable irritations, blemishes, and affronts that occur in the process of relating while maintaining the erotic and loving features in the forefront of the relationship.

The normal wear and tear of daily existence as couples continue to negotiate the vast range of human feelings and emotions while raising their children and conducting the business of life, however, can tax the emotional resources and ego strength of many adults and couples over time. These stresses of everyday life function as stimuli that have the potential to perturb the selfdyad and sometimes the entire family system in ways that can resurrect the antilibidinal qualities that at one time were repressed and projected to the outside of the relationship (Dicks, 1993; Fairbairn, 1944). To the extent that these antilibidinal features are reactivated and now found in the partner—what Fairbairn has called the "return of the repressed"—marital or couple discord is more likely.

When Harry Met Sally

Harry, a 55-year-old married man, called to make an appointment for himself. He greeted me in the waiting room with a forced and uncomfortable smile, a feeble handshake, and sweaty palm. He was visibly anxious, interrupting himself in midsentence, searching for a place to begin telling me about his predicament. He repeatedly shifted his gaze from the floor to my eyes as if asking for my guidance about how to proceed. I reassured him that he need not worry about what he spoke about because I would listen and ask questions where I felt that it was appropriate. Finally, Harry said that he could not be certain when his anxiety and depression actually had begun because he had been anxious throughout most of his early life up until the time he left home and entered college. Recently, it seemed as though he had experienced an increase in anxiety, but he was not sure why. He went on to say that he first met Sally in college and that they were married shortly after graduation. He commented that, for the most part, he had been content in his marriage, until more recently.

Their four children were grown and out of the home. Recently, he and Sally had become quite involved in dealing with Sally's aged father who, although still quite independent and in reasonably good health, was a demanding and surly individual who easily provoked Sally. He said that the almost constant conflict between Sally and her father, over time, had negatively affected her mood, in turn intensifying Sally's unhappiness with Harry. He added that, more recently, Sally had expressed her unhappiness with their sexual relationship. Harry then proceeded to give me a litany of the various arguments that Sally had been having with her father. Here I noted that Harry's perseveration on the arguments between Sally and her father might have been in response to the emerging anxiety as he touched on the issue of his sexual relationship with his wife. Already noting his excessive need for my approval, I wondered if Harry's difficulty in pleasing Sally might actually be one source of his anxiety and a factor in their sexual difficulties.

Reluctantly, Harry proceeded to tell me more about his sexual difficulties. Although Sally was at times supportive of him, she intermittently would shock him with vituperative outbursts conveying her disappointment and anger. His tentativeness irritated her. When she would bring it up to him, he became more anxious, often resulting in losing his erection. Harry proceeded to describe other interactions with her in which she would criticize him for various issues that came up with their adult children. He emphasized how hard he tried to be what she wanted, but that his efforts were seldom appreciated. When I asked Harry what he felt that Sally expected of him, he replied that she had become intolerant of his difficulty in asserting himself with her and her father and their children.

In college Harry had been popular and had dated a number of girls and he also was a member of campus organizations in which he held high offices. Harry seemed to be offering this piece of history to demonstrate that before meeting Sally he had little or no difficulty in asserting himself. He went on to describe his relationship with his parents. His father was a successful businessman who was away from home much of the time. Harry got along well with his father, but emphasized that he especially admired his mother, who had been "a firm disciplinarian, but one who was always fair," sounding a bit protective of his mother.

"Did you work to please your mother?" I asked, picking up on his defensiveness. Harry paused momentarily and then proceeded to tell me about his mother's frequent tirades when dealing with Harry and his siblings. He added that he eventually learned to deal with her by avoiding and placating her during her bouts of anger. He eventually established a tolerable relationship that had prevailed up until the time of her death.

Harry and I continued over the course of several sessions to explore the ways in which he had changed since he had met Sally many years earlier. In the beginning he found her exciting. She was intelligent, lively, outspoken, and always able to handle interpersonal situations in a way that he admired. When I asked him why he found those traits admirable, he easily recognized them as qualities that he lacked in himself, when as a child he resorted to submission and obsequious behaviors in response to his mother's outbursts. When Harry and Sally began having children of their own, he felt that he then began to change. Although early in their marriage he was more easily able to maintain a sense of himself as equal to Sally, he now began to feel less capable in the face of her criticism, especially when she would point out his difficulty in asserting himself and holding the line with their children.

It was now becoming clear that, over the years, as Harry had worked to accommodate to Sally's criticism, he had experienced a gradual erosion in self-esteem. The pressures of family life, which included raising children and dealing with an aged parent, had triggered a loosening of the unconscious antilibidinal relationship with Harry's mother, who was full of rage and to whom he had originally responded with anxious submission. With Sally now as his resurrected critical mother, surfacing since his mother's death, Harry had been unable to maintain a sense of himself as a competent and potent man. His loss of self was in part his solution to maintain a relationship with a wife whom he had come to experience as critical and domineering, while having to repress his rage at both her and his mother. His difficulty in attaining an erection unconsciously represented his desire passively to withhold pleasure from Sally, at the expense of incurring an even greater loss of self-esteem.

RUDIMENTS OF SEXUALITY FOR THE LOVING PARTNERSHIP

In Freud's original writings the libido was proposed as a hypothetical construct to explain the motivational basis of human behavior and emotion. Revolutionary and shocking to the conservative European scientific community at the time, Freud's understanding of sexuality was yet rudimentary, although compatible with the prevailing physical science of his era. In Freud's time, of course, there were no laboratory tools to observe or measure the libido. Instead, his tools were those of clinical observation and inference without the benefit of our now relatively advanced laboratory assay methods and neuroimaging technology.

With today's technology we are possibly now able to better differentiate the libido into component parts: attraction, excitement, and arousal, with attachment as a related yet different phenomenon; each has its own characteristics and sometimes overlapping neural correlates. Although Freud viewed the libido as originating in the various erogenous zones of the body, contemporary neuroscience and developmental psychology suggest a more complex origin and relationship among the various components of sexual experience. In addition, modern psychoanalytic theory, which at one time was based almost exclusively on clinical studies of psychoanalytic treatments, now also takes into consideration the laboratory findings of the psychological and biological sciences. Together, these areas of science are now contributing to a far richer and more comprehensive understanding of sexuality and the functions that it serves.

Otto Kernberg has defined sexual excitement as a composite of primitive affective experiences that includes but is not limited to the stimulation of erogenous zones. The sexual drive is subjectively felt as a "total field of psychic experience" (1995, p. 21) that recruits early experiences of comfort, nurturance, affection, and merger with the caretaker. These are further combined with the vicissitudes of aggression that originate in early experiences of withdrawal of and deprivation by the caretaker. Throughout development, these affects are progressively differentiated and organized within the brain and the unconscious mind into a rich and varied tapestry of psychic states linking affects with object and self-representations (Kernberg, 1995). Finally, at adolescence, with various hormones and neurotransmitters as catalysts and combined with both an aim and a desired other person, sexual love emerges.

Although in classical psychoanalytic theory it is the mother who is most usually referred to, "caretaker" perhaps more comprehensively describes the variety of figures or objects that influence the child. These include siblings, grandparents, aunts, uncles, and cousins, as well as the mother, father, and the unconscious internal couple of a father and mother combined. The internal couple develops as a composite of the child's accumulated experiences and developing perceptions of the parents' relationship (Scharff & Scharff, 1991). It includes how the parents negotiate conflict; how they feel about each other; how they manage power, control, and respect for one another; and even how they assign masculine and feminine roles to one another and to the child.

Importantly, the child's internal couple also contains within it a perception of the parents' sexuality that is based on a composite of expressed affection and the unconsciously communicated qualities of the parents' sexuality. Also recruited into the child's developing sexuality are the subtleties of family life, including the extent to which the child has access to the inner sanctum of the parental bedroom. All these influences occur in synergy as the child simultaneously observes how the parents make interpersonal contact through vocal tone, eye contact, and the various modes of tactile and kinesthetic communication, whether loving, aggressive, or indifferent.

Finally, a discussion of the couple's sexuality would not be complete without a consideration of Melanie Klein's rich psychoanalytic contributions in understanding the primitive infrastructure of the Oedipus complex. From analytic treatments of young children, Klein demonstrated that the child, in association with the parents, develops primitive fantasies of a mother and father who are combined in an exclusive relationship while enacting aggressive sexual intercourse. Portrayed in these fantasies is an intermingling of various body parts that include breasts, penises in vaginas and other orifices, devouring, incorporating, and merging—all in conjunction with the more reality-based parental relationship (Klein, 1945).

Together, these variables leave their imprints on the emerging sexuality of the developing child, which, during adolescence, is again revised and given greater definition through a combination of psychosocial experience and biological maturation. Understanding Klein's contributions to the Oedipus complex and to sexuality is useful for the clinician, especially when working with those patients or couples who struggle with issues in which the vicissitudes of aggression appear to enter into their sexual functioning. Common examples are those who have been sexually traumatized at an early age or whose relationship with a parent was otherwise ambivalent, angry, or hurtful in some way and now appears to resurface into the sexual arena of the relationship.

WHY HAVE SEX IF NOT TO BREED? SEXUALITY AND AUTISTIC-CONTIGUOUS MODE FUNCTIONING

Why do couples desire sex? Biologists offer us well-rehearsed but insufficient explanations by often ascribing its motivation to evolution—that is, perpetuating our species. Yet people have sex all the time without any intent to bring a child into the world. The answer to this question, then, is simple at its surface and profoundly complex at its depth. Simply put, sex feels good. But what feels good about it? How does it feel good and why does it feel that way? And if sex does feel good, where does that feeling come from? Is it just one feeling or are there many, and is it a physical sensation, is it mental, or is it both? Why do most people in general find greater pleasure in sexual intercourse than in masturbation? And is sex equally pleasurable with different people, or more satisfying with one who is special? Does it ever hurt and, if so, how can it feel good too?

Most people have never seriously considered these questions and, if asked, will typically shrug them off, punt them to the philosophers, or summarily ascribe it all to "hormones." In this section I will attempt to answer these questions by providing case studies to illustrate the range of experiences and complications that exist when attempting to understand the role played by sexuality in the loving relationship.

Although it is the androgens that catalyze the intensity of sexual desire, the sexual drive is more comprehensively influenced by the myriad of social, interpersonal, and unconscious factors discussed throughout this writing. When considering the neuroimaging studies differentiating attraction, desire, and arousal and having established the importance of the attachment system and the selfdyad in partner selection, we now have a more complete though complicated understanding of the couple's loving experience.

In this section I will attempt to integrate what psychoanalysts and couple therapists have come to understand about the total experience of sexuality and its unconscious meanings, demonstrating how these become important in marriage and in other permanent partnerships. This takes us into the realm of subjectivity and the unconscious meaning of each partner's sexuality, the couple's unique Oedipal configurations, the selfdyad, and the couple's relationship to the wider society in which it lives.

To understand the essence and purpose of sexuality in the adult partnership, we must address the nature of sensory experience, affects, and their connection to the drives and internal object relations. In a thoughtful exposition pertaining to this topic, Kernberg asserts that affects are developed through a succession of reward and aversive experiences for the infant in interaction with the caretaker, forming structures that are internalized, layered, and progressively differentiated. Some are augmented, while others are dampened in the context of relational encounters with others. A rich network of internal object relations conjoined with affects is eventually formed that now becomes installed in the various drive states participating in adult sexuality (Kernberg, 1995).

According to Kernberg, the fundamental purpose of adult sexuality, apart from its procreative intent, is founded on a wish for pleasure through sensory experience. It involves a recruitment of another person into that experience such that the varieties of sensation occurring through touching and being touched express derivatives of libidinal and aggressive drive states linked to early object relationships and their corresponding affects.

Thomas Ogden's conception of the autistic-contiguous position as the most basic mode of generating experience assists us to understand the primordial essence of sexuality more comprehensively. Preceding the paranoid-schizoid position in its ascendancy for the infant, Ogden adds this as a third mode to the traditional Kleinian paranoid-schizoid and depressive positions. Unlike developmental stages, which are essentially successive, a position recurs throughout the life span and, while in its ascendance, reigns supreme over the others, whose influence on the person is now minimized by comparison (Klein, 1964; Ogden, 1989). Because sexuality with another represents a combined experience generated from all three modes, with shifts in dominance of mode throughout the entire sexual experience, a brief review of each position and its role in sexuality is warranted.

In the paranoid-schizoid position, the infant's preoccupations center on survival of the ego and the self, with a preponderance of splitting defenses involving a division of good and bad experience. In the depressive mode that follows, the individual's concerns center on preserving good internal and external objects as the infant now recognizes that the good and bad objects are really one and the same. Projection is now reduced as splitting defenses diminish, changing the fundamental fear in the depressive mode to that of guilt with its accompanying desire to preserve good internal objects.

When in the paranoid-schizoid and depressive modes, the individual is fundamentally preoccupied with the relationship with objects; in the autistic-contiguous mode, the person is immersed in a field of complete sensory dominance. Here the infant's most basic experiences are presymbolic and without thought or reflection; instead, he is preoccupied with shape and enclosure, beat and rhythm, and hardness and edgedness (Ogden, 1989). There is a rudimentary emergence of a self that is forming at the boundary of surfaces as the infant continues to encounter shape, texture, hardness, softness, warmth, and cold, as well as sound, movement, and rhythm. With these experiences, the infant develops an increased awareness of a sense of the body and the self as merged but also separate from inanimate things and animate others.

Sexuality, perhaps as much as any experience of adult life, is characterized by an immersion within an autistic-contiguous mode in which the individual is absorbed in a total field of sensory dominance. Although aspects of paranoid-schizoid and depressive mode functioning enter in (for example, sometimes conscious fantasies are entertained or distractions occur), sexuality is predominantly governed by sensations and feelings within the body self. During sexual intercourse, there is an encounter with another person as both partners become steeped in a sensory-dominated domain that ultimately completes and governs the psychosomatic partnership. Aspects of paranoid-schizoid functioning might intermittently enter into the sexual experience at intense moments of passion and sensory immersion as one shifts into a realm dominated by aggression or even contempt.

During times when these paranoid-schizoid experiences are activated, their expressions through behavioral gestures or vocal channels can become potentially disruptive for a partner if that specific feature of the sexual encounter is experienced as aversive and incompatible with that partner's internal world. At this moment depressive mode functioning might instead prevail for that partner. When a specific action becomes compulsory for erotic stimulation, gratification, or orgasm for one partner but is noxious or reprehensible for the other, an interruption or breakdown of autistic-contiguous mode experience might be more likely, with the potential to disrupt the selfdyad. This can possibly become problematic for those couples who have a great investment in remaining together but who are otherwise unable to reconcile their preferred sexual practices.

Importantly, aspects of depressive mode experience must always enter into the couple's sexuality, even though expressed within an autistic-contiguous mode. Examples of depressive mode expressions include, for example, demonstrations of loving concern at times at which an individual might concede to having sexual intercourse when fatigued or preoccupied with external concerns. Additionally, there might be occasions when the individual, again out of concern for the partner, feels a desire to provide pleasure, even when that sexual activity, gesture, or vocalization is outside the individual's preferred repertoire or moral code. In each of these situations, the individual is focused predominantly on a concern for the partner and the individual's pleasure becomes secondary.

Although intermittent and overt expressions of paranoid-schizoid functioning can occur at any point within the province of the couple's sexuality, it is the predominance of autistic-contiguous mode functioning—the individual's and the couple's immersion in a sensation-dominated mode of experience, but in the overall service of depressive position functioning—that ideally governs the entire range of sexual expression. It is the absorption in this sensory field, influenced by unconscious object relations, that determines the nuanced gestalt of the couple's sexual relationship. Furthermore, it is important to recognize that reasonably healthy sexuality for the loving couple must entail an optimal balance and flexibility of movement among all three modes of experience. To the extent that a partner becomes stuck in one mode—becoming rigidly fixed in a preferred sexual practice that is incompatible with the other partner's preferred mode, for example—the sexual relationship will more likely falter.

Teresa and Edward

A breakdown of autistic-contiguous mode functioning in the couple characterizes the preponderance of sexual problems appearing in the consulting room. These clinical presentations can be generated by intrapsychic conflict within one or both partners or as a function of overt or latent couple conflict between the partners. Sexual disjunctions, the chronic disagreement on the frequency or preferred sexual activities, can present with such salience for the couple that one partner experiences an erosion of the self while the other partner *appears* to dominate and sometimes even flourish. The case of Teresa and Edward is an illustration.

Teresa and Edward, a married couple in their mid-30s, called for an appointment because of their increasing difficulty in getting along. Although their stated purpose for the consultation initially seemed vague, it became apparent that their increased interpersonal strife had resulted in both experiencing depressions that were related to their marital dissatisfaction. There was now little joy in being together, and their conversations frequently took the form of arguing about their unsatisfactory sexual relationship. Edward remarked that it seemed ironic that the only thing they could now agree on was their mutual dissatisfaction with their sexual life.

Teresa and Edward had been married for 10 years. Prior to marriage they both enjoyed their sexual relationship while generally agreeing on its frequency and timing. In the early years of their marriage they continued to have daily sexual intercourse—sometimes more frequently when Edward was able to arrange opportunities to leave work to come home for a brief encounter. Although during their early years Teresa continued to comply with Edward's rigorous schedule for sexual intercourse, she began to feel that the frequency represented "something compulsive." In a tone of exasperation Teresa said:

> I came to realize that it was never enough for him. It's like he is a machine. Sometimes he doesn't even ejaculate, and then he wants to do it again. I can't and won't keep up with this, Ed. Sometimes it seems like I'm not there with you. It's the weirdest thing; it's like you're masturbating, and yet we're having sex.

Teresa went on to tell me that recently their relationship had grown "mutually antagonistic," describing what she felt was Edward's intolerance of her feelings and preferences regarding their sexual life. Recently, when she flatly refused him, Edward became overtly enraged and verbally abusive, augmenting Teresa's anger and deepening her resentment.

Wanting to explore what appeared to be Edward's compulsive orientation toward sexuality, I fully expected a defensive reaction in light of Teresa's diatribe and harsh criticism. In contrast, Edward appeared approachable and willing to address the issue that Teresa had introduced. Although he at first described what he felt was his "high sex drive," his trite response and defensive posture gave way to a more open discussion about what was emerging in my mind as a breakdown in autistic-contiguous mode functioning.

I was especially struck by Teresa's comparison of their sexual relationship to masturbation. She described a feeling of being excluded from the encounter, while Edward seemed to be locked into an experience of solitary confinement. I began to consider that Edward's compulsive approach to sexuality, including its incessancy and its frequency, might represent a hypertrophy of autistic-contiguous experience as a defense against closeness and intimacy, with depressive mode functioning largely absent. If that were the case, then most certainly Teresa would feel excluded from the sexual encounter, while Edward was defensively sequestered within an autistic-contiguous mode.

Edward somewhat tentatively and shamefully began to speak about his background. He had been raised in an isolated rural area, living in a communal religious community. Although close to his mother, he was not close to his father. It was the norm within the community for the men to take several wives. Edward's father had four wives, the first being Edward's mother. Edward had 26 siblings, although he was unsure how many were full siblings and how many were half-siblings. His father, the patriarch of the cult, wielded considerable power and influence in this community in which he was highly respected but also feared by most, including Edward.

At an early age, both the boys and the girls in the community were drafted into a form of sexual indoctrination in which they were required to engage in sexual acts with several of the most powerful male leaders of the community. Edward was no exception. Although most of the teenagers were compliant with these culturally prescribed requirements, Edward's close relationship with his mother, a woman who had been known to be opposed to these requirements, encouraged his rebellion, and he eventually fled from the compound. At the age of 15, Edward ran away to live with an aunt and an uncle who raised him through high school, subsequently sending him to college where he then met Teresa.

Although incredulous when Edward first told her about his background, Teresa was compassionate. Edward swore her to secrecy that the details about his early life would never be revealed. Over the years they rarely spoke about it, while they established a life together that was mutually fulfilling, with one exception. The compulsive quality of their sexual relationship was now affecting Teresa in such a way that she had become averse to intercourse with Edward. If she continued to agree to Edward's requirements for frequent sexual intercourse, she was in danger of losing a sense of herself as a separate individual. If she instead asserted her right to define the parameters of their sexual relationship, she might be in danger of provoking Edward's rage and his retaliatory attempts to control her. It was not only the frequency of sexual encounters that troubled her, but also Edward's force, all at the expense of her pleasure and her autonomy.

As couple therapy proceeded, supplemented by individual sessions with Edward and Teresa, we were able to elaborate and eventually work through the sexual trauma that Edward encountered while living in the community in which he had been raised. Through the course of treatment we came to learn that Edward had consciously rejected the values of his father's cult and its sexual practices by repressing his anger at his father for inflicting the sexual abuse upon him. But in the regressive atmosphere of the sexual relationship with Teresa, there was now a return of the repressed (Fairbairn, 1944).

Forcing Teresa into intercourse became a revised version of the abuse that Edward originally encountered; he was now treating Teresa as he had been treated during the years before he had fled the compound. For Edward there had been no room for the nurturing, loving, and reparative aspects of sexuality that are characteristic of depressive mode functioning. Instead, he expressed split-off aspects of paranoid-schizoid functioning, while remaining defensively isolated within a total sensory field of experience walled off from the imagined dangers of closeness and intimacy.

ADDITIONAL FEATURES OF SEXUAL EXPERIENCE

We have by now established that sexual pleasure involves an immersion within autistic-contiguous mode functioning in which near total sensory dominance is recruited in the service of expressing concern and love for the partner. Although supervening during the sexual encounter, autistic-contiguous mode experience allows for transitory infusions of paranoid-schizoid functioning through attenuated displays of aggression in the service of depressive mode experience in which the loving qualities of the relationship prevail and are successfully conveyed to the partner. In this section I will review additional features of sexuality that, through psychoanalytic treatment and couple therapy, have been revealed as fundamental aspects of erotic experience.

Otto Kernberg has described some of the subjectively experienced qualities of erotic desire while linking their functions to their primal meanings and their unconscious connections to early object relational experiences. Although in his formulation he does not specifically address the sensory experiences as functions of autistic-contiguous mode functioning, there is an assumption that the search for pleasure is fundamentally rooted in the sensory modality, as both partners express primordial and developmental needs and experiences.

First, sexual intercourse—the experience of penetrating a vagina or an orifice of another or being penetrated by a penis or other protuberance—always includes the unconscious experience of crossing interpersonal and intrapsychic boundaries when fusing with another. The fantasy of two becoming one manifests within the partnership in a way that the penetrating/being penetrated bodily experience becomes a somatic concretization of its interpersonal counterpart—namely, the oneness that is experienced when exchanging mental contents through projective and introjective identification.

Penetrating or being penetrated recruits the drive state of aggression, providing tactile stimulation and erotic gratification while forecasting an eventual release through ejaculation and orgasm. The reader will note that Kernberg's view of penetration as representative of the aggressive drive reflects his allegiance to classical theory. I believe that a more contemporary view is to invoke the autistic-contiguous position as the fundamental mode through which penetration, tactile stimulation, and orgasm impact erotic desire and the totality of sexual experience.

Second, Kernberg emphasizes that constitutional bisexuality is depicted as each partner identifies with both the penetrating and the incorporating qualities of the experience while eliminating a third party through Oedipal triumph. By successfully defeating a rival, an ingredient of excitement is added to the total sexual experience (Kernberg, 1995). Contributing to the experience of fusion with another is the gratification that is derived when identifying with the partner's excitement. The fantasy of two becoming one enables a transcendence of gender such that each partner becomes both genders simultaneously, thereby attenuating the envy of the other gender. Sexuality serves to dissipate the aggression that inevitably mounts for the couple, while it serves a reparative and restorative function for the relationship.

Third, Kernberg emphasizes that sexuality is in the service of regression as the loving partners are temporarily able to overcome social constraints and prohibitions through the act of taking clothes off. In this way the vicissitudes of civilization and shame are defied. Getting dressed at the conclusion of the sexual encounter represents a return to the shame-based civilized world in which the couple lives. The teasing and being teased qualities of sexuality represent a fourth function of erotic love. To provide and withhold erotic and tactile stimulation alternately through the varieties of foreplay always offers the promise of eventual gratification, while the intermittence and the rise and fall of excitement contribute to erotic pleasure.

Finally, the idealization of the partner's body is a fundamental feature of erotic desire. It manifests as a normal but attenuated version of perverse sexuality that, according to Chasseguet-Smirgel, represents a denial of both castration anxiety and the regressed world of anality. It derives from the infant's idealization of the mother's body, which defends against the aggression and envy of her for all the riches that she possesses inside, including her capacity to provide life and nurturance (Chasseguet-Smirgel, 1985).

When considering the myriad of unconscious functions served by sexuality for the adult partnership, we can easily see the potential it holds to enhance the relationship or to undermine and even destroy it. Scharff (1998) emphasizes that good enough sex for the couple serves the general purpose of repair and integration. For this to succeed, both partners must possess a capacity to communicate that love, concern, and desire successfully.

The sexual encounter has the potential to ameliorate destructiveness by conveying that the partner is loved, valued, and cherished. To the extent that this is successful, attachment is restored while the essential mirroring qualities of the relationship are also implemented. By providing pleasure, forgiveness is earned as the partners experience a psychosomatic fusion in preparation for the inevitable separation that will follow. The repeating sequence of separation, sexual tension, teasing, fusion, and penetration/being penetrated, culminating in orgasm, reorganizes and regulates the various drive states while also replenishing the relationship.

6

THE CENTRALITY OF THE SELFDYAD IN THE DYNAMIC ORGANIZATION OF THE COUPLE

A psychobiological foundation for the partnership is established when friendship, romantic attraction, sexuality, and attachment converge in an optimal way. I have described the unconscious processes involved as the two partners become acquainted with each other—processes in which there is a continuous appraisal of fit and complementarity as they establish a medium through which aspects of personality are both projected and introjected. These aspects of character include traits, needs, wishes, relationship scripts, conflicts, traumas, and other features of self-organization. Through these encounters, an individual determines the extent to which the other partner complements the self, providing the potential for further self-development. Through ongoing interactions that include conscious relating as well as unconscious communication through projective identification, the exchange of mental contents continues throughout the courtship as well as the life of the partnership.

COUPLE FORMATION AND TRANSFORMATION

Although we have invoked friendship, attachment, and sexuality as important in partner formation, these variables do not fully account for why one person is chosen over another as the romantic and permanent partner. Recalling that complementarity is a central feature in couple formation, we might still wonder why it is sought in the first place, why it is fundamental in the construction of the selfdyad, and how it functions in holding a couple together—often for better but sometimes for worse.

When Henry Dicks pioneered his studies on marriage and marital dysfunction at the Tavistock Clinic in London in the 1960s, he was initially struck by what he called the "attraction of opposites" (Dicks, 1993, p. 63). He acknowledged that his observations were not new, stating that it was generally accepted that opposites attract in both friendships and in marriage. Dicks cited the literary characters of Don Quixote and Sancho Panza as an example of the "strong, silent man" who found the "outgoing woman." He also cited Carl Jung, who had many years earlier described the complementariness of human relationship. Dicks then issued his proclamation: "When tolerated, it is clear that the complementarity of a functioning dyad adds considerably to its spectrum of relatedness to the world outside, and to the possibilities of psychological cross-fertilization and growth" (Dicks, 1993, p. 63).

Dicks subsequently developed his theory along the lines of the complementarity of inner objects, now going far beyond the more simplistic idea of the attraction of opposites. Here Dicks seemed to be addressing the manner in which both partners' internal worlds, including needs, fears, wishes, and defenses, all organized into unconscious relationship scripts, must mesh while creating an interpsychic fit. Although Dicks provides clinical data to illustrate "complementarity," there remains the question of why, in the process of couple formation, there is a search for a complementary inner object fit as opposed to a search for a partner who is alike or similar. After all, would not a similarity to their own psychological organization seem more logical and practical and even simplify relationships if partners were more likely to behave, feel, and think alike, and even share common interests?

Within Dicks's concept of complementarity or fit, I believe, there exists a primordial and unconscious motivation that underlies the search for differentness. Christopher Bollas's concept of the transformational object offers a compelling theoretical construct that assists us in understanding the motivation to find another whose inner objects complement those of the self rather than replicating them. Bollas reminds us that what is crucial in determining the mother as an object for the infant are the essential functions that she serves. The mother becomes an object through a process involving "cumulative internal and external transformations" (Bollas, 1987, p. 14). She is experienced by the infant according to actions and activities that change the self-experience of the child. She becomes important not just because she is essential for survival, but also because she is a medium through which the infant's self becomes transformed as she assists him toward cognitive, affective, and instinctual integration.

The wish for transformation continues as a memory trace of the original desire for maternal transformation and will manifest itself throughout the life cycle as the person seeks new objects and new experiences. Bollas cites persons, places, events, and ideologies as offering the hope for transformation or enhancement of the self, all of which he believes derive from the original transformational mother.

The search for a romantic and permanent partner is an object relationship of adult life that offers the prospect of transforming the self. Following Bollas's line of thinking, if the psychological organization of the potential partner was too similar to one's own, the possibilities for self-enhancement and transformation would be reduced. By contrast, finding a romantic partner who complements the self greatly enhances the possibilities for self-growth and change, providing that the criteria of selfdyad functioning are adequately met.

CRITERIA FOR SELFDYAD FUNCTIONING

Permeability, flexibility, and optimal dynamic functioning are essential criteria for the well-functioning selfdyad. When these are achieved in a good enough way, the possibility for relationship satisfaction is vastly increased. Once the partners have moved toward permanence and have either married or defined themselves as permanent partners through ongoing interpersonal encounters and unconscious communication, their roles will become distributed as the intersubjective space of the selfdyad continues to acquire greater refinement and definition. In the following sections I describe each criterion and provide a case illustration of each. I will revisit several cases discussed in previous chapters, while now applying concepts pertaining to the couple's selfdyad functioning.

Permeability

For the selfdyad to function optimally both partners must possess sufficiently permeable self-boundaries. Permeability is defined by the degree of openness and fluidity of conscious and unconscious communication occurring between the partners. It refers to the boundary between the self and the self of the partner; through communication, both conscious and unconscious, aspects of self-experience will be transported into the self of the other partner. Within this communication network is included the diffusion of affects, cognitions, attitudes, intentions, needs, and desires—all while the partner receives and contains them in a reciprocal way. With an optimally permeable boundary, the partner is able to express himself with reasonable transparency while sharing thoughts, ideas, feelings, and intimate expressions with the other partner that are beyond what is shared with all others.

Individuals who are more limited in self-expression—for example, those who are taciturn, reserved, or otherwise isolate affect—might have increased difficulty in establishing or maintaining an interpersonal connection with the partner, then limiting communication and the interpenetration of self-boundaries. When this occurs, there is an inadequate exchange of mental contents that has the potential to devitalize the relationship and compromise closeness and intimacy. Conversely, when a partner continuously encroaches on the other's autonomy, a hypertrophied selfdyad may develop while it occludes or eclipses the self of the other partner, increasing the potential for relationship dissatisfaction, sexual dysfunction, emotional symptoms, and even somatic problems (Kerr & Bowen, 1988). When the selfdyad suffuses the self of the partner, the possibilities for personal growth are attenuated. Fundamentally, being a couple erodes selfhood.

Figure 6.1 depicts several relationship possibilities. In each figure, the partner is designated as a circle. The selfdyad is the common overlapping and darkened area of the two circles. Through projective and introjective identification and the assignment and arrangement of roles,

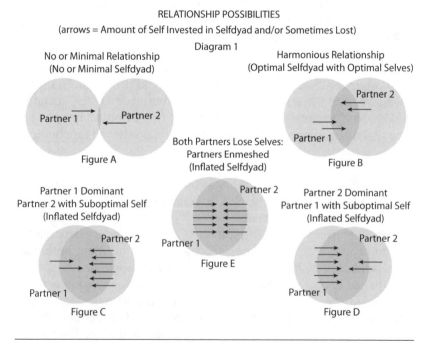

Figure 6.1 Relationship possibilities.

the selfdyad is formed as an interpsychic system that is distinct from the individual selves. The number of arrows designates the amount of self invested or sometimes lost to the selfdyad by each partner. This is in part determined by the openness or permeability of self-boundaries of the partners, as well as individual features of the partners affecting the urgency of projection.

Figure 6.1A depicts suboptimal permeability and a minimum of diffusion into the selfdyad, creating a distant and devitalized relationship. Figure 6.1B shows optimally permeable self-boundaries and an optimal diffusion of self into the selfdyad, creating a well-functioning selfdyad. This characterizes the harmonious relationship. Figures 6.1C and 6.1D show exaggerated permeability and interpersonal urgency to project the self, creating a hypertrophied selfdyad that eclipses the self of the other partner. In Figure 6.1C partner 1 is dominant, and in Figure 6.1D partner 2 is dominant. In both, the nondominant partner is unable to sustain a subjective sense of self-functioning, giving up too much of self in support of selfdyad. Figure 6.1E depicts an approximately equal but exaggerated projection of two selves into the selfdyad at the expense of autonomy of both partners. This often defines enmeshed partnerships. Frequently, the boundaries between the partners are too permeable, while there is too much projection or diffusion of self into the selfdyad.

Sara and William   Sara and William, presented in Chapter 3, are an example of a couple who had an insufficiently permeable yet mutually acceptable selfdyad for many years; it became problematic at the death of William's mother. Without the support of her mother-in-law, Sara began to require more openness and intimacy with William, but in a way he was unable to provide. Originally, they had established their selfdyad on the basis of safety and protection. Because Sara had grown up in a chaotic family environment that included parental substance abuse, William's passivity and quiet nature were especially comfortable during their courtship and early years of marriage. They provided an antidote to Sara's previous emotional trauma. Sara also felt embraced by William's extended family, especially his mother, who served the function of a surrogate parent.

William's family background consisted of an environment whose day-to-day functioning centered on caring for William's developmentally compromised twin siblings, whose medical problems created an anxious family atmosphere. With both parents' focus on the twins' rehabilitation and serious health problems, William lacked essential mirroring as he developed an insecure attachment. Ironically, his unobtrusive style and the social inhibition that emerged from William's early environment provided a field of safety for Sara.

Upon the death of William's mother—the person who, for Sara, provided considerable nurturing, but who, for William, was experienced ambivalently—the couple's relationship began to deteriorate. Now Sara was no longer content or reassured by William's quiet and unassuming style, but instead began to experience him as depriving her of closeness. The loss of the sustaining surrogate mother served to resurrect in Sara the rejecting inner object relationship with her emotionally absent alcoholic parents. Although Sara's demands for more communication certainly signaled William about what she needed, the intensity of her feeling states only pushed him further into withdrawal, augmenting her anger and depression while leaving them both bereft and abandoned.

Couple therapy would focus on assisting Sara and William to grieve the loss of William's mother, while helping them to elaborate the unconscious meaning of this loss and its implications for their relationship. This would create a forum for more open communication while increasing the permeability of their self-boundaries. Complex attachment functions would then hopefully emerge as they both learned to provide support for each other within an atmosphere of safety.

Flexibility

Flexibility, the second criterion of selfdyad functioning, refers to the couple's ability to react, adjust, and behave with each other in response to what is communicated and needed in the relationship. This includes the capacity to give of oneself, to compromise when there are differences, and to yield control freely during times of disagreement and charged affective exchanges. An ability to comfortably work out preferences, needs, and the various roles that are required for a comfortable coexistence determines the flexibility of the selfdyad.

Couples who are capable of making easy give-and-take decisions without undue deliberation or conflict usually exemplify flexibility of the selfdyad. A lack of flexibility, on the other hand, is indicated in relationships in which, no matter what might be considered, the partners seem to argue endlessly about minor and often irrelevant details. There is often difficulty in making decisions and in distributing roles within the relationship. The desire to win, be right, or get one's way sometimes takes precedence over the actual content and substance of the interaction. When the selfdyad lacks flexibility, the partners are less able to compromise or to yield comfortably at times when differences arise within the relationship. Here a partner might fail to recognize the impact of his behavior on the behavior of the other partner.

An example is the husband who, in describing his wife to the therapist, presents an interaction in a rigid and one-sided way, with no apparent awareness or acknowledgement that his communication has influenced, much less motivated, the very behavior or characteristic that he describes in the interaction. For him, the wife's behavior stands alone, while he fails to recognize that her behavior was at least partially in response to the communication between them and what he had projected onto her. Here the husband's anger might prevail while he insists that the wife's behavior represents one thing or another, although, from the therapist's standpoint, the behavior in question has a very different meaning from the one assigned by the husband.

As another example, the therapist observes that a wife's anger at her husband shows a lack of empathy and understanding of his motives. She complains that he is affable and jocular when he is around their friends, but when he is alone with her, he is sullen and withdrawn. Focused on this disparity and feeling the rejection, the wife describes the husband as oppositional and passive-aggressive, seemingly to convince the therapist that her husband's behavior represents a fixed trait that has nothing to do with her or the relationship. Convinced that her husband's intrinsic personality disorder is really at the root of the problem, she is able to disavow an awareness of the impact of her behavior on their interaction, while she now has ample justification for her anger.

Georgette and Liam   Georgette and Liam, a couple in their 30s, had been married for 6 years. Liam was a physician and Georgette an attorney who had been working part-time for the 3 years since the birth of their baby. Now that their daughter was 3, Georgette and Liam felt that she was ready to enter daycare while Georgette returned to work on a full-time basis. Liam had originally agreed that he would pick up their child at daycare by 5:00 in the afternoon so that Georgette would be able to see her clients late in the day. Recently, Liam had been considering the possibility of undertaking additional postgraduate training that would involve a significant financial expenditure. He now thought that he should work additional hours for them to meet their expenses for his training. When Liam suggested to Georgette that he was concerned about leaving his office so early in the day to pick up their daughter, proposing instead that they hire a babysitter for an additional 2 hours, Georgette became furious and accused him of reneging on their agreement. She remarked that she would have never agreed to get pregnant in the first place had she known that Liam would back out of their agreement.

Initially, I was struck by the way Georgette and Liam spoke about their relationship. It had the quality of a business transaction that had been negotiated but was now null and void because of a breach of contract. Georgette spoke in a loud voice, explaining herself logically as if speaking to a jury. She said that it was Liam's idea to have a baby and that her willingness to have children hinged on his willingness to help out so that she was able to continue her career. Their agreement, Georgette reiterated, included a cutting back of his hours to accommodate her schedule, while leaving time at the end of his day to spend with their child. In an angry tone Liam interrupted Georgette's oratory, accusing her of being unwilling to listen to reason and to consider his simple solution. He remarked that he had found a sitter in the neighborhood who was able to help out for a few hours each day until one of them arrived home.

Within the first few minutes of the consultation, it became apparent that Georgette and Liam were merely arguing rather than describing their concerns in a manner that might help them understand their situation and achieve a solution to their problem. Furthermore, it seemed that their arguments were actually attempts to enlist me in support of their respective positions so that I might determine who was right and who was wrong. An attempt to engage the therapist as an arbiter of truth and justice is not unusual in couple therapy, especially when a specific life event is presented as a fundamental impasse for the couple.

Accusing Georgette of being unreasonable, Liam pointed his finger in her face as he proceeded to give other examples of how she had to have everything her way. He commented that it was Georgette who always determined when and where they would travel, how their money would be spent, and with whom they would socialize. In rapid-fire response to Liam's tirade, Georgette responded defensively that it was Liam who had insisted that they remain in this area of the country while he completed his residency. She went on to explain that Liam had promised her that after his residency they would return to the East Coast, where her family resided. She further lamented that it was ludicrous for Liam to suggest that she had been rigid, when instead she had been quite conciliatory by agreeing to have a baby and remaining here for him to complete his training:

> Why shouldn't I make some of the decisions about how we lead our lives and spend our money when you call all the shots in the really important areas of our lives? After all, I'm the one who is trained to understand money, so it only makes sense that I should take the lead in making the financial decisions.

Liam retorted by reminding Georgette that she too had expressed a desire to remain here, rather than returning to her home where they would then have to deal with her mother, who would try to control their lives.

Both Georgette and Liam were vying for control, which I sensed was not confined to this one area of their relationship. The oscillation of my sympathies from one person to the other while neither of them seemed to consider compromise as a potential solution suggested that power and control were components of a rigid selfdyad organization. Georgette and Liam were stuck, mired in anger at each other as they both attempted to justify their respective positions.

In formulating this couple's difficulties, it is useful to consider my reactions as I observed and listened to their opening dialogue. During these initial exchanges I first sympathized with Georgette as she eloquently attempted to convince me of Liam's betrayal of their original agreement. Subsequently, I considered Liam's solution to the impasse as reasonable and well considered when I experienced Georgette's remarks as condescending and supercilious and she declared that she deserved the principal power in the relationship. My sentiments and support for one and then the other shifted from moment to moment as I listened to both persons' strong opinions and equally strong rebuttals. This kind of countertransference is quite usual when working with couples with insufficient flexibility. The therapist momentarily becomes caught up in the content of the material rather than the style and the process of the couple's relating. To regain therapeutic equanimity, the therapist might listen and search for any references or associations that would shed light on the very inflexibility that is demonstrated in the interaction.

Observing my countertransference-driven reactions, I noted Liam's reference to Georgette's mother, who would control them if they moved close to her. With control and inflexibility at the heart of Georgette and Liam's relationship, I regarded the remark about Georgette's mother as likely significant. I hypothesized that this might represent an internalized object relationship on which Georgette and Liam had constructed their selfdyad—a mother introject as a central feature in their rigidity. If this were so, addressing the impact of Georgette's mother would provide a route for deepening an understanding of their difficulties while attempting to gain some leverage in working with this obdurate couple. Treatment would then assist them to acquire a better understanding of their needs for control as attempts to protect their autonomy, as we linked these relationship paradigms to Georgette's early relationship with her mother and perhaps others, too.

Optimal Dynamic Functioning

Optimal dynamic functioning refers to the couple's capacity to maintain the dynamic quality of movement, balance, and fluctuating equilibrium within the relationship system. Although permeability and flexibility certainly contribute to the dynamic functioning of the couple, this feature describes the way in which couples develop, distribute, and maintain their various roles and corresponding role responsiveness to each other. It includes the subtle behavioral and emotional accommodations that are made with respect to the partner to preserve and enhance the functioning and the efficiency of the selfdyad. Included is the unconscious accommodation to the partner's affects and level of emotional intensity as both partners assimilate and contain projective identifications of an appropriate magnitude to sustain communication, achieve intimacy, and fertilize the relationship for continuous growth.

Martin and Janet   Martin and Janet, presented in Chapter 1, provide an example of a couple who had been unable to achieve and maintain optimal dynamic functioning, especially around the distribution of roles within their selfdyad organization. Martin had become the more dominant and apparently competent partner while Janet assumed a more subordinate role in their relationship. This is illustrated in Figure 6.1C. Over the years, as their relationship and family life progressed, Janet became more subservient and deferential to Martin while relinquishing her autonomy to facilitate family life, Martin's career, and even Martin's self-esteem.

Although at one time Janet had been quite successful as a teacher, as the years went on and she continued to support Martin and his career, her self-esteem progressively declined as she gave up her needs and personal strivings. Encouraged by her friends to pursue her talent of writing, she decided to launch a new career as an author, precipitating an eruption of marital conflict. Janet's success had effected a change in the dynamic organization of their selfdyad. With Janet no longer in the role of the supplicating partner, Martin could no longer maintain an image of himself as dominant and capable.

Martin and Janet had settled into roles in which both had been unable to adjust to the nuances of each other's needs. Martin was unable to recognize and adjust to Janet's new career, while Janet had shut herself off from the communication that was necessary to effect change in their distribution of roles. Although many couples are able to modify their relationship structure comfortably at junctures calling for change, the couple with a selfdyad that is unable to accommodate often requires the therapist's active interventions.

In summary, with the vicissitudes of life serving as stimuli, including the raising of children, maintaining a social life, dealing with extended family, and managing a career, there is a continuous influence on the couple's relationship. As a function of these ongoing impingements, including changes occurring throughout the life span, the dynamic organization of the couple will ebb and flow, affecting the flexibility and permeability of the selfdyad. To the extent that both partners are able to maintain an optimal dynamic equilibrium of role responsiveness to each other with a minimum of conflict and while supporting each other, the chances for achieving and maintaining a rewarding and loving relationship are vastly increased.

THE ADULT LIFE CYCLE AND THE SELFDYAD

The couple's presenting problems in treatment are frequently influenced by the stage of the couple's relationship, the stage of life of the partners, and other special features pertaining to the partnership itself. Because each stage of life is characterized by requirements that are to be met, there are associated vulnerabilities and risks for the couple when negotiating these tasks. For example, unmarried cohabiting couples who are unable to agree on marriage at some point in the course of their relationship will be faced with having to resolve their disagreement.

Same-sex partnerships and unmarried cohabiting opposite-sex couples must often deal with extended family members' attitudes and biases about their relationship. For some couples and their extended families there is little difficulty, while for others treatment is sometimes sought to help sort out the complications of dealing with the extended family vis-a-vis the partners. The grounds on which the extended family might object to the relationship are often moral, religious, or both. Not infrequently, opposition from the family or from a family member can become so intense that the couple's relationship becomes threatened.

In this section I discuss three cases: a beginning couple, a late-life couple, and a same-sex couple. In each I will show how the interplay of the selfdyad with the self of the partners is affected by the unique life circumstances of the couple—specifically, the sexual orientation of the partners or the life stage that the couple is in. Once again, I will revisit cases presented in previous chapters, while this time emphasizing the life phase as a contributor to the presenting problem.

The Beginning Couple

Although we have established that assessing the goodness of fit and complementarity of the partner begins early in the relationship while continuing as the partners relate through conscious and unconscious communication, the partners might be at variance with one another as they consider the possibility of marriage or moving to the next stage of family life. When, because of these circumstances, anger, disappointment, or exasperation with the relationship occurs, treatment is sometimes sought to resolve the impasse. One partner, for example, might be convinced after a relatively short courtship that the other person is the love of his life and wants to get married in the very near future. The other partner, however, might be much less certain and more ambivalent because of an unresolved love relationship from the past, concerns about the current partner, or fears of intimacy that include anxiety about the potential loss of autonomy.

Tricia and David, a couple described in Chapter 4, had been living together for 2 years. Shortly after they began their relationship they moved in together, though neither of them expected to marry in the future. They enjoyed each other tremendously while maintaining an active sexual life. They both had good jobs that allowed them to support their home, travels, and an active social life. After a year of cohabitation, Tricia casually brought up the possibility of marriage. Although David would engage in these conversations, he maintained a more fanciful attitude about Tricia's comments. Later, while they were on vacation, it was David who brought up that they should get married. He even mused along with Tricia about the prospect of having a child. The matter was dropped, however, until they returned home several weeks later. At a gathering at Tricia's parents' home several months later, Tricia's father, who was a devout Catholic, remarked at dinner that he wondered when the couple would be announcing their engagement. He embarrassed both Tricia and David when he commented that it was time to stop living in sin.

Tricia described this incident as a "show stopper," referring to the shock and anger that David experienced in response to her father's remark. During Tricia's description of this poignant moment, David interrupted her in obvious agitation. "Your father's remark was uncalled for, Tricia. It is none of his business," David said angrily. Tricia was initially quiet as she listened to David's concerns. I interjected, "Although this might be true, David, it has been my impression that the prospect of marriage frightens you, and perhaps this is something that we should talk about." Tricia then proceeded to remind David that when they were away on vacation it was he who had initiated the conversation about marriage but then dropped the subject. These initial exchanges then allowed us to move into an exploration of David's anxieties about commitment, his fears of losing autonomy, and what it means to give up one's youth while moving on to another life stage.

Here was a couple whose conflict erupted over the decision about whether to get married. Over time, their relationship had worked well, with sufficient permeability and optimal dynamic functioning of their selfdyad. Their struggle in making a decision about marriage, however, suggested some difficulty in maintaining necessary flexibility. While focusing on their fears, wishes, and hopes for marriage, we were able to learn that David's hesitancy was related to his mother, who in his formative years had dominated and controlled him through her dependency. As long as he and Tricia were cohabitating he could more easily maintain his sense of independence. To marry, however, meant that he might again subject himself to a woman for whom he would have to assume responsibility. As David and Tricia explored the developmental circumstances fueling their impasse, they were able to move forward into marriage.

The Same-Sex Couple

Lara and Debra came for therapy because of a conflict that erupted between them over Debra's parents, who were planning a visit to their home. Lara and Debra had recently purchased a house together and moved in as permanent partners. While Lara's family had known about her sexual orientation for several years, Debra had never openly addressed the issue with her parents. Rather than talking candidly with them about her relationship with Lara, Debra asked Lara to move out of their house temporarily while she hid all evidence of their partnership by removing Lara's belongings. When Debra proposed the plan to Lara, an argument ensued with Lara threatening to leave permanently. Outraged by Debra's secrecy, Lara insisted that Debra immediately announce their relationship to her parents in her presence.

Treatment centered on exploring Debra's shame about her sexual orientation and the prospect of having an open discussion with her conservative Southern Baptist parents. Lara's demands on Debra, on the other hand, were another target for treatment as they represented a propensity to become aggressive and demanding at times when she felt narcissistically injured or threatened. Lara at first spoke in vague terms about her background, especially her relationships with a father and older brother with whom she fought bitterly to attain what she called her "personal rights for freedom and equality."

Although at first Lara's descriptions resonated with ideological plati-
tudes, we would eventually learn more about the origin of her style and
how it pertained to her relationship with Debra. For example, it was
discovered that it was this very quality of Lara's assertion mixed with
rebelliousness to which Debra was attracted. Throughout her life Debra
had been hesitant, passive, and inclined toward self-doubt, especially in
dealing with her strong and opinionated mother.

Debra and Lara had organized their selfdyad around an unconscious
agreement that Lara would assume the more dominant posture in the
relationship while Debra followed her lead. With Debra's diffidence
bolstered by Lara, Lara could also experience a sense of satisfaction by
caring for Debra and fighting her battles. Simultaneously Lara would
then experience a sense of familiarity and a connection to her family of
origin while in a relationship that supported her dominance. Now, as
Debra's unresolved issues with her mother surfaced, her passivity came
into direct conflict with Lara's propensity to confront and control.

Because Debra's parents would be visiting in just several weeks, treatment was initiated with short-term goals. These included pointing out
to Lara that her demands on Debra were unproductive in assisting her
in coming to terms with her sexual orientation. This permitted Debra
the opportunity to work through her feelings about her sexuality while
paving the way for her to deal more openly with her parents. The tension between Lara and Debra and the risk for a breakup were successfully ameliorated as Debra came to deal more openly with her parents
around these issues.

Following this successful short-term therapy, Lara and Debra decided
to continue treatment. We would now shift our focus by addressing the
lack of flexibility and problematic dynamic functioning in their partnership. A more equitable balance of roles and styles might emerge if
Lara were able to establish more tolerance for Debra's passivity, while
lessening her need to dominate and compensate for her. Simultaneously,
Debra would be allowed and encouraged to establish more assertion
and power in their relationship.

Working with Lara entailed an exploration of her early experiences with her brother and father, both of whom she experienced as
demeaning and cruel. Her hatred of both had been fundamental in
her intrapsychic life, and superiority and authority over others became
ways to defend against the possibility of ever again subjecting herself
to the dominance of others. Debra, on the other hand, was now faced
with coming to terms with a mother whose control over her had been
remarkably similar to what she and Lara had created together. Although
idealizing and depending on her mother during childhood provided

her protection and safety, it had given her little opportunity to develop her autonomy when she entered adolescence. Furthermore, her father's passivity and his inclination to remain in the shadow as he acquiesced to his wife's dominance provided a role model of a parent who inhibited his power as he unconsciously encouraged his wife to take charge. This couple paradigm was now repeated in Lara and Debra's relationship. As Lara and Debra deepened their insight into their relationship with their parents and families of origin, they were able to increase the flexibility of their selfdyad functioning.

The Couple in Later Life

The couple in later life encounters challenges that are unique from those inherent to other stages of adult life. Retirement is sometimes a momentous event and yet one that can proceed smoothly when the partners are able to provide support for each other while coming to terms with the loss of careers, alterations in social status, and changes in physical functioning. The central developmental task at this stage of life becomes the replenishment and reorganization of meaning and fulfillment, which for many couples was at one time provided by work. The partners are frequently faced with more free time that must now be divided between new or renewed interests and being with each other. How the two individuals respond to these changes provides a new set of developmental challenges that the couple must now negotiate.

In general, couples in later life who have maintained a reasonably flexible and permeable selfdyad and for whom work and careers have been comfortably balanced with intimacy and play will manage the transition of retirement while more easily coming to terms with the psychological losses and changes that are entailed. There are couples, however, for whom the process of retirement is confronted and managed in a less fluid way. For these couples, career and/or work may have historically assumed such importance for the individual or for the selfdyad that the partners have been less able to integrate intimacy, play, and work comfortably. Now, with one or both partners ending their careers, the dynamics of the relationship change and a problem emerges.

Mattie and Art, a couple who had been married for 55 years, called for a consultation. Mattie had recently retired from her active career in philanthropic work. Although Art had sold his successful engineering company several years ago, he had continued to travel throughout the world to various engineering firms by serving as a consultant.

Mattie and Art, now just a few months short of 80 years of age, were having difficulty in their relationship, ostensibly around issues pertaining to where, when, or how they would travel. Their four children were grown and married and had children of their own, all living in distant areas of the country. Although Mattie had remained interested in their children and grandchildren over the years, Mattie and Art had not been especially close to them because of Art's unwillingness to drive by car to visit them. Mattie's fear of air travel had prevented visits to their children except by automobile or train. Art, on the other hand, refused to travel by car because it represented a waste of his time. Art's recently informing Mattie that she simply needed to "tough it out and get on that airplane" was met with considerable anger and resistance as the conflict between them now became unmanageable.

Upon meeting Art and Mattie I was impressed with their vigor and keen intellects. Mattie took the lead during the first session while Art sat impatiently throughout her introduction. He intermittently glanced at his watch as he looked out the window. Although Art's distractibility was quite apparent, Mattie did not comment, instead continuing to explain herself in laborious detail. Although I too noted that it might be easy to become distracted from Mattie's elaborations, I felt irritated with Art for his flagrant but nonverbal dismissal of Mattie's concerns. Had he come to the appointment simply to placate his wife, I wondered, and did my annoyance with him represent an identification with Mattie, whose complaints about travel were merely a symptom of a more pervasive problem in the relationship?

Mattie described her anger at Art for his unwillingness to drive to visit their daughter and family, who were having a party to celebrate their granddaughter's 16th birthday. Art had instead made plans to travel to Japan on business, and although he would attend the gathering, he would be arriving late that evening. Art insisted that, if Mattie was unwilling to fly on her own, she should have her sister drive her. Upon hearing Art's suggestion Mattie became even more furious, commenting that Art only considered his needs and that it had never been any different throughout their entire marriage. While listening to an escalation of Mattie's anger, I suddenly noticed Art attempting to stifle his yawn as he turned to me to inquire how long their appointment would last. He added that he had to leave later that day to catch his plane. With Art's display of derision I now wondered about the extent to which his unwillingness to drive his wife might represent a more enduring narcissistic feature. Or was his behavior a passive-aggressive reaction to Mattie's persistent nagging? I would wait to see.

Here was a juncture in couple therapy where a wife's angry complaints and concerns were met by a husband's disregard and thinly veiled disdain. While Mattie's whining behavior was certainly irritating and unproductive in accomplishing its goal, Art's contemptuous behavior appeared equally infuriating. Suddenly responding to my own annoyance with Art, I remarked, "Art, you are making an effort not to yawn, but I think that your apparent boredom might convey your disregard of Mattie's concerns." An uncomfortable silence followed. I glanced back and forth between Mattie and Art during this pregnant interval as both stared at me for what appeared to be an eternity. Suddenly, Art broke into a broad grin while Mattie remained stony faced. "You know, son," Art said, "I don't think anyone has ever said anything like that to me before. But I *am* bored and I am also damned mad." Although Art acknowledged the accuracy of my observation, addressing me as "son" was condescending and seemed yet another attempt to wield his superiority over others.

As treatment unfolded, we were able to learn a great deal more about Art and Mattie's selfdyad functioning and how it had sustained them during the 55 years of their marriage. Art and Mattie first met at a debutante ball given in Mattie's honor by her parents nearly 60 years ago. Mattie had grown up as an only child in privileged circumstances and, by her own admission, was spoiled by her parents and grandparents. Art had been on the service staff for the party. Mattie had been impressed with his good looks and charm, a style that both Art and Mattie acknowledged had been his ticket to success.

Art had been raised in impoverished circumstances by a single mother, and he left home at the age of 14. At 19 he began working for a catering agency that provided service to the socially elite. Although Art had only worked for the agency a short time, he paid his manager to acquire the job at the mansion in which Mattie lived, where the party would be given. Mattie remarked that although Art tried hard to impress her, she was initially appalled by his "low brow" status. When Art finally persuaded her to go out with him, Mattie's parents objected, making active attempts to break up their relationship.

In spite of her parents' objections, Mattie began dating Art and, after a brief courtship, they were married. With the financial support of Mattie's parents, Art was able to attend college, obtain a degree in engineering, and eventually start his own company. Mattie for the most part had raised their children alone while Art grew his company into prominence. He had little involvement in the lives of his children during the years they were raised, which seemed acceptable to Mattie. As the children grew older, Mattie became more involved with her philanthropic work. Although Art and Mattie would attend social events together, their relationship remained distant, regulated and maintained by their respective careers and the structure of the high society in which they lived.

By this time in the consultation I had the impression that this was a couple who over the years had led separate lives while maintaining their marriage and raising their children. Intimacy and even physical togetherness had been minimal. And yet it did not seem as though intimacy was especially sacrificed because neither of them seemed to want it. Mattie and Art had constructed their selfdyad in a way that had promoted their self-interests while they were able to avoid closeness and intimacy. Their relationship structure is depicted in Figure 6.1A in this chapter. Both had found partners who would respect their narcissistic needs, while not burdening each other with desires for closeness or intimacy. Mattie's recent retirement, however, seemed to add a dimension of need to the partnership that Art was unwilling to negotiate.

Art and Mattie, a couple in late life, illustrate some important points pertaining to the selfdyad and how it functions vis-a-vis the individuals in the partnership. Couples can be quite capable of maintaining the relationship over time, assuming that the selfdyad functions to preserve the selves of the partners. Although many illustrations throughout this book have described couples for whom the selfdyad had encroached upon the self of one or both partners, Mattie and Art exemplify a couple whose selves were fully supported by their selfdyad for many years. They had unconsciously agreed to take and demand little from each other, instead using each other to enhance themselves narcissistically as individuals. Now encountering retirement, Mattie's need for additional support from Art introduced a change in their dynamic functioning as a couple, setting their conflict into motion.

Couple therapy would require that we address their previously functional narcissistic selfdyad, while slowly addressing issues pertaining to compromise and flexibility. Whether we would eventually broach issues pertaining to their lack of intimacy and sexuality would remain to be seen.

7

CONTEXT, RELATIONSHIP
MAINTENANCE, AND REPAIR

In previous chapters we explored the psychological, biological, and social factors involved in the process of partner selection and the formation of the couple. We addressed how finding the partner is based on both the need for attachment and an unconscious yearning for transformation, while the relationship is developed and maintained through a continuous process of unconscious communication. We have emphasized the importance of internal object relations and how these relationship scripts become congealed into the selfdyad—a conjointly constructed system operating synergistically as a function of two selves that are in communication with each other both consciously and unconsciously. And, finally, we have discussed how relationship satisfaction depends on whether the selfdyad functions to support and enhance the selves of the partners.

In this chapter we will turn our attention to the specific factors involved in maintaining this intricate balance between self-expression and a mutually loving and enriching relationship. We will attempt to define those features of relating that distinguish partnerships that are successful in enhancing the self versus those that tend to vitiate the self and, ultimately, the selfdyad. We have thus far developed a model for understanding the formation and development of the intimate partnership and its impact on the self. Here we will extend our understanding of these processes by addressing the nature of interpersonal connection and its relationship to attachment and how these are mediated by the subtleties of communication occurring between partners. With the use of a clinical vignette I will illustrate the ways in which unconscious conflicts and relationship scripts impact the selves to influence communication between the partners and within the selfdyad both consciously and unconsciously.

TWO SELVES, THE COUPLE, AND COMMUNICATION

Although all clinicians and writers in the field of couple and marital therapy likely agree that the quality of communication is fundamental to achieving relationship satisfaction, what actually constitutes that quality and how support or lack of support of the partner is ultimately conveyed might divide psychological experts according to theoretical allegiance. Clinicians oriented in a psychoanalytic direction, for instance, largely believe that communication between two individuals, whether in an intimate partnership such as marriage, parent and child, or therapist and patient, is predominantly unconscious. Indeed, words and actions matter considerably. But of far greater importance are the unconscious emotions, wishes, and needs conveyed through words, actions, subtleties of tone, inflection, facial features, eye contact, and posture. And to complicate matters even more, what is ultimately conveyed is determined not just by the one who sends the communication but also by the one receiving it.

Most self-help books on the market today focus on communication through conscious relating. These authors will sometimes provide suggestions and recommendations about how to speak to one's child, one's student, or one's partner, and they might even provide insights about gender-specific attributes or suggestions for improved sexual functioning (Gordon, 1970, 1974; Gray, 1995). In most of these works, little attention is paid to the unconscious processes that are operating and to how crucial developmental antecedents are repeated within the partnership.

Although self-help books can be enlightening, sometimes even offering hope by encouraging treatment, they are usually insufficient in assisting couples with their difficulties in communication. The fundamental reason for this is that what is actually communicated between partners is often quite different from the words and behaviors occurring within the communication network. Thus, the prescription that is provided fails to address what lies at the root of the communication difficulty. The one-size-fits-all approach contrasts with the thesis of this discourse: that what is actually communicated within the intimate partnership is predominantly unconscious, flowing from deeply held convictions about the self and others and in the service of connection, attachment, and the unconscious desire for transformation.

This prelude takes us into the realm of affects, self-needs, and the communication process itself. In discussing some of the important features of communication, we will consider the valuable contributions of the self psychologists, the group of psychoanalysts who have expanded our understanding of self-needs and their importance in human development and in psychotherapy.

Heinz Kohut made a radical departure from the existing nomological network of traditional psychoanalytic theory as he attempted to reformulate the essence of psychotherapeutic treatment. His ideas have also contributed to a better understanding of the nature of communication and, importantly, to a better understanding of the universality of human psychological needs and how they are conveyed from one person to another. First and foremost are the basic needs that include care, shelter, food, and interpersonal involvement. Other self-needs include knowledge, skills to be learned, or skills that are sought from those who possess a credential for providing that skill. The teacher–student, doctor–patient, clergyman–parishioner, and parent–child, as well as intimate partners, the subject of this writing, are all examples of relationship pairs in which each individual within the dyad requires something important or essential for the self—what we define as a self-need.

Although the primary purpose of the teacher–student relationship, for example, is to provide the student facts and skills, educators are well aware that when there is a basic rapport and mutual respect between teacher and student, learning will likely be enhanced. The purpose of the relationship is facilitated when essential selfobject emotional needs are met within the partnership. This includes a communication style and an interpersonal environment consisting of empathy and affirmation that adequately provides what is needed.

Kohut originally defined the selfobject as a person in the infant's environment that the infant, as a function of immaturity of the self, is as yet unable to distinguish from the self (Kohut, 1977). These objectively separate others (the mother and father usually) provide necessary functions for the infant by fulfilling basic needs, the selfobject functions, that the child is not yet able to provide for himself. Having only a rudimentary sense of self that is entirely dependent on parenting figures for the fulfillment of basic physical and psychological needs, the maturing child gradually incorporates these selfobject needs into a self-structure that eventually becomes independent of the original selfobjects.

Kohut emphasized that the self that finally emerges will be a composite of the child's constitutional makeup and what the selfobjects have transmitted. Through psychological merger with the selfobjects, these selfobject functions eventually become installed within the mental organization of the child. Kohut emphasized that the developing psyche of the child is also influenced by the way in which the child is able to participate in the selfobject's subjective experience of him or her, which is again a function of having psychologically merged with that important other person. What is conveyed by the selfobject to the child is transmitted through words, but also through tone, inflection, touch, gaze, and the subtleties of communication—all while empathically attuned to the child as if these experiences were the child's own. At maturity, this emergent adult ideally will have incorporated a sufficiently coherent and resilient self-structure that is now independent of the original selfobjects.

Kohut originally conceptualized a psychology of the self as a paradigmatic elaboration of the existing psychoanalytic theories, but also as an expansion of developmental psychology. Because the mechanisms by which the child develops a sense of self involve ongoing experiences of being subjectively merged with a caretaking selfobject, the concept of empathy was conceived and elevated to a position of preeminence. Although the self psychologists originally emphasized the essential role of empathy in psychoanalytic therapy, its prominence in effective communication has been a more recent discovery. Here I assert its importance in the communication between intimate partners where, through affirmation and support, the attachment bonds of the couple are formed and maintained (Hazan, Campa, & Gur-Yaish, 2006; Shaddock, 2000).

In developing his expansions of psychoanalytic theory, Kohut did not address projective identification as a mode of communication between the selfobject and the child or between partners. His contributions instead centered on the conveyance of empathy for the developing child and for the patient in the psychoanalytic situation. While emphasizing the selfobject's responsibility for imparting a psychologically salubrious environment, Kohut did not place a great deal of emphasis in his writings on how the child or other recipient takes in the communication and interprets it according to his or her psychological structure. Although I believe he presumed this, he emphasized the inevitability of the parent's or analyst's empathic failures as instrumental in communication difficulties and, ultimately, the root cause of failure in the self. For our purposes, empathic failures are explained as the selfobject's defensive efforts to rid the self of an unwanted quality by projecting it outside the self and into the other person. Here the selfobject's intended empathy is contaminated by parts of the self that must be urgently evacuated, however, now creating a distorted version of the other partner's actual experience.

THE SYSTEM AND THE SELF

Although I have made an attempt to remain theoretically equidistant among the various psychological schools of thought, I lean toward an object relations paradigm supplemented by systems theory and a psychology of the self. While some might argue that object relations theory contains within it a theory of communication that renders a systems theory unnecessary, a systems model additionally posits that, as couples develop their partnerships with their idiosyncratic patterns of communication, both partners will provide stimuli serving to modify, sustain, and regulate the behavior and emotional functioning of the other partner. The concept of projective identification has exceptional explanatory power in helping us understand how partners experience an urgency to evacuate an unwanted part of the self by placing it into another.

A systems model, however, adds another dimension by enriching our understanding of how two individuals influence each other by shaping each other's feelings and responses. What is actually conveyed to the other person—in the form of wishes, needs, and affects, for example—comes to have a regulatory effect on the couple system as the partners develop an interlocking stimulus and response sequence that becomes both the cause and the effect of each other's functioning. This synergism provides the dynamic movement and balance of the selfdyad, creating features of the relationship that are often unique from the personal traits of the two partners forming it. This accounts for the well-known phenomenon in couple therapy that the character style and personal qualities of an individual patient might appear to the clinician as quite different from that same person's style of relating when seen in conjoint therapy with the partner.

The following vignette illustrates several important points I have been making: the importance of affect states transmitted without words, how a couple's communication style can lead to a selfdyad unable to provide needed selfobject qualities, and how essential reparative qualities of a relationship can be undermined when the selfdyad fails to regulate feelings of anger and strivings for control.

Ginny and Frank

Ginny and Frank, a couple in their 40s, appeared for their appointment in such a state of palpable anger that just moments before their session was to begin my assistant urgently stepped into my office to speak with me. Several other patients in the waiting area seemed to be uncomfortable in the presence of this couple. My assistant, Cheryl, was also apparently uncomfortable with what appeared to be this couple's resounding emotions, an uncharacteristic reaction for this seasoned professional who had worked with me for many years. When I asked Cheryl what had actually transpired in the waiting area she responded, "Oh, nothing actually." So I asked, "Well, what was said"? Again she responded, "Nothing. They're just so angry and cold with each other. Well, I guess for one thing he is rattling his newspaper and she…well, she just looks mad. They are sitting faced away from each other and the other patients are watching them."

Concerned and intrigued with what had been conveyed to me, I repeated to Cheryl the essence of what she had said: "So the people who are waiting to see me are quite angry with each other, but nothing has been said between them; yet, the other patients in the waiting room are uncomfortable." Cheryl looked at me, now puzzled by her own observation and my summary of what she had just told me. At this moment she and I both realized that here was a situation in which the intensity of emotion between two people who had come to see me had mounted to such a threshold that, even without spoken words, their affects had been projected into the reception room and invaded the mental space of others.

This interaction between two people who had uttered no actual words but whose feelings toward each other pervaded a therapist's reception room provides a fascinating introduction into the realm of nonverbal communication. Having established that projective identification lies at the base of unconscious communication of the couple, the selfdyad, and the feedback loop, which for the couple becomes regulatory, we will now consider how this system of communication has the potential to undermine the well-being of the couple or to support and enhance it. Without a single word spoken between Frank and Ginny, there had been a transmission of affects of such intensity that others within their range were able to experience their feelings as if reading their minds.

This illuminating introduction to a couple whom I had not even met but whose emotional functions I had already glimpsed through nonverbal communication provides an example of how affects are communicated between and among humans with or without words. Schore has demonstrated that communication patterns between mothers and babies develop through entrainment, a psychophysical process by which the right hemispheres of the brain decode and store information while developing a synchrony with each other according to vocal tone, olfactory cues, posture, gestures, and mannerisms. What is conveyed are subtleties in affect that come to regulate each other's emotional states and responses (Schore, 1994, 2003).

Schore's work provides a psychobiological model for the concept of projective identification as the fundamental mode through which intimate partners come to communicate as they transmit affective states, needs, and desires. The concept of entrainment also provides an explanation for the mutually sustaining quality of the selfdyad, which then becomes regulatory for the couple while providing a foundation for attachment. As each person becomes intimately acquainted with the partner's nonverbal cues and mannerisms, for example, the couple develops a synchronization of affects that then has the potential to diminish or to enhance the couple's intimacy.

Ginny and Frank's most apparent affect was anger, at least when presenting as a couple. Were they, however, inherently angry people? If so, how did they find each other as partners and what was the original attraction that provided a foundation for their once loving connection? If they were not intrinsically angry people, or perhaps one was and the other was not, how had they settled into a chronic state of rage toward each other that now brought them into treatment? What was it that each wanted and needed from the other and why was this not satisfied? And, finally, embedded within their expectations, what were the parts of the self that had been repressed and were now projected? These questions become the principal guideposts for the therapist as the couple's story unfolds.

As I proceeded into the reception area to meet this couple, Frank remained seated as Ginny got out of her chair and walked toward me. As I stood in the doorway Ginny whispered that she would like to speak with me alone. I quickly glanced at Frank, who was seemingly preoccupied reading his magazine. Because there had likely been an agreement between them, at least unconsciously, that Ginny alone would initiate the consultation, I motioned for her to enter, leaving Frank in the waiting area. I wondered now why they had come in as a couple while choosing Ginny to begin the consultation.

Ginny sat down and without delay said to me that she felt that she could no longer remain in the 20-year marriage to Frank. She said that their three children had encouraged them to seek treatment, primarily Ginny thought, because they were quite attached to their father and were afraid of losing him through a divorce. Their 12-year-old daughter had recently been diagnosed with irritable bowel syndrome, which her physician thought was likely due to the marital discord. Ginny's tone and manner with me appeared to be thoughtful and considerate as she expressed her concerns and worry about the impact of their troubled marriage on their daughter. Momentarily, I lost sight of the introduction that was previously given to me about the infectious anger that this couple had purveyed in the reception area. Here with me now was a woman who spoke softly and carefully as she expressed her guilt that her troubled marriage was at the root of her daughter's medical problems. So far there was no hint of the intense anger that had been previously described.

I said to Ginny that I would like to hear more about the difficulties between her and Frank and how they had agreed that she would come in alone. She responded that she felt that I could get a clearer picture of their problems if she first came to give me some background information. Ginny's response seemed conspicuously superficial, I thought. "Is there any other reason?" I asked. Ginny became silent as she dropped her head. Her jaw tightened in response to my inquiry about why they had not come in together. She went on to say that for many years she had felt that her marriage was in trouble. Because raising their children to become well-adjusted adults was a common goal for both her and Frank, they had decided to continue their marriage in spite of their unhappiness with each other.

I asked Ginny how she had understood the difficulties between her and Frank. "We can hardly be in the same room with each other," she responded. "I've gotten to a point that whenever he opens his mouth I become furious. And I want to argue with him, no matter what he says. And he is the same way with me." Ginny seemed to be describing a chronic pattern of interaction in which they had come to respond to each other with intense and immediate anger and that was easily provoked by the other one. Ginny's comment that she becomes furious "whenever he opens his mouth" suggested that, through entrainment, this couple had likely developed a selfdyad that had become rigid, reactive, and mutually regulatory for their angry interactions. I responded by asking if the intensity of their anger at each other might be a reason they chose not to come in together.

She went on to say that she and Frank had grown so intolerant of each other that even their couple friends no longer wanted to be around them. "There is no other person in the world that can provoke me into rage so easily," Ginny said. She proceeded to tell me that they had come to a point where they were unable to be civil to each other, much less provide support for each other. Frank, for example, had been experiencing some work-related difficulties, which he no longer discussed with her. "He doesn't really talk to me about anything anymore, and I don't really care. The coldness that I feel for him isn't really like me, though. When we are with others we are both very pleasant people. It seems that when we're together, we become instantly hateful," Ginny said, clearly puzzled by the changes in their affective states that she was describing.

Ginny appeared to be describing a selfdyad that had come to be experienced by both her and Frank as alien to their individual selves. Both appeared to have lost the capacity for selfobject relating, while intimacy and connectedness had deteriorated over time. It was here that I sensed an opportunity to deepen our understanding of their situation by asking a question about Ginny's background. "Ginny, you remarked a moment ago that there is no one else that can provoke your anger so easily. Has there ever been?" I asked. After a brief pause Ginny replied, "Well, maybe my father." She went on to inform me that as a child she had been especially close to her father. When she moved into adolescence, however, her father could not tolerate her independence. Whenever she took issue with her father's position, he would either become enraged or punish her with silence and withdrawal. Here was the first hint of Ginny's internal world—a history that contained clues for an eventual understanding of her and Frank's relationship difficulties.

Now that I understood the basic difficulty for which this couple had come to see me, there was a question of how to proceed. It was clear that Ginny had come in alone because of the difficulty that she and Frank had in being together. To avoid each other might minimize the intensity of anger that was easily generated between them, but in a way that would also diminish the opportunity for resolving the conflicts between them.

Suddenly I noted my slight anxiety about Frank being left in the waiting room. They had originally scheduled a couple consultation, I reminded myself. And yet I seemed to be more concerned about this than was Ginny. So what did it mean that I was experiencing anxiety about the way this couple had presented for the consultation—concerned that Frank would feel left out? I tuned into my musings to understand something that was occurring in their relationship. Faced with the issue of Frank's inclusion, I now conveyed my struggle to Ginny. "Ginny, there are just about 20 minutes remaining, and I am aware that Frank has not yet come in. What are your feelings about this?" I asked.

Ginny replied in a manner that seemed dismissive of Frank. She responded that Frank really had not expected to come in anyway, and that his coming to the appointment was merely his attempt to "dominate" her. Here Ginny seemed to be ascribing an image of control to Frank, while it appeared as though *she* was also attempting to take control by dismissing him from the session. Aware that Frank might possibly be squeezed out of the session and in a way that could compromise treatment, I said to Ginny that, because Frank had accompanied her to the session and it had been my understanding that they were coming in as a couple, it seemed that he should be included. Reluctantly, Ginny conceded that she understood my position.

Frank entered the consultation room looking somewhat apprehensive. As he sat down beside Ginny, I immediately began to experience the mutuality of contempt that my assistant had described. After a brief introduction I asked Frank how he understood their difficulties. Working to be tactful, he commented that he and Ginny had grown "intolerant" of each other's views and opinions. He proceeded to describe himself as "a very opinionated person" and then referred to his family of origin, in which he was the eldest of five who had been put in charge of the younger children while his parents worked nights. Frank was clearly saying that he had been placed into a position of leadership at an early age, implying that he had earned the right to demonstrate his authority in the family. "She always knew that I had strong opinions on most matters, and at one time she really liked that about me," Frank said. He continued, "But as time has gone on, she feels that I am controlling her, even when I give my opinions about politics and things like that."

Proceeding in a somewhat oratorical way, Frank said that Ginny was very "controlling," but that she refused to acknowledge it. "Now she just ignores me, and I guess I've come to ignore her too," Frank said, with bitterness in his voice. Here I was struck by Frank's observation that Ginny ignored him and that she was controlling. It captured how I had experienced Ginny's attempt to dismiss him from the interview as she attempted to take charge of the session. Hearing Frank's description of their difficulties, Ginny suddenly abdicated her composure. "If you didn't always bitch about how I don't listen to you, or how cold I've become, or how I'm just like my father, maybe I wouldn't ignore you," Ginny said in fury. Although I had spoken with Frank for only a few minutes, it seemed that he could indeed be experienced as critical and imperial. And yet it was Ginny's attitude of disregard that provoked his complaints, as she had over time become less willing to provide Frank the affirmation that she once had given him. The more Frank voiced his complaints about what he was not getting from Ginny, the more Ginny felt attacked and controlled by him. Over time their intimacy had eroded as they both increasingly failed to respond in ways that would nurture their relationship.

DESTRUCTIVE AFFECTS AND THEIR REPAIR
THROUGH SELFOBJECT RELATING

With couples in crisis the therapist is faced with having to make a rapid assessment of the central difficulty by sometimes verbalizing the dynamics of the problem in a way that diminishes the tension and anger and staves off the destructiveness that has been brought about by the couple's aggression. This becomes a monumental task when considering that all this must be accomplished while simultaneously assisting the couple to muster hope and motivation for continuing the work of therapy. This, of course, is not entirely different from working with individual patients. But for the couple in crisis, it might be even more urgent for the therapist to provide immediate feedback that assists the partners in containing their rage, despair, and other affects that are undermining the relationship.

Especially important are those affects that fuel the resistances and threaten the couple's willingness to return for treatment. But it is not just the anger and the incendiary quality of the interaction that require the immediate attention of the therapist. Anger or even a proneness to volatility by itself does not usually carry the most destructive potential for the relationship. What provides the greatest risk for the relationship and threatens its survival is the anger between the partners that undermines the necessary selfobject qualities of relating that are required for the repair of the relationship.

With especially volatile couples whose rage has settled into a chronic pattern of relating, it can be even more difficult during a single hour to assess the central problem in a way that addresses the crisis while providing interventions to help contain the couple's affects and simultaneously garner motivation for treatment. Because couples in crisis will frequently leave a session while still experiencing intense feelings, they will often continue to discuss and even argue over the issues lingering from the treatment hour. In these situations there is risk that the couple will amplify their most destructive feeling states, in spite of the therapist's best efforts to provide the necessary containment.

Furthermore, in sessions in which there is considerable emotion displayed and projective identification is especially apparent, the therapist is at risk for becoming emotionally disorganized as a function of the couple's affective overflow. The therapist's clinical equanimity can become compromised, undermining the capacity to provide interventions that will assist in containing the couple's most destructive emotional states (Zeitner, 2003). More will be said about this later in the chapters dealing with technique.

Previously, we established the importance of the attachment functions for the intimate couple. We have expanded our understanding of projective identification as a fundamental mechanism by which couples communicate as they place into each other qualities of the self requiring containment by the partner. To the extent that both partners are able to accept the projections of the other, the selfdyad formed will likely enrich the relationship in such a way that both partners experience a sense of being enhanced and transformed (Bollas, 1987). But what are those specific features of interpersonal relating that are required for the self to flourish? And how are they manifested behaviorally?

Kohut taught that selfobject needs must be supplied for the child by the mother to ensure a healthy development of the self. He extrapolated his theory of development to the treatment process by emphasizing the importance of selfobject needs in psychotherapy and, by implication, in all forms of human intimate relating throughout the entire life span. Although Kohut did not formulate a psychology of attachment per se, Shaddock (2000) has described selfobject functions as "windows" into attachment.

THE COUPLE'S SELFOBJECT FUNCTIONS

When a couple's anger and other destructive affects have congealed into the selfdyad, both partners will be less able to communicate in a manner that nourishes and allows for the repair of intimacy. In this section we will expand upon the selfobject functions that are especially pertinent for intimate partners and without which the partners will be compromised in their ability to repair the inevitable injuries and the vicissitudes of aggression that occur as a function of intimate relating. Where possible I will refer to Ginny and Frank as a way of illustrating the quality of selfobject relating and its implications for their ability to maintain and repair their relationship.

Listening

Although for Kohut listening was not specifically a selfobject function, for our purposes it represents an essential mode through which couples communicate their needs and wishes. The *New Lexicon Webster's Dictionary of the English Language* (1989) defines listening as using "one's ears consciously in order to hear." To listen to another in an intimate encounter, however, is a behavior that extends far beyond this literal definition. For intimate partners, there is the implication that truly listening to the other person involves conveying to the partner that what was heard was also understood. For this to occur, there must be a behavioral signal, verbal or nonverbal, that reveals to the partner that the communication has been recognized as important. Here we again note that within all intimate partnerships empathy is a necessary feature of the interpersonal encounter that is probably always present in some form for true listening to occur.

For example, it is not unusual for a partner to accuse the other partner of failing to listen, when instead that partner feels misunderstood. Similarly, couples can easily become embroiled in arguments and impasses that have nothing whatsoever to do with whether one has been listened to. Instead, what is indicated is a lack of empathy for the partner's position. Conversely, when the partner is able to convey an understanding of the other's position or message, even in the face of a disagreement on the actual issue, the likelihood of an argument or impasse is frequently lessened. A capacity to listen, to understand, and to convey empathy for the partner's position or feelings, then, lies at the heart of the communication between intimate partners.

Ginny and Frank had evolved in their relationship such that listening to each other with a capacity for empathy was severely compromised. A most glaring example of this occurred when Frank commented that Ginny had come to a point in their relationship where she ignored him. Using this innocuous word instantly unleashed Ginny's fury to the extent that she was unable to hear his concerns about feeling lonely and missing the intimacy that they once had.

There was also an implication that at one time Frank had reaped considerable affirmation in knowing that Ginny appreciated his strong opinions on many matters. Now she had come to experience Frank's opinions as intolerable and she felt controlled by him. The more Frank would explain his position and let her know what he wanted in the relationship, the more she felt criticized and controlled by his attempts to reestablish some form of interpersonal connection. As Frank became more identified with the controlling qualities of her father, Ginny withdrew more, and she was now unable to hear Frank's fears of losing the connection that they once had.

Empathy

The concept of empathy by now has a long and illustrious history within psychology and psychotherapy (Rogers, 1961). It was Kohut and the contemporary self psychologists who made it central to the psychoanalytic task by showing us its place in the development of the self and in the process of communication (Kohut, 1959, 1971, 1977). While empathy is one of the psychotherapist's most essential tools because it allows the therapist to understand the patient's inner psychological life through vicarious introspection, it is also a central feature of interpersonal relating that facilitates attachment (Shaddock, 2000). Empathy allows intimate partners to come to know each other's inner lives and motivation by facilitating the interpenetration of mental boundaries that create and maintain intimacy and attachment, while simultaneously becoming a fundamental feature of the well-functioning selfdyad.

For the couple whose relationship has settled into a chronic state of anger or other negative affective states, it can be assumed that the capacity for empathy has similarly declined. This was the case for Ginny and Frank. Although early in their relationship Ginny had admired Frank's self-assured style and strongly opinionated nature, over time she had come to experience him as trying to control her in almost every way. Because Frank had become identified with an unconscious representation of Ginny's father, who had threatened her autonomy as she moved into adolescence, she was now unable to sustain her empathy in a way that would allow her to hear his complaints as a desire for closeness and a wish to restore the admiration he once experienced from her.

Similarly, Frank's urgent need to recover this admiration, driven by his need to reinstate the position of authority he once had within his family of origin, made it difficult for him to understand that his complaints were experienced by Ginny as his attempts to control her. Over time, there had been a deterioration of empathy for each other's position, and Ginny and Frank were now locked into a mutually reinforcing selfdyad of anger and control—characteristics they experienced as alien to their individual selves.

Having empathy presumes that one is able to apprehend the essence of the partner's experience in a way that is relatively uninfluenced by one's own sensitivities. Although all of us possess vulnerabilities related to our relationships with early caretakers and significant others, a toxic relationship paradigm that has not been resolved but merely sealed over through repression has the potential to ignite a relationship conflict when a quality or an action of the partner too closely resembles the early relational paradigm. The toxic relationship from early development represents a psychic lesion that carries with it a potential to destroy empathy as the partner becomes experienced as the original hurtful other.

Mirroring

While listening and empathy operate interdependently and are essential for all intimate relating, they simultaneously function as characteristics of effective communication and as modes through which essential features of selfobject relating occur. Although Kohut's original definition of the selfobject was a central construct of self psychology, with implications for the analyst's relationship to the patient, we now consider the concept of selfobject to have even wider application in understanding the essence of communication that occurs within all intimate partnerships.

Kohut's original definition of mirroring referred to the selfobject mother who reflects and confirms the infant's expansive and excited states while the child grows and transforms through an accretion of developmental achievements. The concept of the mirroring selfobject is easily extrapolated to the psychology of the couple. For our purposes, mirroring refers to the individual's attention to the partner by effectively conveying that partner's affective state. What is central to the experience of mirroring is the partner's ability to respond to the other partner's emotional state in a way that confirms and delineates that affective state while conveying that the other partner is central and important to the first partner's experience. Fundamental to mirroring are behaviors that convey a participation in the excited and expansive states of the partner, while simultaneously recognizing the most salient affect, whether the mirroring partner offers verbal support, advice, or ongoing conversation.

What is critical and unique to mirroring, regardless of the specific kind of verbal or nonverbal exchange, is that the selfobject is able to participate in the partner's affective experience. What is essential is the transmission of positive affective contact within an atmosphere of acceptance. This might take the form of providing an insight or clarification of something that is experienced or said by the partner, merely listening attentively as the partner gives an account of something, or simply maintaining eye contact while one is interpersonally involved. The term "mirroring" implies that one self reflects the experience of the other through listening, watching, engaging, or actively interacting with the partner. Through this process, the self-experiences of the partner become more clearly defined. Through the mirroring experience, attachment becomes solidified, while the experience of the self as being both connected and separate is confirmed.

Apparently, Ginny and Frank's ability to provide mirroring experiences for each other had deteriorated significantly. The cold and icy atmosphere they had created in the reception room as they turned away from each other while Frank rattled his newspaper conveyed their mutual hostility. Burdened with inner conflicts relating to unresolved early relationships, both Ginny and Frank were unable to appreciate each other's behaviors as representing their needs to be mirrored, affirmed, and understood. As Frank experienced Ginny's rejection, he felt justified in pontificating in a way that he hoped might make him understood. In doing so, Frank's identification with Ginny's father introject only reinforced her inclination to take flight from him as she grew more angry and cold. Now stonewalling each other's needs and wishes, essential mirroring had declined, while both were now locked into a selfdyad of rejection, hostility, and mutual control.

Idealizing

Kohut's original formulation of the idealizing selfobject function stemmed from his observation that patients require an experience of being psychologically merged with one who is admired for qualities of strength, calm, safety, and soothing, and who possesses a capacity to guide and inspire. Although one might easily recognize idealization as essential for the child's growth and development and a necessary ingredient in the helping professions, it is perhaps less immediately apparent that idealization is vital for the couple's relationship. Inherent to the couple's idealization is the unconscious experience of safety that is reminiscent of the security that was originally achieved with parent figures. This unconscious representation of parental attachment now, however, provides a slippery slope—a relationship that has the potential either to sustain attachment or to repair or repeat wounds from early development (Clulow, 2001).

To establish a secure attachment through intimate partnering, idealization must remain in ascendance, without which there will likely follow a reduction in passion and intimacy. As with the other selfobject functions, the more unresolved conflicts and early developmental failures are evoked within the individual and unconsciously represented in the partner, the greater the chances are for failures in the idealizing selfobject functions.

The idealization that originally drew Frank and Ginny together had waned as both partners had become associated in each other's minds with early developmental failures. Frank's strongly opinionated style had at one time been admired by Ginny, while he experienced her admiration of his intelligence and take-charge qualities as essential for maintaining his self-esteem. Growing up in a home in which he had been in a leadership role as he took charge of his siblings, but lacking guidance from parents who were largely unavailable, Frank had come to regulate his self-esteem by establishing himself as a leader of others. Although in the beginning of their relationship Ginny had admired him for his authoritative qualities because they represented those admired features of the Oedipal father, eventually she had come to experience Frank's criticism as the controlling qualities of her father during her adolescence, who had stifled her autonomy.

Although it is highly useful for the therapist to inquire of both partners what it was that was originally valued and admired in the other partner, it was unnecessary with Frank and Ginny because it was offered spontaneously. When the therapist observes an abrupt shift in the partner's perception of a once idealized quality that is now resented or even despised, it can be hypothesized that the partner has now become identified with a toxic inner object from early development. Armed with this understanding, the therapist is then in a position to address the mutual projection process as it unfolds in the treatment.

THE DEVELOPMENT OF SELFOBJECT RELATING

By now we have established the importance of selfobject relating for all permanent partnerships, without which intimacy, affection, and the various ingredients of attachment for the couple will likely falter. We have demonstrated how selfobject functions that at one time fueled the couple's intimacy can erode and become dysfunctional when early conflictual object relationships are reactivated within the partnership. When these selfobject functions are no longer an integral part of the relationship, the couple will be crippled in its capacity to repair the emotional injuries that are inevitably experienced in the course of everyday life. Without these readily available functions, the stage is then set for an accumulation of aggression and other destructive affects that might then congeal into a selfdyad that fails to support the selves of one or both partners.

Although selfobject functions are crucial for maintaining the loving qualities and intimate involvement of the couple, they cannot be directly taught or coached in the process of treatment without addressing both partners' developmental histories. It is through this process that the therapist becomes aware of developmental needs and wishes that likely have been thwarted and were then sought in the intimate partnership. This, of course, differentiates psychodynamically focused couple therapy from treatments of a behavioral or other orientation. As both individuals are encouraged to explore past relationships in the presence of the other partner, with a concentration on each individual's unique circumstances, early relationship patterns, and developmental obstacles, the therapist is then positioned to assist the couple in coming to understand the dynamic underpinnings of their relationship.

It is only then that the selfobject functions might be restored to the selfdyad, as both partners gradually and systematically detoxify problematic perceptions and experiences of each other while coming to understand their own and the partner's internal world. Within the consulting room, in an atmosphere of understanding and empathy that is provided and modeled by the therapist and through the continuous process of interpretation, both partners are assisted to expose and eventually work through their unconscious relationship scripts. Here they will gradually internalize the selfobject functions provided by the therapist, while gradually restoring these functions to their relationship.

8

WHEN THE SELF FAILS TO FLOURISH

Having laid the foundation for how the couple relationship develops and how both partners enter into this contract with a desire for transformation and a need for self-definition, we will now address the various ways in which these goals might fail to be realized. In previous chapters we described the social, psychological, and biological variables that are involved as couples enter into a relationship of permanence. In doing so, the couple establishes its unique interplay or dance as each self is inevitably modified through the ongoing cycles of projective identification. As the couple's roles are more clearly established, the selfdyad is formed and continues to function through conscious and unconscious communication while sustaining and supporting the selves of both partners. Whether the selfdyad supports and transforms each partner to a different and fulfilling level of selfhood will determine the success or failure of the relationship.

TRANSFORMATION: THE SELFDYAD AND THE LINK

Although our emphasis thus far has been on the intricacies of partner formation through unconscious communication, in this chapter we will focus our study on these processes and their impact on the self-experience of the partners. We will consider the various ways in which a faulty or unstable selfdyad can undermine the self and the various clinical outcomes that can emerge.

Recalling that experiences of transformation within the mother–infant pair are precursors for desiring new and different experiences throughout the life span, it is useful to consider some of the theoretical expansions that have emerged from the psychoanalytic work conducted in South America and parts of Europe. Isidoro Berenstein, an Argentinean psychoanalyst and family therapist, has enlarged our understanding of the dynamics involved in the formation of couple and family bonds by extending some of Pichon Riviére's original ideas pertaining to interpersonal dyadic functioning (Riviére, 1971). For Berenstein, the *link* is a superordinate construct that involves two interrelated processes that together define the dimensions of interpersonal connectedness. The first process refers to the familiar projective and introjective identificatory cycles that have been consistently emphasized throughout this writing. He calls the second the "interference between subjects"; which according to Berenstein, this applies to any two members of a family system.

Berenstein emphasizes that because any two individuals in an intimate partnership or a family system are unable to identify completely with each other, they must make a psychological space for "otherness" within the dyad. It is within this space that both partners can be different from what they would otherwise be if alone or if each were with another person in another dyad. Berenstein calls the influence of otherness within an interpersonal relationship the "effect of presence" and contends that it provides the quality of newness that renders that partnership unique from all others.

I believe that Berenstein is defining, although in different vernacular and from a different theoretical model, the essence of transformation that Bollas (1987) has described. He is explicit in saying that these latter processes provide uniqueness to the partnership in a way that is *not* derived from early life experiences, in contrast to the projection–introjection mechanisms, which he reminds us derive from early developmental experiences. He adds that while projective–introjective identifications are based on a concept of absence, "interference between subjects" is based on a concept of presence. Psychotherapeutic treatment, Berenstein asserts, must explicitly deal with both sets of mechanisms. While projection–introjection mechanisms are components of transference interpretations deriving from the past, linking functions are based on each partner's present capacity to make a space for the differentness and uniqueness of the other. Furthermore, it is the link that provides the capacity for the self within the partnership to experience the sense of transformation.

To the extent that both individuals are able to make a sufficient space for the other, the self of each is then elevated to a higher level, and this elevated level of experience in part determines the quality and intimacy of the partnership. This elevated level corresponds to what I have referred to as a revised or more complete sense of selfhood. To the extent that one or both partners are unable to provide a region for sufficient differentness, there is an increased likelihood that the self of one or both individuals will strangulate (I. Berenstein, personal communication, July 30, 2009).

The concept of the link, explained by Berenstein from the vantage point of the subjectivity of the partners, provides a somewhat different slant to our understanding of the selfdyad. Yet his ideas are easily integrated into our conceptualization of the dynamics of the couple. In the previous chapter flexibility, permeability, and the capacity for dynamic functioning were elaborated as central criteria for the effectively functioning selfdyad. Berenstein's emphasis on the partners providing a space for otherness within the present is actually contingent on the partners maintaining the required flexibility, permeability, and dynamic functioning with respect to the other. This constitutes what I believe Berenstein refers to as presence rather than absence. Although he argues that providing "space for otherness" is a present function only, considering that flexibility, permeability, and the capacity for dynamic functioning are essential conditions for providing that space and are at least partially determined by the partners' intrinsic character organization, the pasts of the partners indeed are implicated.

Although there may be some blurring of presence/absence and presence/past in Berenstein's conceptualization of the link, his way of thinking about the partnering process is entirely compatible with how we have conceptualized the selfdyad, and it also has implications for psychotherapeutic technique with couples. In agreement with Berenstein, not only must each partner's past be addressed in the process of therapy, but also the here-and-now interactions that pertain to the selfdyad—that is, making space for otherness—must simultaneously be considered.

Scott and Linda

Scott and Linda called for a consultation because of their difficulty in coming to an agreement on managing their teenage daughter's curfew now that she had turned 16. Scott and Linda easily reflected on their own backgrounds as they attempted to understand their predicament and its implications for setting Allison's curfew. They both had been raised in families in which there had been considerable control exerted by their parents as they entered adolescence. Both had been permitted to date and to move about freely with their friends as long as they maintained good grades and did not get into any trouble. They had early curfews, sometimes ten o'clock on weekends, while neither was allowed to go out on week nights.

In exploring their feelings about their backgrounds, both Scott and Linda recalled the resentment they experienced over the control and the inflexibility of their parents. Their family backgrounds were remarkably similar: Both had grown up in conventional and conservative Midwestern homes and intact families, with no apparent traumas within their families of origin. Neither Scott nor Linda appeared to have any overt psychopathology, and their relationships with their parents and siblings were reasonably close. Furthermore, they fundamentally agreed on most parenting issues and even that a certain amount of parental governance was important in raising healthy and well-adjusted children.

While they initially denied other significant difficulties in their marriage, it appeared as though Scott and Linda's presenting problem centered on a focused deadlock pertaining to a parenting issue that was erupting at a critical juncture of family life. Linda insisted that because she at one time resented her parents for their strict controls over her, she did not want to repeat their mistakes in a way that might cause Allison to resent her. When inquiring of Linda how she dealt with her resentment as a child, she responded that she merely acquiesced to her parents' wishes. She went on to say that Allison's maturity level suggested that she was quite capable of handling a more generous curfew without repercussions. She felt, after all, that Allison was much like she had been as an adolescent—responsible and mature—and that she should be rewarded accordingly.

Scott also recalled the resentment he once had toward his parents. In contrast to Linda, however, he made many pleas for a more flexible curfew, but now today felt that the parameters that his parents once provided him greatly contributed to his character—namely, an appreciation for self-imposed limitations, a sense of moral obligation to others, and a respect for his elders. Strikingly, Scott and Linda presented their differences of opinion on the matter of their daughter's curfew with equal conviction, clarity, and a certain self-righteousness as they laid out their arguments and corresponding rebuttals.

It is noteworthy here to comment on my countertransference, which during the fourth session I used to formulate a hypothesis about their difficulties. Three sessions had transpired during which the same trite arguments had been presented with intransigence. During these sessions I found myself uncharacteristically impatient with both Scott and Linda, wondering when something new would be added. But each time one of them spoke, a mere revision of a previous statement or argument was presented, always elegantly.

Suddenly, I was taken back to my school days, during which I learned to debate. During a brief pause I asked if either of them had ever been debaters in school. Both immediately shot me glances of incredulity. "How did you know that?" Linda asked. She went on to say that they both were debaters during college and had actually met during a debate tournament. Although this couple had remained rigidly fastened on this one problem pertaining to Allison's curfew, I now wondered whether their inability to yield might pervade other aspects of their functioning, in spite of their mutual denial of other significant problems in their relationship. It appeared that my hunch paid off as Scott now spoke about the way in which they had difficulty in negotiating other aspects of their relationship.

During the 19 years of their marriage it had been difficult for them as a couple to make decisions about many things, including how finances were managed and how to deal with extended family. Scott commented that, even on inconsequential matters, they would sometimes debate endlessly. Providing an example, Scott spoke of a recent family outing that he had arranged on the previous weekend. Although he had taken considerable time to plan a bicycle trip for the three of them, Linda objected strongly, insisting that her route was better.

Now Linda interrupted Scott. She commented emphatically that there was no doubt in her mind that the 4-mile ride that she planned more clearly met their specifications, while Scott's proposed route had more hills and would take them longer to complete. Again, there was urgency in Linda's voice as she resurrected her logic-based rhetoric in an attempt to convince Scott and me that she was right.

Predictably, Scott cut Linda off in midsentence, prepared with additional data pertaining to the size of their bike tires, which he said Linda was not taking into consideration. Now, according to Scott, Linda's argument was effectively nullified. This debate between Scott and Linda, the outcome of which was inconsequential by comparison to the kinds of negotiations and decisions that couples will make over a lifetime, was striking to me.

As Scott and Linda continued to volley argument and counterargument I continued to experience moments of exasperation as I listened to them become bogged down into minor details that were accompanied by a heightening of their tension and anger at one another. Importantly, both seemed strikingly unaware of their interpersonal process; instead, they were intent on proving who was right.

Here was a couple with a circumscribed problem that related to setting a curfew for their adolescent daughter. Their backgrounds and histories were remarkably similar and without apparent pathological contributions from family circumstances, trauma, or unresolved parental relationships. Both Scott and Linda felt generally satisfied in their partnership, including their sexual life. Yet they were experiencing significant difficulty in permitting a space for the others' wishes, needs, and preferences. Although another therapist might have managed this couple by providing just one or two appointments during which they were advised on how to handle the curfew, my assessment involved experiencing a sector of their relationship that seemed without significant developmental contributions, but instead represented an insufficient flexibility in their selfdyad, with an inability to permit a region for each other's ideas and preferences.

A CAVEAT ON COUNTERTRANSFERENCE AND THE SELFDYAD

Throughout, I have emphasized the manner in which the clinician must listen to illuminate the couple's most salient difficulties in relating. This mode of listening, of course, applies to individual patients and to couples alike, and yet there are differences. The use of the therapist's countertransference in understanding the patient is a familiar concept for practitioners of a psychoanalytic persuasion, but may be somewhat more foreign for those practicing couple therapy from other theoretical vantage points.

Fundamentally, the use of countertransference refers to the therapist's ability and willingness to respond internally to the patient affectively and cognitively, while simultaneously subjecting his internal reactions to his private intellectual processing. The ultimate purpose, of course, is to understand the emotional functioning of the patient or the couple and, on this basis, formulate and deliver an intervention that is helpful and mutative. Because the therapist's countertransference reactions develop through the same projective processes that transpire between the partners, the couple therapist is in an advantaged position to understand the couple's impasse by studying his responses to both partners, while coming to understand the structure of their selfdyad and the partners' characteristic ways of relating to one another.

Although the couple therapist's countertransference reactions are sometimes more personally disorganizing than those experienced within an individual treatment setting, they are nonetheless useful and even essential in coming to understand the problem areas for which the couple seeks treatment. The therapist's fluctuating and sometimes chaotic countertransferences are emphasized here because they always reflect some aspect of what is projected or introjected by the partners, as well as their failure to be contained adequately. More will be said about this in a later chapter in which the technique of therapy is discussed.

THAT VITAL BALANCE

A flawlessly functioning selfdyad in congruence and constant support of the self of both partners is a psychological impossibility. A more realistic goal for the couple is an optimal but sometimes conflictual distribution of roles, along with intermittent interpersonal conflict and distance. What is essential, however, is the couple's ability to remain engaged and committed as damage is repaired, while then restoring intimacy. This defines the couple's subjective sense of oneness and merger, and the alternating separateness that determines the experience of transformation. There is a dialectical movement between a selfdyad that performs the tasks of intimate relating and family life and then in turn supports the individuality of both partners.

Conversely, as the partners experience sufficient space for differentness and support for their roles, both are in turn motivated to enhance and support the relationship. Maintaining this dialectic interplay presumes that the partners have been able to establish their selfdyad with a requisite permeability and flexibility that permits an optimal intrusion into the psychic space of the partner through projective identification, while not usurping the self of the other.

Haydée Faimberg has formulated an extension of object relations theory by describing a concept she has called the "telescoping of generations" (Faimberg, 2005). In her writing she attempts to account for the psychic mechanisms by which internal objects are passed through the generations, especially as a function of a family history that may include disavowed secrets. To the extent that the family members (often parents and grandparents) have colluded to remain silent about facts and information, there is an increased likelihood that even several generations later the residual effects of this history will become installed within the child.

Adding to our understanding of how identifications occur through the intergenerational transmission of unconscious links to forebears, Faimberg describes two processes, which in their extremes become characteristic of narcissistic relating between parent and child. She feels that tracing these processes is essential in liberating a patient whose identity has been strangulated by the constraining forces of these narcissistic links. Here it is important to note that Faimberg's definition of the link is fundamentally different from that of Berenstein. She appears to define it along conventional lines, used synonymously with "connection" while attempting to account for the unconscious transmission of intergenerational influences on narcissistic functioning.

Fundamental to Faimberg's theory is that the child or patient functions according to a "split identification of the ego, insofar as its cause is partially found in the history of the 'other'" (Faimberg, 2005, p. 10). Her model appears to be compatible with Fairbairn's endopsychic theory of internal object relations, although Faimberg does not so methodically describe the splitting process of the object and the ego that Fairbairn (1944) painstakingly addresses. Instead, she expands a more traditional object relations model by demonstrating how split identifications develop as a function of both conflictual relationships and attachment problems with parents and the disavowed influences of previous generations. For Faimberg, the child identifies not only with the other, but also with the interpersonal processes that have existed within the family, including its disavowed secrets and its dramas.

Characteristic of narcissistic relating between parent and child is a twofold process in which the parent appropriates the positive attributes of the child's identity, feeling entitled to the child's devotion and love, while simultaneously expelling or intruding into the child the parts of the parent's identity and family heritage that have been rejected. The child's love is demanded by the parent while simultaneously the child is hated because he is different from the parent and because he shares the parent's personal history. Most importantly, because of these paradoxical processes of appropriation and intrusion, the child is trapped by the parent's narcissism wherein his identity is not his own. Instead, it belongs to another—one who has both incorporated and projected a disavowed history from a previous generation.

The appropriation and intrusion functions of which Faimberg speaks describe a process of narcissistic relating that destroys the child's separateness. These functions can also be observed in intimate relationships in which a partner demands to be loved by the other, thus appropriating the identity of the partner, while simultaneously intruding and projecting into that partner those rejected and disavowed parts of the self. Thus, the second partner's self and sense of agency are usurped, while he is sometimes unaware that it is the partner who has contributed to loss of self. The second partner may feel trapped within a relationship in which love is both given and taken, but for the price of separateness and selfhood. An example is the battered wife whose husband needs her to love him unconditionally, while she is simultaneously loved and hated by him. She is loved for what is appropriated by him while she becomes a repository for an identity he wishes to disavow. Here the self of the wife is eliminated and replaced by the projected and unwanted self of the husband.

APPROPRIATION, INTRUSION, AND LINKING

Frank and April

The appropriation and intrusion functions so characteristic of couples who have constructed a narcissistic selfdyad are illustrated in the 2008 film *Revolutionary Road* (Mendes, 2008). Sam Haythe's film adaptation of the 1961 novel by Richard Yates features Frank and April Wheeler, a young married couple, who move to the suburbs to pursue the typical postwar 1950s American dream. Frank takes a job that provides a modest living and April becomes a bourgeois housewife and mother of two, giving up her aspirations to become a professional actress. Although commonplace in its theme, the film contains some profound psychological nuances for understanding the collapse of a self and the implications for human tragedy.

In the film April finally recognizes and subsequently speaks to Frank about their vapid lives. Blaming Frank for settling for a job that was beneath his original aspirations, she announces to him that to change their lives he should quit his job and they would then move to Paris. Her plan is to work in Paris while Frank will now have the time to find out what he really wants to do with the rest of his life. She presents this to Frank as a creative solution to her boredom, his go-nowhere job, and her accelerating disappointment for his lack of ambition; Frank becomes angry at April for her dissatisfaction and her failure to appreciate her life.

As their disagreements over these issues mount, they progressively torment each other with mutually accelerating blame, endless arguments, and ruinous extramarital liaisons. Neither Frank nor April looks within himself or herself, much less their relationship, to understand their mutual unhappiness; instead, they spiral downward into marital despair.

What perhaps is missing in the film is a clearer elaboration of a man and woman who together had created their mutual misery, culminating in the demise of a self and in April's self-destruction. Instead, the film simplistically explains the tragedy as due to Frank's complacency, April's chronic dissatisfaction, or even suburban living itself. What is merely hinted at in the film is the way in which this couple's mutually constructed selfdyad had gone awry, unable to support the selves of both, including coming to terms with April's unrequited ambitions to become an actress and Frank's need to take the path of least resistance by remaining employed by a company where he was almost assured of no advancement.

In a scene toward the beginning of the film in which April and Frank are discussing her stage performance of that evening, Frank disparages the production in a not so subtle manner; he then unconvincingly attempts to compliment April as having given the best out of a host of mediocre performances of the evening. Later, in her dressing room following the performance, April asks Frank to cancel their dinner plans with their friends, presumably because of her shame about and disappointment in her performance. When he continuously balks at canceling their plans, April declares emphatically that if he does not do it for her she will do it herself.

It is here where we are able to observe Frank's lack of sensitivity to and empathy for her, as well as his passivity in their relationship. Frank's lack of assertion is additionally highlighted as we come to understand that the job he detests is with the same company in which his father had spent his entire work life. The irony of remaining employed by the same company that provided his father no advancement, which Frank at one time said he would never himself tolerate, hints at his fears of surpassing the Oedipal father, resulting in a languor covered by false self-assuredness and feeble ambition.

As the film progresses, April's emerging disdain for Frank becomes more apparent as she comes to realize that this "most interesting person that I have ever met"—an endearment to Frank at the beginning of their courtship—was merely an illusion. What is progressively revealed to April is a man whose bravado and ambition were mere defenses against his fears and his shame for his personal failures, now replaced with complacency.

Denigrating April's performance was just one example of Frank's intruding into her fragile and inadequate sense of self, while simultaneously appropriating her love, loyalty, and self-sacrificing qualities. Taking in these projections, April eventually transforms from a self-confident and aspiring artist into a defeated and desecrated woman. Her eventual plea to move to Paris represents an inept and last-ditch effort to reclaim her self, while simultaneously attempting to rescue Frank and their relationship by providing him an opportunity to find a better existence.

With little persuasion Frank agrees to relocate, but he subsequently reneges when a glimmer of hope arises that he might be elevated to a more prestigious position with a higher salary. Ironically, there is here an implication that, after all this time, Frank is just now able to command some respect because he is finally taking a more affirmative stance with his employer by asserting his intention to leave.

Once again disappointed, April now arranges a one-time sexual liaison with their neighbor in retaliation against Frank for his previously confessed extramarital affair. Although we have the impression that up to the present time Frank and April had preserved at least some semblance of sexual intimacy, April now becomes pregnant, leaving the viewers and April, too, uncertain about the paternity of her unborn child. Regardless of the father's identity, her pregnancy now represents the death knell for the possible liberation of a self. Shockingly, while at home, April induces her abortion after sending Frank off to work and deceiving him that all has been forgiven. In the final scene Frank is summoned to the hospital, where he learns that April has hemorrhaged to her death.

Perhaps most importantly for our purposes, what is illuminated in this film is the complexity of the dynamics occurring between a man and a woman, which ultimately culminates in the destruction of a self and a wife's "accidental" suicide—April's self-induced abortion. Although the title of the film, *Revolutionary Road,* is the actual street on which the Wheelers live, it metaphorically refers to the path on which a couple's marital journey is taken. On their chosen life course, symbolic for Frank and April's mutually constructed selfdyad, April executes a revolution to regain her sense of agency, although failing miserably. The calamitous ending of the film becomes an evocative portrayal of a self that lost its transformative potential and then literally died.

IMPLICATIONS FOR PSYCHOPATHOLOGY

Throughout previous chapters clinical examples have been provided to illustrate the ways in which the selfdyad must support both selves for the partnership to be experienced as fulfilling and loving. For this to occur, the boundaries of both selves must be sufficiently permeable to permit a flow and mutual exchange of mental contents. When the boundaries of one or both partners are insufficiently permeable—sometimes exemplified by a difficulty in relating to the partner openly or sharing few interests or values in common—the result may be a sense of boredom, aloneness, or disinterest in the partner.

When one partner experiences a significant life event, there is always a corresponding psychological resonance within the dyad. Because of this it is essential for the therapist to be alert to recent and remote changes and shifts that have occurred within the present network of nuclear and extended family relationships. This would include losses, traumas, or crises that might be contributing to interpersonal rever-berations within the family, as well as the couple relationship itself.

It is not unusual in the beginnings of therapy for a couple or individ-ual patient to minimize, deny, or even overlook a loss or a contributing significant relationship disruption within the extended family. Unless these contributions are specifically addressed, it might be sometime later before the clinician discovers an event within the extended fam-ily that has been contributing significantly to the presenting problem. This might be something as important as a death of a parent, as in the case of Sara and William in Chapter 3, or an illness in an aging relative that profoundly affects the patient or the couple. The case of Marilyn in Chapters 1 and 2 illustrates how a woman's decision to retire in order to care for her aging mother had intrapsychic consequences for both the patient and her husband, causing reverberations within their selfdyad. This life event set into motion Marilyn's previously latent conflicts with her mother, while simultaneously alerting her to how she had subordi-nated her sense of self to others, including her husband.

THE IMPACT OF TRAUMA

Much like the impact of acute illness and the encroachment of the aging process with its accompanying deterioration of a loved one, traumas within the nuclear or the extended family will frequently create a ripple effect through the entire family system. Whether one family member sustains the brunt of the impact or there are distributed effects on all or some family members will be determined by a host of factors. These include the nature of the trauma or injury itself, the potential for recov-ery of functions, the coping skills of the victim and family members, the dynamics of the couple and family, and a variety of other practical factors, including the availability and quality of support systems for the victim and family.

A trauma sustained by one person within the dyad will always affect the relationship system of the couple, while having the potential to affect the self of the other partner profoundly. Ironically, to the extent that the couple has achieved the necessary permeability and flexibility in their selfdyad to experience a transformation by the relationship, the uninjured partner may be more likely to experience the reverberating effects of the trauma. Although inconveniences and disruptions sur-rounding the practical details of caring for the victim or the person who is ill are almost routine, here we will discuss the impact that the crisis has on the selfdyad and its implications for the uninjured part-ner's emotional functioning.

Martha

Martha called for an appointment to address the depression she had been experiencing for the past 4 years. Her psychiatrist had tried her on a number of antidepressant medications, most of which were either unhelpful or caused her uncomfortable side effects.

Martha had been living with Curtis in an unmarried partnership for the past 10 years. She recalled that for the first 5 years of their relationship she had been happy and content. Both she and Curtis had rewarding careers. They had agreed that they would not marry or have children so that they could immerse themselves in work and have the time and money to travel. Five years ago, while Martha and Curtis were rock climbing in the mountains, a boulder was dislodged under Martha's foot while she was scaling a canyon wall. Curtis was some distance below her when a large fragment struck him in the head and he plunged downward to the bottom of canyon.

Although it took some time for Martha to descend, another climber saw the accident and summoned the paramedics, who soon appeared by helicopter. Curtis was flown directly to a nearby emergency room for treatment; however, his brain injury was significant, leaving him with aphasia and other cognitive impairments. He sustained numerous fractures from the fall, which eventually healed, but he was left with some limitations in mobility. Curtis was now considered completely disabled, although he was able to care for himself throughout the day while Martha was away at work.

Martha's story entailed a most tragic life event that had obvious negative consequences for both her and her partner. We can also say that a serious accident and life-changing tragedy such as this would tax almost any person, putting that individual at risk for a depressive state. What seemed especially pertinent in Martha's case, however, was not the tragedy itself, her guilt over the details surrounding the fall, or even the specific life changes that had occurred since the accident. Especially relevant for Martha were the changes in Curtis's personality and the impact on her sense of self.

Although Curtis had recuperated physically with the help of extensive rehabilitation, this once assertive, active, and vital presence in Martha's life had now become a sedentary and passive man who offered little initiative or spontaneity in action or in conversation. While at one time Curtis had been experienced by Martha as a formidable partner who excited her with his zest for life and ebullient energy, he was now relegated to a quality of life and a style of relating that were just barely more than mere existence.

After first hearing Martha's tragic story I asked her how all these changes in her life had affected *her* as a person. The phrasing and the nuances of this question are especially important when assessing the impact of trauma, changes in life circumstances, and their impact on the person and the couple. At first Martha began to itemize the various changes in her social life and day-to-day activities that had occurred since the accident. Wanting to understand more about the structure of their relationship and its impact on Martha's sense of self, I reiterated my question.

Martha went on to say that she was now a much different person from the woman she had been 5 years ago. She proceeded to describe herself as a shy and somewhat fearful person throughout her formative years. After meeting Curtis and establishing their relationship, her sense of security grew and she no longer felt uncomfortable in social relationships. Martha went on to explain that Curtis had always been patient and tolerant of her cautious approach to life and her anxious attitude about the world and its potential dangers. "He actually changed me," she said. She added, "Now, without the same guy I used to love, I feel I'm forced to be outgoing, but it's not the same. It's like I'm not really the same person without the Curtis he used to be."

The case of Martha and Curtis once again underscores the profound impact of the selfdyad on the self of the partner. Here was a woman whose personality and character style had been fundamentally avoidant and phobic throughout her early development. Curtis's extraversion and expansive energy level, projected onto Martha, prompted an experienced change in her from an anxious and hesitant woman into one who felt more secure in her world. Martha further offered that although in the beginning of their relationship Curtis was somewhat inconsiderate and obnoxious with others, her steadier and more laid back nature enabled him to develop a sense of restraint and consideration for others.

Martha had described an optimal way in which the projective–introjective dynamics between her and Curtis had set into motion a positive transformation for both. They had been able to affirm each other by providing sufficient space for each other's uniqueness, while leaving ample room for the residual qualities of Martha's shyness and Curtis's vivacity. As a couple they possessed the necessary permeability and flexibility of self-boundaries to exchange their mental contents, contributing to an adaptive and smoothly functioning selfdyad. Curtis's accident, however, resulted in significant changes in his personality and his temperament. Now this once outgoing man had become apathetic and inert, while Martha experienced both the actual loss of Curtis's exciting qualities and the loss of herself as the person who had been transformed by their relationship.

The case of Curtis and Martha vividly illustrates the impact of tragic circumstances and physical trauma on the individual and the couple. Although a trauma affects the victim most directly, its effects on the intimate partner and the entire family are almost always present. To the extent that the dynamic equilibrium of the couple is disrupted, even when that balance has previously been optimal, there may be a significant impact on the self-functioning of the partner that sets into motion a depression or other symptom disorder.

CHILDREN AND THE COUPLE

When working with children and adolescents it is essential for the therapist to view the problem areas of the child as a manifestation of a combined picture of the child's temperament and biological and developmental factors, as well as the myriad of psychological factors and family dynamics. Depending upon the therapist's training and orientation, there are differences in the extent to which a clinician will emphasize a child's difficulty as a representation of a dynamic disturbance in the family system. Therapists versed in object relations theory or family systems models are perhaps more inclined to conceptualize a child's presenting problem by considering the family's unconscious processes and projections as fundamental to the child's difficulty (Ackerman, 1958; Bowen, 1978; Scharff & Scharff, 1987; Shapiro, 1979).

A variation of this is the child whose presenting problem is an outcome of a chronic disturbance in the parents' couple system, unconsciously displaced and projected onto a child who carries a valency for the parents' anxieties. An example is the child with a specific learning disability or attention deficit disorder who draws the parents' attention and emotional energy, while deflecting the focus from their marital problems. Here the couple's anxiety about their relationship is diverted and projected onto the child and his problem areas, albeit in an exaggerated way. The couple's relationship is then precariously preserved and protected from overt conflict as the heightened concern and attention on the child's problem creates an intensifying spiral of shared family anxiety. Over time, the anxiety may become progressively installed within the child, augmenting the child's difficulties (Bowen, 1987; Haley, 1980). The end result is a child whose learning impediment is exacerbated by anxiety and/or other psychological factors, which additionally inhibit his motivation to work through or compensate for his limitations in learning.

Child and adolescent therapists and family therapists alike frequently encounter children who are especially attuned to their parents' relationship difficulties. It is not uncommon for these children to become stalled developmentally, sometimes unconsciously sacrificing themselves to remain closely observant or even involved in their parents' troubled relationship. The child may harbor a fantasy that monitoring and staying close to one parent and to the family will preserve its unity. Sometimes the child or teenager who presents for treatment is the one with whom the parent is strongly identified. These children are at risk for developing more serious emotional problems, a psychosomatic illness, or even a disorder of self-control, which then allows the parents to deflect the focus from their troubled relationship by immersing themselves in their child's problem or enmeshing themselves in the child's life.

In *Leaving Home*, Jay Haley has written about adolescents and young adults who have developmentally stagnated because of dynamic disturbances within the family system (Haley, 1980). One variation of this is the parent who unconsciously communicates his need for the child to remain dependent by projecting onto the child his anxieties about independent functioning. As a result the young person is unable to achieve the necessary coping skills and self-esteem to attend college, to get and hold a job, or to move out of the parental home and into society. Here the couple's troubled relationship is effectively rescued while the child is prevented from moving toward a healthy differentiation of the self and into the world of the independent adult. Haley demonstrates how, in understanding the structure of the family, the therapist is able to address the sometimes subtle dynamics that serve to restrict the young adult from the trajectory of emerging adulthood.

In general, child and adolescent therapists who are trained or at least versed in family dynamics are more inclined to work with the entire family or its subgroup or to use a combined approach in which the child is seen in individual therapy and the family is seen in family therapy. In a previous era it was more common for child analysts and therapists to see the child individually while the family therapist worked separately with the family. The child and family therapists would then collaborate to address the child's problems and the family dynamics sustaining or augmenting the child's difficulties more comprehensively. Perhaps with the contemporary expansion of object relations theories and family systems theories, therapists are better equipped today to deal more comprehensively with the range of children's difficulties and their connection to family processes without the involvement of multiple treaters.

Considering the importance of family dynamics and their impact on the child and given how pervasively unconscious communication operates within the family, one can easily understand how disturbances within the parental relationship can be unconsciously funneled onto a vulnerable child or adolescent who carries a valency for the parents' or a parent's projections. The child effectively serves in the role of symptom bearer for the couple or family system by carrying the parents' projections.

Julie

Julie, a 17-year-old, was referred by her pediatrician for chronic nausea and a host of vague and medically unexplained aches and pains that had interfered significantly with her school attendance and performance. Julie was the third child in a family of three children, with one brother in college and another who had graduated and was now living on his own. She had been an exceptional student and a talented musician until this past year, when she began to experience her symptoms. Importantly, her symptoms began just weeks after receiving her letter of acceptance to a prestigious university located in another part of the country. Although Julie had been turning in her makeup work at school and was having no difficulty in understanding the academic material, she was continuing to fail her tests and her grades were plummeting. Leslie and Fred, Julie's parents, were unable to explain this marked change in their daughter, who had no history of emotional problems, had been popular with peers, and was considered by all who knew her to be intellectually gifted and destined for success.

Fred was a commercial airline pilot who over the years had been away from home for periods of time; Leslie had recently retired as an elementary school teacher. It is noteworthy that my first attempts to schedule a family consultation were met with difficulty. There were several cancelled appointments, two related to Fred's sudden change in his work schedule and two because of Julie's precipitous attacks of nausea and vomiting. Speculating about the family's resistance to therapy, I finally suggested that they call me to reschedule when they felt that their situation had settled down. Within a week they called back to schedule an appointment, which this time they kept.

Upon meeting the family I was immediately struck with Leslie's formidability and Fred's lassitude. Leslie began by describing the progression of Julie's medical problems, providing details about their many visits to specialists to find an answer to Julie's difficulties. There was a thinly veiled insinuation that the many physicians they had consulted simply missed the diagnosis and for that reason the family should not have been referred for therapy. Striking to me was Julie's inarticulateness in describing her illness and her life as an adolescent. Because Julie had been labeled by her parents and her referring physician as "gifted," I thought this contradiction to be significant. Her physical appearance was somewhat waif-like, and she maintained poor eye contact as she glanced nervously between the floor and her mother as if looking for guidance on how to respond to me. Julie's frequent hesitations and halting speech prompted Leslie to reply for her as Fred sat passively on the sidelines, appearing vacant and uninvolved.

Already my countertransference to this family was relevant in coming to understand Julie's problems and the related family dynamics. Simply put, I felt excluded and irrelevant to this family, while the mother by contrast seemed highly essential—at least for Julie. Because I am usually able to establish myself quickly as someone who is helpful and who has expertise in working with families, there appeared to be a force operating within this family that created my sense of being eliminated and feeling unimportant. It was here that I assembled some pieces of the puzzle to inform a provisional hypothesis about the functioning of this family.

Here was a gifted teenager whose emerging autonomy had taken a regressive downturn during her senior year in high school. Under the sway of the imminent separation from the family unit or when other dynamics are operating within the family, the final year of high school in preparation for college is frequently a time during which the adolescent with a fragile self-structure is at greater risk for developing emotional problems. The codependent quality of Leslie and Julie's relationship was easily recognized.

Equally noteworthy was the father's passivity in this family in which the mother had likely overfunctioned for their teenage daughter while the father was relatively remote. Experiencing myself as unimportant to this family represented a concordant identification with Fred, who quite likely also experienced himself as irrelevant to his wife and daughter. Furthermore, his lack of involvement in the family probably served to reinforce the enmeshment between the mother and daughter, further undermining Julie's individuation.

Now hypothesizing a strained marital relationship that would need to be addressed, I turned to Fred, who had thus far contributed very little in the interview. Inviting him to give his view of Julie's problems was met with some tangential remarks about Julie's brilliance in comparison to their two older children. Fred then mentioned that he would soon be retiring and that he thought it ironic that Julie would develop her problems at a time he was retiring and as she was preparing for college. Now addressing the entire group, I commented that Julie's going off to college, with Fred retired and at home, would undoubtedly represent a significant change in their family life that would take some getting used to. With this intervention I wanted to highlight that what Fred had identified as an irony actually spoke directly to the problem. These two events occurring simultaneously confronted Fred and Leslie with togetherness in a way that had not existed since the birth of their children.

Now Leslie spoke. With a tightened jaw and forced smile she remarked that Fred had not been around for the past 25 years and she wondered if he would be able to tolerate retirement. Fred was conspicuously silent, as Julie turned to her mother and broke out of her silence. "Maybe *you* won't be able to tolerate his retirement, mother," Julie said sharply. Surprisingly, Julie was confronting the latent strain in her parents' relationship by introducing her perception that her parents' apprehensions about being together might be a factor in unconsciously restraining her independence.

So here it was: a pivotal juncture in a family session in which the family dynamics had unfolded, paving the way for me to address the dysfunction of this couple's relationship as a factor in their teenager's stagnated development. This was a mother who had lived her life to care for her daughter, possibly in part as a distraction from her concerns about her relationship with her husband.

Observing Fred's passivity, I now wondered about his contribution to Julie's inhibitions. I found myself speculating about the way in which his career had affected his lack of involvement in family life. Those families with members who travel for a living must develop their relationships and family life around the periodic absences. Having worked with many patients and families in which a member's absence was a feature of family life, I was aware that most will develop compensations for these factors. Furthermore, I noted that although Fred was often away for 2 or 3 days at a time, he would subsequently be home for 4 or 5 continuous days, during which there was ample opportunity to be available to his wife and daughter.

Yet Leslie's comment that Fred had not been around for 25 years communicated a bitterness that seemed to reflect a sense of having being abandoned by him. Certainly Fred's career as a pilot had been a relevant factor of family life, but perhaps one that simultaneously provided a convenient avenue for maintaining an emotional distance for this couple, while sustaining family life. The price paid, however, was a daughter who had been unconsciously recruited into the role of mediator and sacrificial lamb, compromising her emerging autonomy.

A WORD ON FAMILY THERAPY

When a fragile parental relationship is discovered underlying the manifest problem in a family—especially when a child is represented as the identified patient—the therapist must be cautious, tactfully and sensitively making interpretations pertaining to the dynamics of the family and the couple. It is important to remember that the symptomatic child is unconsciously chosen by the parents, while that child also becomes a participant in enacting the complexity of the family drama. Not uncommonly, the therapist can fall into the trap of viewing the child or adolescent as either the blatant cause of the parents' relationship problems or the innocent victim of the couple's dysfunction.

Family relationships are structured as a complex tapestry of interrelated components that are more than the mere sum of individual personalities. Furthermore, they are organized according to unconscious group dynamic processes that frequently are approximations of both parents' intergenerational histories, recruited into interaction with each family member's unique temperament, conflicts, needs, and character traits. In addition, the subgroups and alliances that are formed within the family function as compensations and defenses to protect family members from the real or imagined dangers that threaten an individual, the couple, or both.

The inadvertent or technically premature interpretation of the couple's latent difficulty when a child or adolescent has been presented as the main concern for the family is fraught with risk. Remembering that the identified patient in a family system functions as a distraction and a defense against other, more potent threats for the family or the couple, the therapist will be alerted to the importance of carefully and tactfully addressing the underlying difficulties in the couple's relationship.

Julie, who had otherwise presented as an inhibited teenager, abruptly spoke to the parents' fears of intimate relating. Although this represented a potential turning point in the treatment, it was simultaneously a juncture at which the family might be at risk for a premature termination of therapy. When the threat of exposing the latent marital problem is too great to bear for one or both partners, the family may more readily interrupt treatment, rationalizing that the therapy has been unhelpful or that the therapist has not adequately addressed the problem in the child.

We learned in Chapter 3 that couple and family bonds are formed in the service of maintaining attachments. To that same end subgroups within families, including the overly close or enmeshed alliance between a parent and a child, can serve a defensive purpose that provides a place of refuge or support for the parent and/or the child. An example is the

Oedipal constellation in which a close alliance exists between a child and the opposite-sex parent, while the child simultaneously maintains a distance from the same-sex parent, sometimes resisting identification with that parent.

Also, various subgroups can be formed within families out of anxieties, uncertainties, or fantasies pertaining to other relationship pairs existing within the family. In families in which the intimacy of the couple is severely lacking, a constellation might possibly be formed in which a parent appropriates the self of the child while the attachment between the parent and child eventually becomes mutually parasitic. Assuming the child remains in the codependent role, the symbiotic dyad extrudes the other parent, while the selves of both parents *seemingly* stabilize. Here the selfdyad effectively regulates itself by eliminating intimacy from the relationship by sacrificing the child's autonomy.

CONCLUSION

In this chapter we have focused on the variety of ways the self can collapse and manifest psychological difficulty when the selfdyad is faulty. In considering the film *Revolutionary Road* we addressed the tragic ramifications that are possible when a self is appropriated by the partner. Finally, in extending our discussion to the family, with a clinical example we illustrated how a troubled parental selfdyad can attempt to salvage itself when one partner emotionally fuses with an offspring, while the child in turn becomes developmentally frozen. It is the hope that the examples and discussions provided in this chapter have illustrated the complexity of dynamics that exist within couples and families, while emphasizing the importance of maintaining the dialectic between a fluidly functioning selfdyad and the selves of both partners.

9

INTROSPECTION AND ITS ENEMIES

Each of the various schools of psychotherapy emphasizes different phenomena and seemingly divergent criteria for patient improvement. A common ingredient shared by all modalities, however, is some variation of self-awareness as a route for achieving emotional growth. The therapist's guided inquiry into the patient's difficulties initiates an emerging verbal–cognitive–affective process through which an increasing awareness of the self begins to take form as the patient puts into words experiences that have possibly never previously been formulated or verbalized.

Although a psychodynamic approach encourages introspection as the preferred mode through which self-understanding unfolds, other approaches also promote self-awareness, although often in a more abbreviated way. For example, the cognitive approach encourages the patient to understand his own distortions of mind, within the frame of reference of faulty reasoning, while the therapist demonstrates how those difficulties have been created and are maintained. The understanding of the patient's experience that unfolds in the interaction between therapist and client becomes the path for emotional healing, whether the therapist's preferred theory is cognitive behavioral, humanistic, client centered, or otherwise. This book espouses a psychodynamic way of thinking about patients, their relationships, and their marital difficulties. This theoretical system provides the most comprehensive way to achieve the introspection required for the client's learning about the self and the self within the context of his relationships.

THE CASE FOR INTROSPECTION

All patients, whether presenting for individual or couple treatment, seek psychotherapeutic assistance because they have encountered a level of mental discomfort that has finally exceeded a threshold of tolerance. They seek the assistance of a professional who they hope will shed light on the nature of the emotional pain, toward the goal of relieving it. Simply put, a patient who consults the psychotherapist always wants to feel better, but no longer knows how to do so. We clumsily call the various ways in which our patients present their pain symptoms, conforming to a sociocultural paradigm that by now is ancient—that of medicine and the doctor–patient relationship.

This doctor–patient paradigm, which subsumes the psychotherapies, is unique within the spectrum of services that attend to the various ills and needs of humanity, although counseling services of all kinds exist in our Western culture, including legal, financial, social welfare, spiritual, and others. Some might even argue that several of these services include within their parameters a psychotherapeutic aspect, especially if one defines "psychotherapy" by the verbal actions and activities used to achieve its aims—the end goal of feeling better at the conclusion of the service.

The psychotherapeutic and psychoanalytic tradecrafts, however, are unique among the counseling professions. What distinguishes psychotherapy—and, especially, the dynamically focused treatments—is the emphasis on introspection and insight as modes through which the client's mental health improves or personal growth occurs. As discussed in Chapter 1, an individual presenting to the psychotherapist will frequently describe his concerns through a lexicon of dissociated affect or cognition: "I feel depressed," or "I feel so confused that I can't think," or "I hear these voices in my head that tell me...." The psychotherapist always knows, however, that these are merely surface manifestations or shorthand communications of a complicated convergence of what has become problematic in the patient's life in conjunction with his inner self, including character style, defenses, and instinctual organization.

Psychological symptoms or complaints are always end products that, for the psychotherapist, should *never* be confused with etiology. This is where a dynamic orientation of behavior and emotion departs from the paradigms of biological psychiatry and behaviorism, both of which by and large tend to view the presenting symptom, the affect, the distorted cognition, or even the interpersonal problem as the target for treatment. In these latter paradigms it is presumed that the etiology of the symptom lies within the cognition, affect, or behavior itself or the neurological structures within the patient's body. The dynamic view of human behavior and emotion, including relationship and couple difficulties, presumes instead that what has finally converged into a symptom might well have recruited a biological proclivity through which the patient's life issues and unique psychology have become represented. This might include a vulnerability in synaptic firing or an anomaly in the balance of neurotransmitters, for example.

But for the psychodynamically trained therapist, the target for treatment is always the subjective experiences of the patient's past and present relationship difficulties. Here the clinician's focus is not limited to the end product or surface manifestation, but instead centers on the troublesome past and current life issues as they intersect the personality style and unique functioning of the person. Dynamically oriented treatments always include a focus on the patient's developmental history and the manner in which representations of past relationships, what psychoanalysts call "inner objects," are organized within the person—those recalled, forgotten, disavowed, and outside his awareness.

Added to this mosaic of mandatory psychological foci for the psychotherapist are the patient's current close and intimate relationships and their connections to pertinent early relationships, developmental experiences, and traumatic happenings. These include past relationships with parents, siblings, grandparents, aunts, uncles, cousins, and the unique networking among them. These experiences with formative others have left neural traces within the brain and relationship scripts and characterological propensities within the mind that now effect the problematic experiences and symptoms for which the client is seeking help. Furthermore, present-day happenings and relationships activate familiar patterns of relating to these important others from the past, carrying the potential for the person to adapt to his present circumstances and relationships with others or interfering with his relationships or his psychological and/or psychobiological functioning.

Finally, returning to the central thesis of this book, couple therapists especially recognize the importance of the relationship selfdyad and its intrinsic ability to effect changes in the individual. Here I am making a subtle but important distinction between the relationship of the intimate couple, which is a conscious and observable phenomenon that is mostly apparent to others and even to the couple, versus the selfdyad itself. It is this mutually constructed dynamic entity, the selfdyad—a private psychological space in which two have become one—where both persons are transformed from who they were as individuals and recast within the intimate partnership. Furthermore, it is this private space that accounts for the partners' subjective experience of having been changed from what each was without the other to what each is within the intimate partnership.

Turning one's attention toward the selfdyad, especially when working with patients whose initial concerns center on the client's experience of the partner, is fundamental to the treatment process. Assessing the partner's impact on the client (e.g., how the client feels changed, constrained, or affected in mood or a reference to a conflict between giving in to the partner versus adhering to his own position) provides important clues in coming to understand the dynamic interplay of the partners.

Understanding the interlocking system of the selfdyad and its impact on the individual is different from the more traditional paradigm of linear psychology—the "that causes this" paradigm. When considering the contribution of the selfdyad to the client's or couple's prevailing problem, we are instead maintaining a dynamic systems focus that more comprehensively and accurately addresses patients' difficulties—that is, how and why the presenting symptoms, including relationship difficulties, have been constructed and reinforced and are now maintained within the intimate partnership. When the therapist thinks within a dynamic systems model, the stage becomes set for the introspection that is essential for the client's or couple's growth.

EMOTIONAL INTENSITY AND INTROSPECTION

In couple therapy it is important for the therapist to assist both individuals to establish insight into self-motivation as both come to understand their respective roles in perpetuating their difficulties. This statement may seem pedestrian to some readers, perhaps especially to those who actively practice couple therapy. And yet, because the couple treatment setting is frequently of high emotional intensity, sometimes with both partners having considerable difficulty in modulating affect, the emotional tension and contagion within the couple consultation often militate against self-reflection and the achievement of insight. Even when there is no apparent conflict within the session, the therapist should be alert to the internal states of the partners because they may be quite different from the partners' overt presentations.

Commonly, a partner might appear to be listening to the other voice complaints and concerns while, however, he is quietly and busily preparing his rebuttal and mobilizing his defenses to counter what is experienced as inaccurate reporting, misunderstanding, or an attack on the self. Because some clients are more proficient at maintaining emotional control within the session, even when experiencing considerable internal turmoil and/or aggression, the lack of self-reflection, a difficulty in listening, and a dearth of empathy for the partner can go unnoticed by the therapist. Here the therapist might be gaining considerable insight into the couple's problems, while the partners are gaining little or nothing. Instead, there is merely an appearance of achieving insight, while aggression continues to mount and introspection fails to develop. By contrast, in the individual treatment setting, there might be periodic eruptions of negative affective states, but the working alliance and the intermittent positive transference states provide a relative quiescence that facilitates introspection and the achievement of insight.

In more theoretical terms, when couples come for treatment in a state of anger, hurt, and blame, sometimes feeling traumatized by the partner, there is frequently a predominance of paranoid-schizoid functioning in which reflection and insight into the self, the relationship dynamics, and empathy toward the other—those manifestations of depressive position functioning—are at low ebb. Splitting phenomena are extant, with rigidly held perceptions of the partner as bad partially mediated by the perceiving partner's projected bad internal object relationships. While they are in a paranoid-schizoid mode, the partners are frequently unable to maintain a balanced and multifaceted view of the other's behavior as motivated by the interaction and affected by each others' perceptions.

Furthermore, because of the high pitch of emotion and rapid-fire action in the treatment setting that, especially in the early stages of treatment, often centers on blaming of the partner, discharging painful affects, and rampant projective identification, the therapist is vulnerable to the same disequilibration of emotion that the couple experiences. This is an especially important and frequent countertransference obstacle when considering that the couple therapist must first and foremost function as a container for the couple's emotions, acting as a shock absorber that processes and metabolizes the affects and internal experiences that are not yet cognitively represented (Scharff & Scharff, 1991).

COUNTERTRANSFERENCE DISINTEGRATION

When used as a way to understand the unconscious of the patient or the couple, countertransference serves a most valuable function. The couple therapist, however, is especially susceptible to a disruption in analytic equanimity when encountering the bombardment of diffuse affects of couples immersed in a paranoid-schizoid mode. Here the therapist is especially vulnerable to a loss of neutrality and impartiality, both of which are fundamental requirements in the therapy of couples. Because countertransference obstacles are common to all the psychotherapies, I reserve the term "countertransference disintegration" for the couple therapist's loss of impartiality, neutrality, and optimal distance; when not recognized and brought under control by the therapist, this can put the entire treatment and the chances for its success at risk.

The most common manifestations of countertransference disintegration occur at those times in which the therapist loses sight of the interlocking mutual contribution of both partners, allying himself with one partner against the other, forming a complementary identification (Racker, 1968) with that partner's internal objects. Here the therapist is temporarily unable to retain a comprehensive view of the couple as a system in which both partners are playing out roles that are partly in response to the other partner and partly a projection of an internalized object relationship (Zeitner, 2003). The introspection required for the couple to process its difficulties cognitively through insight and reflection might then be lost or never developed during the course of therapy as the therapist's identification with one partner's internal objects undercuts his capacity to continue seeing the problem as co-determined. In this way the selfdyad is bypassed, while therapeutic leverage is diminished or lost altogether.

The vignette in the following section is a first session of a couple presenting with a conflict pertaining to their sexual relationship. Because of the intensity of the affect displayed in the session, it seemed especially important rapidly to establish a dynamic framework through which the partners could come to understand their sexual difficulties. Although establishing a dynamic formulation of the presenting problem characterizes all the exploratory psychotherapies, in the treatment of couples it is especially important to establish this focus in a way that gives equal weight to each partner's contribution to the problem.

In the following case example the couple presented almost entirely without an introspective focus, a problem characteristic of couples whose anger and resentment have been building over time. Often the partners will describe their views of the other and their relationship in a narrow, rigid, and concrete way, while openly or secretly blaming the other, with little or no awareness of their own contribution to the difficulties.

In the following case, establishing the introspective framework was at first compromised because of the constraining influence of Justin's anger. Although Lily presented as the more injured party, there was a critical juncture within her individual session that permitted me to assist her in coming to recognize her anger and hostility as contributing features to their sexual difficulties. I will show how I worked with this couple to broaden their focus from an incendiary and repetitive recitation of their sexual struggles to a final achievement of a more compassionate understanding of their complaints as surface manifestations around power, control, and assertion.

Lily and Justin

Justin, a pastor, and Lily, a homemaker, came in at the recommendation of Lily's psychiatrist. Lily had been in treatment for about a year for depression, anxiety, and tension headaches, which had worsened in recent months. Because the focus of her individual treatment had recently taken a turn toward her relationship with Justin, her therapist referred her for couple therapy in addition to the pharmacotherapy and individual therapy she had been receiving. It was Lily who initiated the first appointment; Justin reluctantly agreed to accompany her. He made it clear that there was nothing wrong with him, but that he would come in if it would help his wife.

Surprisingly, Justin opened the session by launching into an angry diatribe about Lily's lack of sexual responsiveness. He remarked that it seemed to him that she "controlled" their sexual relationship. He proceeded to blame her restrictive Catholic background for her views on sex as dirty and forbidden. Justin commented that prior to their marriage the frequency of sexual intercourse had been just barely adequate, but because there were so many other attractive features about Lily, he continued the relationship while thinking that things would change once they were married. Furthermore, he felt that once she converted from Catholicism, she would experience some liberation from her repressive background.

Lily sat quietly through Justin's complaints, appearing somewhat distant and impassive. She failed to elaborate on her background, while merely agreeing that her Catholic faith had been prominent in her formative years. When I encouraged her to reflect on her views of their sexual relationship, she reluctantly offered that she felt that once every 2 weeks was adequate, although she knew that Justin was often frustrated with her. She added that she thought they had worked out their sexual relationship in a way that had been mutually acceptable, although not ideal. My continual attempts to encourage Lily to expand on or to disagree with Justin's views were met with resistance. I wondered what her reticence might represent for their relationship, in light of the fact that she had been the one to initiate couple therapy and had apparently been experiencing considerable emotional pain.

Beginning to feel a bit barraged by Justin's vociferous complaints about Lily, I now wondered if Lily's lack of spontaneity and passivity might represent an unconscious communication that was important in coming to understand their selfdyad. Perhaps Justin's oracular style caused Lily to be unable or unwilling to exercise her own voice. Because of her continued diffidence, I scheduled an individual session with her.

In the individual hour, I was immediately impressed by Lily's openness and fluidity of thought and feeling. Her hesitance had seemingly vanished as she spoke with conviction, but now she openly blamed Justin for their difficulties. At this moment there seemed to be little reflection on *her* contribution to their problematic interactions. Instead, she proceeded with an inflammatory denunciation of Justin for *his* dictatorial qualities. She proceeded to tell me that, over the years, Justin had become renowned for building a large and influential church body, and that he had come to treat her as he did the employees of his church. I commented to Lily that it seemed to her that *she* was controlled by *him*. I specifically chose the word "control," recalling that Justin had used this same verb in describing Lily's unwillingness to have sex with him.

As Lily proceeded to articulate her anger at Justin, she cited numerous examples of what she felt were his attempts to control her. I now recognized that Justin's complaint about Lily's control of sex matched Lily's experience of Justin as a man who was out to wield his power over her. A mutually held conviction that each was controlled by the other appeared to be a central feature of their difficulties. Both had contributed to a selfdyad in which they had mutually projected a quality of control that left little room for what was important to them as individuals. As a rule, when both partners describe the other in similar ways and use equivalent or identical words to describe their interactions, it is likely that projective identification is operating and that features of the selfdyad are being described.

Implications of the Private Space

In practice, it is sometimes difficult for the therapist to remain mindful that features or attributions identified by one partner in the other are not necessarily apparent or observable. This phenomenon is due to the very nature of the selfdyad. The selfdyad develops within an intersubjective and private space of the couple, in which features of the selves of both are unconsciously projected onto the other, effecting a response that simultaneously serves as an ongoing stimulus for the other partner's reactions. Because both partners can unconsciously attempt to rid the self of qualities that have become toxic in the process of development, the relationship becomes a repository into which these qualities of the self can be evacuated.

To the extent that both partners are able to receive these projections and attributions, contain them, and comfortably metabolize them without undue reactivity, the couple will likely develop their private interlocking patterns of communication into a smoothly functioning and adaptive selfdyad that facilitates communication while enhancing intimacy. But because projective identification functions as a mechanism for unconscious communication and serves as a mode for evacuating the effects of toxic unresolved developmental lesions, it can come to function as a defense, setting into motion patterns of communication with the capacity to congeal into chronic couple discord. Just as the exaggerated use of any one defensive strategy for an individual can come to represent psychopathology, for the couple using excessive projective identification to rid the self of toxic issues, the interpersonal realities can similarly become blurred while the couple becomes stuck in a repeating cycle of conflict. This was Justin and Lily's predicament.

Although within the first two interviews little had been revealed about their individual histories, it had become reasonably clear that Lily and Justin had an equal hand in projecting onto each other inner objects characterized by control and inflexibility. Both partners had come to feel as though they had little autonomy in the relationship and were convinced that the other held all the power. Moreover, both had come to feel that the other lacked empathy about what was important to them as individuals.

Having identified the issue of power in their relationship, I also thought it was important to better understand how Justin's complaints about their lack of sexual involvement had impacted Lily. In the individual session I asked her how she had experienced Justin's unhappiness. Now she appeared freer to explore her feelings without the reticence that I had observed in the conjoint session. She remarked that, as Justin had become more demanding of her over the years, she had become more resentful as her interest in sex declined. Her explanation was presented as if it were a natural outcome when one is offended and hurt by another person. To encourage further introspection I said to her, "And when one is angry at another, holding something back that the other one wants seems quite natural, doesn't it?" Following a momentary pause, Lily replied, "Maybe I sometimes hold it over his head because I feel beaten up and powerless"—for the first time appearing more reflective about her role in the interaction.

My assistance in helping Lily clarify that her sexuality was something that she held back offered a subtle but important variation on her more conscious experience of her relationship with Justin. It seemed to prompt a shift from experiencing herself as a passive victim who was merely angry at her husband's offensive behavior to an active participant and a live contributor within the intersubjective field of their selfdyad. In response to my slightly altered version of her response to me, she was able to expand her insight into her more aggressively motivated behavior within their interaction. Now she was able to see her diminished sexual responsiveness to her husband as not just a preference, but also her attempt to achieve her own sense of power within their relationship.

This was a couple who had developed their selfdyad around power and control of the other, both consciously experiencing themselves as victims who were angry at the other's provocations. Although the manifest complaint was Justin's anger over the lack of intimacy, it eventually became apparent that he experienced Lily as depriving and controlling him by withholding sex. Initially, he had little insight into his controlling qualities and virtually no understanding of how his behavior toward Lily had contributed to the lack of tenderness and intimacy in their relationship. Lily's silent treatment and withdrawal from Justin, on the other hand, was both a response to feeling criticized and subjugated and a passive-aggressive expression of her need to assert herself when confronted with his dominance.

Summary

The technique of couple therapy must always include the therapist's attention to the dynamic interplay of *both* partners' contributions—those behaviors and projected experiences occurring within the entire field of communication between them. Within this realm of communication I include not just the actual words and actions between the partners, but also the unconscious communication that is encoded within the chosen words, actions, and total field of relating.

The case of Lily and Justin vividly demonstrates how the anger hidden within Lily's depression and headaches had been serving to undermine the couple's capacity to employ insight into their respective contributions to the presenting problem. Furthermore, although Lily had been the overtly symptomatic partner, Justin, too, had been struggling with his smoldering anger. Although couples coming for treatment are obviously aware that there are difficulties within the relationship, it is usual for each partner to hold the other primarily and sometimes exclusively responsible. This imputed responsibility becomes the most potent enemy of the introspection that is required for the treatment process to move forward and to be helpful.

THE COUPLE'S AVOIDANCE OF INTROSPECTION

In this section we will elaborate on the ways that couples present their difficulties, including the various defenses and interpersonal mechanisms and strategies used that have the potential to hijack the introspective focus. When these mechanisms are recognized by the therapist, it can be safely assumed that they represent the very difficulty the partners have in maintaining a reflective, compassionate, and empathic stance with each other. The therapist's task then is to assist both partners to develop or restore their reflective capacity as they come to better understand themselves within their relationship. To the extent that both partners are able to develop their introspective capacities in the treatment process, there will inevitably emerge an increased empathy and understanding of the partner and the dynamics of the relationship.

Although introspection is both the goal and antidote for the couple's impasse, it is most difficult to maintain in the actual practice of couple therapy. Both partners typically experience their own positions, attitudes, and emotional reactions toward the other as reasonable responses to the injuries inflicted by the other. To come to recognize one's role in the relationship as having a motive other than self-protection—that is, to become aware of one's destructive motivations—is a central and sometimes understated goal of dynamically focused couple therapy.

The various ways that both partners come to blame each other often preclude an awareness of one's own role in either creating or maintaining the difficulty. It is useful for the couple therapist to think of blame and anger and their vicissitudes as defenses that most often involve the projection of a toxic internal object relationship. Regardless of the factual accuracy or legitimacy of the complaint about the partner, what is pertinent is the way in which the reported concern or issue evokes painful affects for the partner. These affects typically have developmental antecedents, which by and large have remained out of the partner's conscious awareness or have never before been considered relevant. Attending to how the partners blame each other, while holding the other partner responsible, must include the use of interventions to assist them both to become aware of their projections and their developmental precursors.

As the individuals come to understand the relevance of these early experiences contained within the projection, the pressure to evacuate these affects by blaming the partner will be reduced. Not infrequently, the urgency to blame the partner serves to protect the self from the shame that would otherwise be experienced. Assisting both individuals to recognize the shame that frequently underlies the blame and anger is often liberating for both partners. Here the therapist's equal empathy and sensitivity to both partners is of utmost importance, for in the atmosphere of intense affects, it can be easily corrupted and abandoned as a function of the couple's projections.

THE THERAPIST'S AVOIDANCE OF INTROSPECTION

Maintaining the introspective focus is arguably one of the most difficult tasks in the practice of couple therapy. Not only does the couple tend to sabotage the essential introspection in the ways we have described, but the therapist is also prone to abandoning this position. In this section we will address the factors that interfere with the therapist's ability to maintain the systems focus required for maintaining therapeutic neutrality and for minimizing the potential for countertransference disintegration.

Establishing Misalliances

A misalliance is defined as the therapist's identification with one partner in a manner that is experienced by the other partner as alienating. Here one and sometimes both partners will experience the therapist as taking sides, with one feeling vindicated, supported, and relieved, while the other feels blamed and misunderstood. Not uncommonly, this is not brought out openly in the session, but instead between the partners following the couple's session. It is at this point that the treatment process may falter, possibly precipitating an impasse or even a premature termination of treatment.

Establishing a misalliance often represents a countertransference-related difficulty in the therapist, which may emanate either from his misunderstanding of the dynamic structure and functioning of the selfdyad or from his personal conflicts activated by one partner's or the couple's issues. The therapist may become pulled into an alliance with one partner by temporarily abdicating his equidistance between the partners. There may be a loss of the perspective that the couple's difficulties are co-determined, with partners' conscious and unconscious features fitting together like a lock and key.

This obstacle is commonly experienced by therapists whose formal training and supervision have been primarily or only in the individual psychotherapies. Although the therapist indeed views couple therapy as a treatment mode in which the two partners are seen conjointly, the actual therapeutic focus within the treatment hour is on the partners' individual psychological issues. Although both individuals are invited to explore their pasts, the therapist fails to demonstrate and interpret the interlocking dynamic arrangement of the partnership as a co-construction of repressed internal objects that, through projective identification, both create and perpetuate the couple's difficulties. The therapist then fails to give attention to the selfdyad as the interpsychic representation of a total couple system in which the perceptions and behaviors of both partners are partially determined by the other—each expressing a projected part object relationship that is both the effect and the cause of the conflict.

Assisting both individuals to accept their individual roles encourages a more empathic and realistic adaptation and an acceptance of the partner's uniqueness. Maintaining this kind of focus within the treatment eventually allows the perception of the partner to become untangled from the projections. Meanwhile, within the process of treatment, both partners will expand their awareness of how and why the other was unconsciously chosen to heal and complete the self by providing a revised and improved version of the original object relationship. To the extent that the therapist fails to appreciate or to retain the focus on the selfdyad or abdicates this perspective as a function of countertransference disintegration, the treatment is likely to falter.

The case in the following section illustrates how a countertransference impasse emerged out of the therapist's identification with one partner's inner objects. In seeking a supervisory consultation, the therapist was able to identify a similarity in his own history to that of one partner. This ultimately helped him to regain his therapeutic neutrality and the necessary equidistance for understanding and working with the selfdyad.

Nora and Hans   Nora and Hans had been in treatment for approximately 1 year with Dr. A, who asked me to consult because of his concern that Nora's recent eruption of anger threatened the continuation of therapy. Dr. A described Nora and Hans as volatile individuals who seemed to have little patience with each other's way of parenting their 16-year-old son. Jeff was a demanding and narcissistic adolescent boy who, according to Nora, was excessively and inappropriately indulged by Hans. Over time, she had grown progressively angrier with Hans, accusing him of pandering to their son's demands; her attempts to bring Jeff under control were perceived by both Hans and Jeff as unreasonably authoritative. The case had many complicating aspects, including Jeff's sociopathic features, drug abuse, and history of learning disabilities. The central difficulty for which Dr. A consulted me, however, was the impasse he encountered as he worked with this couple around their parenting issues, which recently had spiraled downward into a serious deterioration in their marital relationship.

As Dr. A described a sequence of several sessions that included relevant history pertaining to Hans's and Nora's parenting styles, I noted that he made an intervention that seemed to initiate a reverse of the tide into a negative direction. While exploring Nora's volatile relationship with her mother, a woman who had been diagnosed with bipolar illness during Nora's childhood, Dr. A remarked that Nora's behavior with Hans seemed to carry the same quality of explosive affect that her mother portrayed throughout her formative years. Although Dr. A's intervention was not incorrect, I felt that it was unconsciously driven by Dr. A's identification with Hans while inadvertently ascribing blame to Nora for their struggles. There had been several other features of Dr. A's presentation that hinted at his negative countertransference feelings toward Nora and an exaggerated sympathy for Hans. It is important to note that when the therapist has formed a countertransference misalliance with one partner, an interpretation that might otherwise be correct will often be experienced by the other partner as unempathic and insensitive.

Hypothesizing that Nora felt misunderstood as a function of Dr. A's alliance with Hans, I interrupted Dr. A to ask how he felt about this couple. The following issues emerged. First, Dr. A remarked that his mother had been treated for a bipolar disorder and that she eventually committed suicide. He spoke of his conflictual and unresolved feelings about her death—the rage he felt toward his mother for her constant diatribes within the family, but also the profound guilt he experienced over the years following her death. In his own therapy he had come to recognize that the relationship he had with his mother was one in which his anger toward her had coalesced into a sadomasochistic struggle in which Dr. A behaved in ways to provoke her, setting off her explosions. He proceeded to describe how his father and mother would become embroiled in conflict, with his mother attempting to prove Dr. A's culpability and his father in turn protecting him.

Dr. A and I were now able to understand and discuss his identification with the attacking inner object of the couple's selfdyad, with Dr. A allying himself with Hans as his father, while unconsciously impugning Nora as his attacking mother. Although the alliance with Hans against Nora had been subtle, it was experienced by Nora as an attack and a loss of Dr. A's neutrality. As Dr. A became more aware of the source of his countertransference misalliance, he was eventually able to restore the neutrality required to work with the selfdyad.

Here was a seasoned couple therapist who had both the training and the experience to understand and work with the dynamic interplay of this couple. But because an important feature of the couple's selfdyad had activated Dr. A's unresolved family issues, including the conflictual guilt about and hatred of his mother, the treatment process had derailed.

Passive Avoidance of Intense Affect

We have established that the intensity and the persistence of aggression are generally greater in couple therapy than in individual therapy. The therapist's capacity to tolerate aggression is a factor that can significantly alter the treatment process as well as the therapist's countertransference. Therapists who are less tolerant or who are uncomfortable with expressed aggression might be inclined to avoid affective involvement by sidestepping crucial issues or topics that are potentially inflammatory. This countertransference manifestation represents yet another way that the therapist can unconsciously disrupt the introspective focus and inadvertently sabotage the treatment process.

By and large, in contrast to individual therapy and psychoanalysis, couple therapy proceeds less according to free association. Although the couple therapist indeed must provide a structure for the work by encouraging the couple to observe the themes that arise during the intervening days between appointments, the actual issues brought into the consultation room are less frequently from a reflective or introspective vantage point than they are in individual psychotherapy. Instead, it is usual for one member of the couple to bring into the session an observation about the partner that is portrayed as an insight or a concern but is actually a disguised complaint or even an attack on the partner. Here the complainant is often unaware of how the described behavior has been influenced by his behavior or by affects that have been projected into the selfdyad.

In other words, couples are frequently less able to view the partner's behavior as a partial function of the interaction between them, especially during the early stages of treatment. As the partner listens to the other's concern or observation, he may experience it as an attack or criticism and respond with a counterattack or a rationalization for the cited complaint. This common occurrence often precipitates a regression into the paranoid-schizoid mode, which is inimical to the introspective focus that is more characteristic of depressive mode functioning. As a consequence, the couple treatment setting can then become a virtual battlefield to which the therapist responds with his own countertransferences, which are at least partial functions of the couple's projective identifications. These dynamic interactions and affects can invade the therapist's unconscious psychological map, affecting his capacity to tolerate and manage aggression and to intervene and interpret with efficacy (Zeitner, 2003).

Active Avoidance of Intense Affect

A variation in which the therapist who is uncomfortable with aggression passively avoids aggressively tinged issues is the situation in which the therapist actively intervenes to dampen down the intensity of affect. Here the therapist might experience anxiety about the expressed aggression or develop some confusion in understanding the dynamics of the couple. In this latter situation the affect of the couple has actually invaded and disrupted the mind of the therapist, causing a quasi-dissociative process to occur. Although intentionally intervening to soften affective intensity can sometimes represent good therapeutic technique—especially when emotion is potentially destructive to the treatment or when the couple has derailed from introspection—we are talking here about a countertransference-mediated intervention that interferes with the emerging understanding of the couple's difficulties.

Experiencing a sufficient quantity of affect within the session is essential for the couple to maintain intimacy and involvement with each other while simultaneously helping them develop new patterns of relating and understanding. The therapist maintaining the proper balance of affective modulation within the session, as the partners come to better understand themselves in the context of their relationship, represents one of the important features defining the art and science of couple therapy.

When supervising therapists and students in training, I have encountered countertransferences in which the therapist who is uncomfortable with the expressed anger in a session may resort to interventions that soften or evade important feeling states. What can sometimes follow is an interference in the couple's emerging insight into their relationship dynamics. An example is of a therapist I once supervised who acknowledged to me his discomfort with the couple's aggression. To address the couple's difficulties, he provided a behavioral prescription for the partners to talk with each other on a daily basis about their perceived good qualities. This was to be accomplished during the interval between appointments.

Although behavioral interventions and strategies can sometimes be facilitative, this therapist's use of this intervention appeared to be misplaced—emanating from his feelings about the couple's anger. I offer this example as a gentle warning that the dynamic systems focus can easily become corrupted in the heat of aggressive interactions that exceed the therapist's threshold of tolerance when they impinge on his internal world of inner objects and conflicts. The end result may be a defensive rendering of supportive measures that ultimately serves to suppress interactions and affects that have the potential to deepen the introspective focus and develop the couple's empathy and insight into their relationship. Straddling the fence between supportive interventions that appropriately modulate affective intensity of the couple on the one hand, while amplifying and interpreting the sources of these emotions on the other, represents a fundamental goal for dynamically focused couple therapy.

Doctor X Doctor X, a quite talented therapist whom I had previously supervised, asked me to consult on a couple he had difficulty understanding. Dr. X informed me at the outset that, in contrast to his usual comfortable way of working in conjoint therapy with the couple he had come to speak with me about, he felt anxious and unable to understand the dynamics of their interaction. Uncharacteristically for Dr. X, he felt confused in formulating a dynamic construction of this couple's difficulties.

Pedro and Jimmy were a gay couple who had consulted Dr. X because of Pedro's waning sexual responsiveness to Jimmy's overtures. Their sexual problems began at the time they started living together. Prior to cohabitating they had been together as a couple for 2 years, during which time sex had been important to them both. Dr. X emphasized that he was not uncomfortable in working with gay couples. He felt that he was able to listen easily and to work with the details of their sexual relationship much as he was able to work with heterosexual couples. And because he had considerable experience in treating difficult patients and couples, he was genuinely puzzled about what he felt represented a countertransference-based problem that caused him a block in understanding this couple.

Dr. X described the opening session of the couple's treatment, followed by another in which I too found it difficult to find a dynamic thread that would lead to a formulation of this couple's difficulty. Interestingly, I took note that Dr. X's presentation to me was executed beautifully as he described the couple's interactions. He provided me with exact quotes of the couple, along with his perfectly crafted interventions. Because a clear dynamic understanding of couples and individual patients does not necessarily appear immediately, I merely listened to his presentation with an open curiosity as I attempted to understand his impasse. About 30 minutes into the consultation, still with no clarification of what might be going on, I noted that Dr. X was speaking to me in an especially loud voice, a volume that I had not recalled in my previous interactions with him. I suddenly wondered if this uncharacteristic volume might be a clue to understanding the problem for which he had come to see me.

I commented to Dr. X about both his speech volume and the precision with which he had executed his presentation. Dr. X paused for a minute while he considered my observation. He then remarked that Pedro and Jimmy both spoke loudly and always with precision and in good control. Puzzled, Dr. X proceeded to explain that Jimmy and Pedro consistently appeared reflective and thoughtful, but that their emotion with each other appeared "flat and disingenuous." He went on to say that they both used a great deal of psychological jargon "as if they had read the latest pop psychology self-help book." Furthermore, Dr. X added, "When Pedro speaks there is a tightness in his jaw as if he might be angry."

Suddenly, as if it were an afterthought, Dr. X remarked that because these men were so controlled in dealing with each other, he had recently given them a behavioral assignment to be carried out daily before returning for their next appointment. He had asked Pedro and Jimmy to speak with each other for 10–15 minutes each evening, telling each other what had been exciting about the other one during the past 24 hours. Surprised by this seasoned therapist's use of a behavioral prescription, especially one that seemed desperate and even clumsy, I asked him why he had employed this technique. He responded that he had grown increasingly uncomfortable with Pedro and Jimmy's intellectualized approach to each other, especially because the treatment did not appear to be deepening. Finally, Dr. X added that he had increasingly found Jimmy and Pedro's intellectualization and "pop psychologizing" to be irritating.

I now put together a more comprehensive picture of the data. This included Dr. X's loud voice and how it mirrored the couple; the precision of the therapist's presentation, which appeared to be a representation of Jimmy and Pedro's sanitized demeanor with each other; the tightness of Pedro's jaw; and, finally, Dr. X's desperate use of a behavioral technique. I formulated my question: "From where and from whom does all this rage come?" I asked Dr. X. My question contained, of course, my hypothesis about the nature of the difficulty that Dr. X had been encountering. Because projective–introjective dynamics are extant within the therapist's consulting room, flowing among all participants within the therapeutic field, it was now clear that Dr. X had absorbed a defensively projected derivative of the anger that had been contained within Pedro and Jimmy's selfdyad.

Although presenting as an intelligent and enlightened couple who seemed eager to understand and remedy their sexual problem, their civility, control, and carefulness masked an underlying anger that impinged upon their sexual functioning. Unconsciously, both partners had agreed to seal off all aggression from their partnership, which had the effect of emptying their relationship of vitality and genuineness. To explore and ultimately recover those features would now become the therapeutic goal as the therapist came to help this couple understand the stiltedness of their relationship.

Pedro and Jimmy's inhibition of aggression had likely been motivated by a shared anxiety pertaining to its potential dangers. Attempting to eradicate discontent and anger with each other, this couple had projected into Dr. X its residuals. Dr. X's use of the well-intended behavioral prescription represented an abortive attempt to interrupt this couple's emotionless presentation while he failed to recognize that their lack of genuineness was specifically in an effort to avoid the anger that they feared. Pedro's lack of sexual desire was yet another attempt to comprehensively deaden feelings that threatened to interrupt the status quo.

Summary

By providing a homework assignment, Dr. X intended to open up a couple's empty and stale relationship. Ironically, he had chosen to suspend the introspective focus of a dynamically oriented treatment in favor of using a prescriptive device that ultimately failed. Not uncommonly, even well-trained therapists are prone to absorbing the unconscious anxieties of the patient or the couple, sometimes compelling the therapist to take a countertransference detour away from introspection in favor of alternative interventions. The therapist is then at risk for inadvertently inviting the couple to carry out the very thing that was feared and repudiated, thus increasing the couple's resistances while therapeutic opportunities are lost. Here the therapist actually colludes to avoid the very affects that have been crippling the couple's intimate life.

DOMINANCE, ACQUIESCENCE, AND THE EXTRAMARITAL AFFAIR

In relationships in which one partner has assumed an exaggerated dominant role while the other is equally acquiescent, it is likely that the aggression within the selfdyad has been forcefully distributed such that one partner has become the primary carrier of the aggression while the passivity and the capacity for repression are projected onto the other partner. In these partnerships the selfdyad may function smoothly for long periods of time. But, not infrequently, as the couple encounters the variety of life's stresses—especially those events that mobilize powerful affects—repression may give way as couple conflict and even individual symptoms erupt (Fairbairn, 1944). Familiar stressors of adult life include the complications of raising children, encounters with extended family that include parents and siblings, financial and career stresses, adjustment to the empty nest, and the death of loved ones.

Frequently, it is the apparently passive partner—the one less overtly angry and with fewer complaints about the relationship—who comes for therapy in an effort to appease the partner who is more openly dissatisfied. The passive partner may feel confused and sometimes overwhelmed by the dominant partner's anger and sometimes perplexed about how to please the partner, acquire forgiveness, or improve the relationship. At other times, it is the more overtly angry partner, regardless of dominance or passivity, who brings the couple for a consultation because of the partner's transgression.

One of the most common presenting problems for couples who come for treatment is the recent discovery of an extramarital affair. While both dominant and passive partners can become involved in extramarital affairs, it is my experience that the dominant partner is more likely to go astray. Commonly, then, when presenting for the initial interview, it is the passive partner who is hurt, betrayed, and enraged, but currently appears to be anything but passive, while now the dominant partner appears contrite, ashamed, and beaten down.

Frequently, when the presenting problem is the affair itself, any mention of preexisting couple difficulties will at first be avoided. Because of the significant hurt and anger associated with the infidelity, the affair might then remain the focus of treatment for a long period of time during which the rage, shame, and wishes for revenge are repeatedly, if not obsessively, expressed in the treatment process. While some couples will more easily shift the focus from the affair to the long-standing difficulties with intimacy, many will remain locked onto the affair in an effort to discharge painful affects that have been incurred by the betrayal, sometimes hoping to extract revenge or reparation from the transgressing partner.

Because of the guilt and shame now associated with the infraction, the partner who has strayed may collude with the angry partner by remaining vague and silent about any long-standing relationship concerns, masochistically preferring to submit to the angry partner's invectives and needs for catharsis. The obsessive focus on the affair can then sometimes represent the couple's shared defense, serving to protect them from addressing their long-standing difficulties with intimacy or their latent concerns pertaining to the exaggerated dominance and submission existing within their relationship. Furthermore, the couple over time has likely unconsciously colluded to avoid open conflict by taking the path of least resistance. For these couples, anger and disagreement are often considered dangerous, while the partners have smoldered in their resentment, sealing off any hint of conscious discontent. Typically, they have failed to develop essential mechanisms for the resolution of conflict, while repression has set into their self-dyad, rendering it brittle and lifeless.

With such couples, the therapist must be especially alert to the manner in which the partners have defensively extruded aggression from the selfdyad, but that now serves as a resistance to the introspective focus. Part of the therapeutic task is cautiously to assist both partners to recognize their mutual fears of conflict while ultimately encouraging them to relate to one another with the full range of feelings that characterize intimate relating. Toward that same goal, the couple with a selfdyad of exaggerated dominance and submission will need considerable help in redistributing, within their relationship system, features of self that define the dominant and the submissive positions. Operationally, as the selfdyad is worked with in treatment and the partners come to better understand how and why each has assumed an exaggerated role, they are frequently able to retrieve and sometimes even reinvent sides of themselves that have been unexpressed and dormant for many years.

With couples experiencing conflicts over dominance and submission, both partners must be assisted to explore and understand the developmental factors that have unconsciously influenced them to assume their exaggerated positions—both their own and those imposed by the partner. For example, for the passive husband whose wife bitterly complains about his inability to make decisions about financial matters, but when he does take action repeatedly finds fault with him, it is essential for the couple to become aware that her criticism serves to influence and maintain his hesitant attitude toward their financial life.

Similarly, to encourage the husband to explore his past—for example, a family background of poverty in which his mother berated his father for his poor financial decisions, which eventually bankrupted the family—becomes essential in helping both partners to understand the genetic sources of his anxiety. Here it is also important for them to recognize that the husband's hesitancy is also rooted in the anxiety of disappointing his wife, as his father disappointed his mother.

Furthermore, the couple must come to understand that the husband's difficulty in making decisions contains within it anxiety that is simultaneously projected into the wife, further influencing her to take action by anxiously criticizing him. Finally, to address the wife's unconscious fears of losing control of their finances, after she had experienced her father's abandonment of a family of young children and a helpless mother, will assist the couple to understand both the unconscious and the interpersonal influences exerted on each other to create their difficulties around dominance and submission.

It should be noted that the partner in the dyad who readily assumes a position of passivity and who characteristically turns away from assertion, even when the more dominant partner is in full support and encourages autonomy, may be manifesting a pathological dependency or borderline structure that is developmentally rooted in incomplete separation-individuation and/or an attachment disorder. Because of this possibility, the couple presenting with a concern centering on one partner's refusal to assert himself, in spite of genuine encouragement by the other partner, requires a careful assessment. In some cases the passive-acquiescent partner might be more appropriately and effectively treated in individual psychotherapy or analysis than in couple therapy.

DIVORCE

Divorce in our culture is regarded as a recourse and a potential solution for any marital conflict considered intractable. It is perhaps most often considered as an option when there has been a breach of marital fidelity. A partner's persistent threat to divorce can also be used as retaliation against the "infidel" and as a way to attenuate the humiliation of the injured partner by assuming control over the continuation of the marriage. It is essential that these issues and possible motives be carefully explored in therapy, especially when the topic of divorce remains on the table for an extensive period of time.

The extramarital affair is without question a most destructive marital trauma; however, it is not necessarily irreparable. Although many factors determine whether the marital breach can be mended, I have found two factors to be most reliable in predicting a positive outcome and a restoration of the marital relationship. First, the couple's commitment to therapy—often, long-term couple therapy—will be important. Second, I have found that the couple's willingness to understand how the breach might have happened, including its implications for the couple's chronic marital difficulties, to be prognostic for a positive resolution. Intrinsic to both of these factors, I believe, is both partners having or establishing during the course of treatment a capacity for introspection that will enable them to study their relationship in a therapeutic process. For treatment to be successful in restoring the couple's intimacy, the couple must eventually come to experience the affair as the tip of the iceberg—a symptom of their long-standing difficulties, which must ultimately be worked through in the process of therapy.

OPPOSITION, WITHHOLDING, AND CONTROLLING

While dominance and acquiescence represent the opposite ends of the spectrum of commonly observed saboteurs of introspection and are easily observed in the beginnings of therapy, opposition, withholding, and controlling—a triad of interrelated behaviors of couples in conflict—are sometimes less apparent to the therapist until the treatment is well underway. Opposition to the partner, which sometimes appears as a readiness to disagree with or correct the partner over minute or unimportant details, sometimes represents a partner's unconscious desire to maintain preeminence in the relationship. Although this may sometimes be innocuous and at other times malignant, it must always be addressed during the course of therapy.

A more apparently aggressive attempt to control the partner and the relationship usually serves a narcissistic function, which obviously requires a careful exploration in the work. The narcissistic equilibrium of the couple may be assiduously maintained, even when both partners experience considerable discontent in the relationship. Here the therapist's countertransference-mediated sympathy may easily become tilted toward the one who is most obviously controlled or devalued, while the other partner's undermining qualities are eschewed. Once again, it is especially important that the therapist be able to recognize the collusive nature of the relationship, in which both partners have an equal stake in contributing and projecting narcissistic features into their selfdyad.

While the apparently controlling partner projects an attacking part of the self by persistently disagreeing, criticizing, or devaluing, there is frequently a counterpart process in which the other maintains a valency for accepting the projected bad object. As one partner manifests the apparent narcissism, the other partner presents as depressed, piteous, and masochistic while unconsciously accepting the projections. Frequently, as the treatment proceeds, it is discovered that the masochistic partner who appears controlled and devalued wields a more subtle power over the partner by expressing anger in other ways. Not infrequently, this partner may experience a chronic depression or a psychosomatic illness that has a controlling and punishing effect on the more apparently controlling partner.

The persistent control of the partner can serve other purposes as well. Although it might represent a narcissistic need to keep the partner in a subordinate position by projecting a feared and repudiated part of the self, it can also represent a way to withhold tenderness and intimacy, simply because it is desired by the other. Here the intent is to withhold something that is desired, as an unconscious expression of hostility toward the partner, frequently enacting an unconscious relationship script from the past.

It should be emphasized that what becomes problematic in intimate relations is not the occasional eruption of any one of these various dyadic transactions, but instead the exaggerated, continuous, and chronic use of any of these patterns of relating. Couples who appear for treatment are usually those who have developed inflexible relationship scripts that no longer are able to support the self of one or both partners.

SEXUAL AND OTHER PSYCHOSOMATIC PRESENTATIONS

Sexuality is perhaps the most elemental and fundamental component of the intimate partnership. It stands alone as that unique realm of experience for the couple that constitutes a bridge between the selfdyad and all that transpires unconsciously and the bodies of the two partners. Couple therapists describe sexuality as a psychosomatic partnership in which the biological functions of the partners are in communication with two minds, while the sex act is executed in the service of sensual pleasure and/or procreation (Scharff & Scharff, 1991). While pleasure and procreation may be interrelated motivations serving the Darwinian purpose of preserving the species, there are other essential psychological functions served by sexuality (discussed in Chapter 4). Here we will address the couple's sexual difficulties as symptoms that serve as substitutes for or displacements from the relationship conflicts that often, but not always, have been avoided by the couple.

Couples will commonly describe what appears to be an isolated difficulty in their sexual relationship. The problem might be represented as an inhibition in sexual desire, a disagreement about frequency, erectile dysfunction, or vaginismus. The sexual problem frequently remains the focus while other aspects of the relationship are avoided. Although unconscious anxieties and previously existing sexual trauma can be etiologic, for our purposes we will confine our discussion to those presentations in which sexual problems represent a psychosomatic displacement of the couple's relationship problems.

Commonly, the couple's sexuality has become unconsciously targeted to express the difficulties and anxieties in intimate relating, while guarding against the imagined dangers of having a more explicit emotional understanding of their relationship problems. What occurs is a projection of psychic tension into the sexual organs of the partners, impairing the couple's psychosomatic communion and functioning as a stand-in for difficulties within the selfdyad. Although sexuality remains the couple's focus, it simultaneously serves as a resistance to the introspection that must eventually be achieved through effective therapy.

Belinda and Stuart

Belinda called for an appointment because her partner, Stuart, had become angry about their infrequent sexual activity. Although they had been together for nearly 4 years, they had been living together for only 1 year, during which Belinda had developed a host of physical problems that had been recently diagnosed as fibromyalgia. She said that her physician had informed her that her reduced desire for sexual activity was a function of her medical problems. As Belinda introduced her situation on the telephone, it was at first unclear whether she was requesting an appointment for herself or for her and Stuart together.

Listening to her brief introduction, I noted a contradiction in her description of the problem. Although she remarked that Stuart had been angry at her for being ill and about the infrequency of their sexual activity, she subsequently went on to describe him as a "saint" who was "extremely sympathetic" about her medical problems. Stuart had taken over most of the household duties, giving her the opportunity to rest when he knew that she was tired and often in pain. Suddenly, Belinda asked whether I thought she should come in alone or have Stuart come in with her. Because she had already described Stuart's perturbation, but also described him in laudatory terms, it seemed reasonable to speculate that Stuart's unhappiness with the situation was at least one ingredient in the clinical picture. On that basis I recommended that Stuart accompany her to the first appointment.

In the opening session Belinda described in detail her problems with pain and the accompanying fatigue that she had been struggling with during the past year. Importantly, when she paused, Stuart quickly jumped in to clarify, as if concerned that something important had been left out. After listening to their lengthy description of Belinda's physical problems and the various treatments that had been tried, it occurred to me that nothing so far had been said about their problems as a couple, much less the sexual problems that Belinda had spoken about on the telephone.

Furthermore, I was struck with what appeared to be an incongruous quality of excitement, which both Stuart and Belinda seemed to share as they eagerly described her excessive pain and fatigue, its effect on their lifestyle, and the inconvenience of seeing many doctors and taking many medications. Noting this peculiar incongruity, I interrupted what appeared to be an almost euphoric recitation of her medical record by reminding them of Belinda's previously described concern about their sexual relationship. Now, in sharp contrast to what Belinda had conveyed on the phone, Stuart attempted to assure me that he completely understood that Belinda's pain during intercourse was due to her fibromyalgia and that he would continue to be patient with her. Throughout the remainder of this first visit, they held hands while continuing to describe their future plans for further medical tests.

This was a couple who had come for treatment after hinting strongly that they had been having sexual problems. At the time of the consultation, however, they seemed to collude in avoiding an open discussion about this part of their lives. Instead, there was an excited focus on Belinda's physical problems that seemed to hint at the possibility that their sexual excitement had been displaced and projected onto a psychosomatic representation of physical pain, serving to defend against sexual intimacy. This case further illustrates how partners can unconsciously collude to avoid a deeper understanding of their relationship while sacrificing intimacy. Furthermore, because Belinda's medical problems appeared to represent a shared psychosomatic defense, it would be especially important for me to proceed with patience and tact, gradually permitting both partners to unmask the fears and inhibitions underlying their avoidance of sexual intimacy.

CONCLUSION

In this chapter I have addressed the interferences that are common in maintaining the introspective focus of couple therapy. Although the management and interpretation of resistance is at the heart of psychoanalytically based treatments of all kinds, the special nature of the resistances in couple therapy has been the subject of this chapter. Rather than using the term "resistance," however, I prefer to describe these as the enemies of introspection, to denote the special features of the selfdyad, and to outline what is required in helping both partners to understand the unconscious nature of their relationship pact.

A core difference between individual and couple therapy is the therapist's focus on the couple's shared affects and internalized object relations, which have the potential to enhance the partners or to cause emotional disequilibrium. In this chapter I have outlined a variety of dynamic patterns that can occur, all having the potential to undermine the introspection required for effective treatment. Furthermore, I have attempted to illustrate how these interferences can corrupt the technical aspects of treatment, even motivating the therapist to employ supportive or palliative measures that can further undermine the insight that is necessary to enhance the growth of the couple.

In the final chapter, I will continue to elaborate the various techniques of analytically oriented couple therapy and to consider the important technical differences from working with individual patients. In the discussions of technique I will return to my focus on maintaining an optimal dialectic between self-expression and a mutually fulfilling intimate partnership.

10

CONSIDERATIONS FOR TREATMENT

This chapter will address central features of the diagnostic and psychotherapeutic process with couples, drawing on those ideas most relevant to the selfdyad and the thesis of this book. Throughout this writing I have emphasized the importance of the couple's shared space. I have called this construction the selfdyad, an extension of Henry Dicks's joint marital personality, but adding an important feature. By observing and treating troubled marriages, Dicks concluded that through projective identification, or what some have called the interpsychic transmission of mental contents, two individuals forming an intimate and permanent partnership will create a conjoint structure that is different from the two personalities forming it (Dicks, 1993). Through the transmission of these mental states, which include conscious and unconscious needs, wishes, fears, and defenses, parts of the self are projected onto the partner.

This mutual projection process, with a partner who has a valency for that projection, will form an interpsychic fit of two selves, establishing a stable and mutually fulfilling selfdyad. To the extent that the partner becomes unwilling or is unable to contain the projection, couple conflict and dissatisfaction within the relationship will likely ensue. Importantly, the selfdyad is distinguished from the joint marital personality by emphasizing that this conjoint entity must function in continuous support of the selves of the partners for the relationship to remain stable, loving, and mutually fulfilling. In a sense, the selfdyad must function as a selfobject for both partners in order for the couple to continue experiencing a loving and fulfilling relationship (Kohut, 1971, 1977). The central goal of couple therapy is to assist the couple to restore their relationship connection such that the selves of both partners are more fully supported and affirmed by the relationship.

I have consistently emphasized that to be and remain a loving couple with a mutually satisfying intimacy, a couple must be able to maintain a fluidity of movement between the selfdyad and the selves of the partners. There are several ways this process can go awry. The first is when the partner is no longer able or willing to contain a projection. In these situations, open conflict most usually arises and the status quo of the relationship is disrupted. Martin and Janet, a couple presented in Chapters 1 and 2, serve as an illustration. The second type of derailment is when the projection imposed by the first partner is experienced by the second partner as incongruous with the self. Here the second partner may internalize and enact the projection, even while experiencing an incongruity with his core self. In this case the self of the second partner may eventually succumb, as illustrated in the film *Revolutionary Road*. The collapse of the self is aptly explained by the appropriation and intrusion phenomena elaborated in Chapter 8.

A third option is when a partner projects onto the second partner a toxic object relationship from early development. Here the second partner enacts the projective identification while confirming the first partner's perception of her "badness." Often the urgency within the first partner to evacuate the bad object, coupled with the rigidity of the perception itself, is experienced as alien to the self of the second partner. By actively repudiating the projection, the second partner paradoxically enacts the projection through various displays of affect, becoming an approximation of the bad object.

It is important to emphasize that although I am attempting to separate the three ways in which the imbalance between the selfdyad and the selves can play out, in reality and in an actual therapy session, they are not easily separated and are not mutually exclusive. Frequently, in the clinical situation, one sees a mixture of all three, their manifestations emerging and receding at different times within the therapy.

For example, a man who had grown up in a family in which his mother treated him like royalty who was destined for great things married a woman who was highly affirming of his competence and his many achievements in the world of academics. His mother had been consistently supportive of her son's academic prowess, while his father had been highly critical of him, instead wanting him to excel in sports. During the first years of their marriage, the wife demonstrated no particular interest in pursuing a career path of her own. She was quite fulfilled by remaining home with their children as she assumed the traditional role of homemaker. Her mother had been a homemaker and her father an ambitious and successful businessman who encouraged his children to get good grades and pursue higher education. Her father consistently conveyed to her and her siblings that in adult life they should pursue what made them happy.

Strongly identified with her mother, the wife eagerly embraced her role of homemaker—that is, until their two children entered middle school. She now experienced an emerging boredom that prompted her to take a job in the field for which she had originally prepared in college. Now that she was less invested in her role as homemaker and adoring wife, her previously repressed identification with her ambitious father surfaced as her own career success came into ascendancy. Couple dissatisfaction now arose as she loosened her identification with her mother while simultaneously relinquishing her valency for her husband's projected image of his doting and constantly available and affirming mother. As her career began to take more time, she now turned to her husband to take up more of the slack at home, including caring for the children and preparing meals. It was at this point that her husband began to experience his wife as disrespectful, unloving, and rejecting.

We are able to observe that the couple's conflict erupted as their selfdyad destabilized, no longer supporting the selves of either partner. This simplified vignette illustrates the crucial interdependency and essential dialectic between the selfdyad and the self. Furthermore, in this example, we are able to see aspects of all three variations of selfdyad breakdown that were previously described. First, the wife was no longer willing to function as her husband's doting and affirming mother, which disrupted the status quo of their relationship. Second, the ambivalence she felt about her change in role, as a function of her husband's pressure to resume her original role as the solicitous wife and mother, had the potential to create the appropriation-intrusion paradigm that Faimberg (2005) has described. Third, to the extent that the wife remained intent on pursuing her career path while forcefully insisting that her husband slow his work pace to help out more at home, she now had become identified with her husband's projected critical father, who originally disapproved of his academic interests.

Although this example points to a developmental progression of family life as the initiating factor for the eruption of couple conflict, there are many factors that can potentially destabilize the selfdyad. By encouraging introspection and insight, the therapist's goal is to increase the couple's awareness of all dynamic considerations, eventually setting up the conditions for a reorganization of the selfdyad—one that once again is able to support the selves of both. Although a reconstituted selfdyad will almost always be different from the couple's original unconscious pact, for the relationship to be restored, the selfdyad must reorganize in a way in which it is once again able to support the individual needs of the partners. In the next section I will outline some essential features of the assessment and treatment process, making the selfdyad central to our discussion.

ASSESSING THE NEED FOR COUPLE THERAPY

Factors in Determining Mode of Treatment

Because many patients begin treatment individually, initiating the consultation with concerns centering on a relationship difficulty with the intimate partner, making the most appropriate treatment disposition will be facilitated by the therapist's understanding of the selfdyad. When, instead, an individual calls for an appointment for couple therapy, ordinarily both partners have already agreed that the relationship itself will be the focus of treatment. In most cases couple therapy will follow, although sometimes combined treatments will be recommended as the therapist becomes better acquainted with the couple and the particularities of their relationship difficulties.

In making an appropriate treatment recommendation for the couple and those individual patients presenting with apparent relationship problems, we will consider three modalities of treatment: individual, couple, and combined. We will address some of the variables involved pertaining to making referrals to other therapists when combined treatments are necessary or when it might be appropriate for the same therapist to use combined modes involving phasing—at times working with a partner, and at other times working with the couple.

Patient Factors There are many issues to be considered when determining the most appropriate form of treatment for a patient or a couple. First and foremost, the patient's or couple's preferences must always be considered. The patient, for example, who schedules an appointment for herself only but whose main concerns center on her intimate partnership can sometimes present complications when the clinician makes a recommendation for couple treatment. The patient might fear working with her partner in therapy, instead preferring a treatment atmosphere that permits a large space for catharsis and support.

This is especially common with those patients who have already experienced a sense of themselves as having been intruded upon by the partner. To begin couple therapy at this time threatens the patient with the possibility of a further loss of self. On the other hand, a patient might unconsciously fear conjoint therapy because it poses a risk that the other partner will expose the patient's role in the couple's difficulties, exacerbating the patient's shame or other affects. A variation of this is the patient who prefers the individual treatment setting because it protects against the exposure of humiliating secrets that are likely to be revealed in the couple treatment format. Although this latter factor presents a potential resistance for any therapy process, it can represent an obstacle when couple therapy is recommended.

Although individual therapy is sometimes initiated when couple therapy might be more appropriate, the patient commonly often improves through the supportive aspects of the therapeutic relationship. But sometimes as the therapist comes to better understand the patient's symptoms and their connection to the couple's relationship, it becomes clear to the therapist that the patient might be unable to sustain those gains in a relationship with a partner whose projections aggravate the symptoms. The therapist in the assessment or early treatment phase might even recognize a selfdyad in which the patient characteristically submits to the partner's wishes and projections by disavowing her own initiative. Without the benefit of the partner's presence in the treatment, it is difficult to determine the extent to which the partner's projections might be influencing the patient to remain unassertive.

As long as the permissive atmosphere of individual therapy encourages a more engaged and assertive position, the patient's self-esteem is supported. She feels valued and respected by the therapist as a function of a solid working alliance. The therapist and patient might even continue to work toward achieving self-understanding as the therapist supports the patient to become more assertive at home. But when she returns to her partner or after therapy has been terminated, she is then unable to be the person she was striving to become while working with her therapist. It is in these situations that we are able to witness the centrality and the resilience of the selfdyad. In spite of therapy going well and the patient achieving considerable growth, reentering the selfdyad with the partner erodes the gains that were achieved in the treatment setting.

One might argue that, if individual therapy had continued over a longer period of time or the patient had made sufficiently "deep" changes in her readiness to accept her partner's projections, she might have eventually broken out of the role that she and her partner had co-created. The counterargument here is that if she *were* actually able to have made these changes, the selfdyad would likely have become disrupted, with the partner now developing his own difficulties—possibly discontent, anger, or depression. Although individual therapy can sometimes be helpful for a couple's problem, especially if the patient in therapy is able to implement a complementary modification in the partner, this kind of even-keeled resolution is rare without couple therapy.

It is important for the therapist to bear in mind that the stronger the absent partner's need to evacuate a toxic object relationship while having it contained by the partner who is now in treatment, the poorer are the chances for a favorable resolution of the problem without couple therapy. It is in these situations that separating from the partner or divorce becomes the other available solution to the impasse; both of these are often considered by the patient and the therapist to be less than favorable outcomes that might have been achieved without the therapist's help.

Although the patient's preference of therapeutic modality must always be respected, a choice of one treatment over another can represent a resistance to therapy. When the therapist believes that a particular treatment mode will likely yield the greatest benefit to the patient, but the patient insists on another form of therapy, it is important for the therapist to explore the concerns and fears that lie at the root of the preference. It is not uncommon for the therapist to assess that a problem in the patient's relationship is a significant contributor to the patient's presenting difficulty. But because the patient objects to a couple consultation or therapy, the therapist acquiesces while proceeding to work with the patient in individual supportive therapy. Furthermore, the patient might improve as depression and anxiety are lessened; this now provides a rationale for continuing individual therapy and bypassing couple therapy.

The problem here lies in the clinician's definition of and criteria for improvement. Certainly, a reduction in objective symptoms defines one level of improvement. And yet it is common for patients to begin feeling better in the early phase of treatment, assuming that the patient has established a solid working alliance with the therapist. For managed care consultants within the insurance industry, symptom reduction is a sufficient criterion for successful therapy, and once it is achieved, the reviewer most often requires that the treatment be terminated.

Dynamically informed psychotherapists, however, are well aware that mere symptom improvement is not enough without sufficient character change and/or fundamental life changes, which sometimes include alterations in the patient's intimate partnership. In the absence of more comprehensive changes, symptom improvement will often be short lived. For these reasons, when the therapist is confronted with a patient whose symptoms are connected to a problem within the patient's intimate partnership, the selfdyad should always be considered when making a disposition and recommendation for therapy. The therapist must then be prepared to address any resistances that might emerge from the recommendation.

Individual, Couple, or Combined Modes of Treatment Not infrequently, the recommendation for couple therapy represents a threat to the patient who has come for individual therapy, especially when it foreshadows the loss of the supportive relationship with the therapist. At these times it can be useful to refer the couple to another therapist who practices couple therapy, while the current therapist continues working with the patient individually. Assuming that the patient accepts the recommendation and the couple therapy proceeds reasonably well and provides a solid holding environment for the couple, the individual therapy is sometimes terminated at the request of the patient. At other times the patient might wish to continue in a combined mode of treatment for the duration of the couple therapy.

When the couple is referred to another couple therapist and the patient remains in individual therapy simultaneously, the individual therapy is often useful in assisting the patient to contain the anxiety that might be experienced in or about the couple therapy. Concurrent individual therapy also provides an opportunity for the patient to address personal issues related to the couple's difficulties. Alternatively, individual therapy can occasionally become a bastion for subtle resistances into which the patient siphons off feelings and experiences that should appropriately be taken into the couple therapy. Here it is important for both the couple and individual therapists to be aware of this possibility, which, when discovered, should be brought to the patient's attention to assist in reestablishing a more workable frame for the combined modes of therapy.

Aware of the frequent usage of combined treatment modes and the potential complications that can arise when interfacing these modalities, Graller and his colleagues have provided a systematic model for the collaboration of the couple therapist with the individual therapist or analyst when combined therapies are utilized. Fundamental to their thinking is that the individual therapist or analyst and the couple therapist can potentially become entangled in various countertransferences and misalliances with their respective patients, as well as with or against each other in a way that potentially sabotages the other therapy and the therapists involved. They outline some of the possible dynamic considerations when concurrent therapies are used, proposing a systematic collaborative method that therapists can implement to attenuate the possible negative effects of combined therapies (Graller et al., 2001).

Inherent to their model is the awareness that not only is there a potential benefit to concurrent individual therapy and couple therapy, but also one or both partners frequently require simultaneous analysis or intensive therapy to address fundamental characterologic or other intrapsychic issues that impact the couple's difficulties. This model provides a creative system that potentially enables therapists to remain clear of their own biases and potential for colluding with their patients in ways that might obstruct both the individual's and the couple's growth.

Although Graller and his colleagues do not specifically address the construct of the selfdyad, their format suggests an intrinsic awareness that the intersubjective features of the couple relationship must be considered by all therapists involved, without which the individual therapist, especially, is at high risk for taking the side of his patient, unconsciously agreeing with his patient that it is the partner who is the problem. The therapist thereby overlooks his patient's role in what is actually a mutually constructed difficulty in the couple's relationship system. It is at these junctures that the couple and individual therapists can easily begin working at cross purposes as a function of the unconscious rivalries and countertransferences that exist among the patients, couple, and the therapists involved.

Finally, it is important to consider the potential complications that can arise when the individual therapist and patient who are currently working together consider a change in treatment mode in which the individual therapist now becomes the couple therapist. In this situation there is no referral to another therapist, thus obviating the need for collaboration between therapists. Not infrequently, even when well past the assessment phase and into the treatment phase, it can become clear to the therapist and to the patient as well that the couple relationship is at the foundation of the patient's difficulties. Often, the therapist and patient might have come to discover the prominence of a selfdyad that underlies the patient's difficulties or, for financial reasons or because of time or other practical constraints, it is determined that couple therapy will be a more expeditious mode of treatment and should now be substituted for the individual treatment.

Regardless of the reasons for the change in treatment mode from individual to couple therapy, there are important considerations that can sometimes be overlooked by the therapist. Commonly, when a change of mode from individual therapy to couple therapy occurs—especially when the individual therapist continues as the couple's therapist—there can be a glossing over or mutual disregard of the significance of this change by both therapist and patient. This often represents a patient–therapist collusion, a mutual denial of the loss of the therapeutic relationship. It is often presumed and frequently rationalized that because the therapist is still involved with the patient, although now in the role of couple therapist, the relationship will continue with no loss incurred. What is indeed lost, however, is the unique alliance between the therapist and patient; adding a third person represents an intrusion that will alter the previously existing therapeutic relationship.

The unique way in which this loss is represented for the patient should be carefully explored prior to making a change of mode. What is frequently underestimated by the therapist and patient alike is that, when the partner is insinuated into the treatment, the patient as previously known and understood by the therapist will be forever changed as a function of the selfdyad that now moves into therapeutic focus.

There are some additional implications when the selfdyad becomes the focus of treatment and the relationship between the individual patient and the therapist is accordingly altered. In addition to the patient having the opportunity to work through the loss of the therapeutic relationship and change of modality, any concerns about adding the partner should also be addressed. Sources of apprehension might include the patient's fear that the partner will come to be preferred by the therapist or that the therapist will eventually discover that the partner is right and the patient is wrong. The couple therapy format might then subsequently be at risk of the partners competing for the therapist's favor. This then becomes linked with the original patient's disappointment and sometimes outrage when the therapist maintains his neutrality and an unwillingness to take sides.

Lastly, it is important to discuss the implications for the partner who begins the process of couple therapy as the newcomer who is now added to the treatment situation. Frequently, this partner harbors a belief that he is entering therapy at a disadvantage and that his partner, the original patient, already has special favor with the therapist. Additionally, he may fear that the therapist holds a bias against him at the outset, having already been clued in by his partner. These conditions can easily set up a paradigm in which the newcomer is entering the treatment situation feeling hypersensitive to any criticism by the partner and sometimes to the imagined criticism of the therapist too, both serving to inhibit communication. The newcomer's heightened defensiveness can then come to represent a resistance that prompts a readiness to flee treatment in the face of conflict or the therapist's interventions.

When there is a change in treatment mode from individual to couple therapy, which adds the second partner, it is useful for the therapist at the beginning of the first conjoint session to explore carefully both partners' feelings about coming to the session together and changing the format. It should be expected that one or both partners' response to the therapist's inquiry will be terse, sometimes reeking with superficiality and denial. Anticipating this kind of response, the therapist might be prepared to say to the couple that he imagines that it must be somewhat anxiety provoking, strange, or otherwise disconcerting for them to come to a session as a couple when Mary (or John) has been seeing the therapist individually. An empathic intervention that assumes and makes the couple's discomfort explicit will often give both partners permission to discuss their true feelings more openly. This will assist both to work through the resistances that occur when making a transition from individual to couple therapy.

Clarifying, questioning, and even looking for opportunities to link and interpret the partners' reactions to developmental issues that might already be known—making explicit any transference-based fears of being less preferred, left out, disliked, or replaced, or of rivalry with the other partner—will assist in making the transition from an individual treatment mode to couple therapy, while an analytic mode is steadfastly maintained. Attending to these crucial variables pertaining to change of mode by addressing the specific anxieties of both partners, the therapist is simultaneously laying the groundwork for attaining the neutrality that is required in working with the selfdyad.

Therapist Factors   In this section I will address some of the variables that directly influence the therapist's decision making as he conducts the assessment, makes the recommendation, and finally implements the treatment with patients whose difficulties center on the intimate partnership. I will also address some of the obstacles that psychoanalysts and dynamically oriented therapists sometimes encounter in the practice of couple therapy when reconciling this way of working with an individual model of treatment (Zeitner, 2003).

The Therapist's Biases and Previous Training   Ideally, we would like to think that with competent professional training, mental health professionals would be sufficiently acquainted with all or most therapies, guaranteeing a proper disposition and recommendation for the best treatment. What we find instead is that therapists are greatly influenced by their formal education and previous training and intrapsychic conflicts, including personal biases, unconscious resistances, and therapeutic or analytic ideals—all of which contribute to how clinical decisions are made and, ultimately, how treatment will proceed.

An example is the analyst's or therapist's bias that analysis or intensive individual psychotherapy is the gold standard of treatment, while the goals of couple therapy are considered to be less ambitious, entailing mere guidance and advice to the individuals about how to improve their relationship. Still today, the term "marital counseling," rather than "therapy," is widely used by laypersons, physicians, and analysts alike, while as a treatment mode it is commonly denied by insurance companies as a covered benefit. Both of these reflect and sometimes confer its second-class status. Our universal diagnostic system, the *Diagnostic and Statistical Manual of Mental Disorders IV*, relegates a couple problem to the status of a psychosocial stressor that is designated on the fourth axis, frequently scripted as a "family relational problem" (American Psychiatric Association, 1994).

Also, it is unusual for therapists to be trained competently in analytic methods and couple therapy, too. This often makes it more difficult for the therapist to evaluate the pros and cons of multiple treatment modes for any one patient objectively. Therapists schooled in an individual model might be more likely to conceptualize the presenting problem of a patient whose difficulties are rooted in a relationship problem by focusing on the patient's affective, cognitive, and behavioral repertoires as manifestations of the individual's ego, self, or psychobiological pathology, even when the partner is thought to be a contributor to the patient's problems. Even therapists who practice from an object relations orientation, but who lack an appreciation of the selfdyad as an entity that has an organizing function for the individual's sense of self, will be limited in their ability to understand fully the mutual shaping process that occurs, as well as its implications for the patient's relationship difficulties and related symptoms.

As a consequence, for many therapists and analysts and certainly for those clinicians practicing from a biological orientation, the presenting problem with the intimate partnership fades into the shadow as a mere contributor to the patient's problem, rather than taking center stage as a focus of therapy. It is often here that the decision for individual therapy is made, with the presumption that individual treatment will reveal and finally resolve the intrapsychic sources of the patient's difficulties. It is often later in the treatment that the therapist and patient will together decide that couple therapy should be initiated to address the couple issues that cannot be effectively addressed in an individual treatment format.

The Therapist's Emphasis on Transference　I have often observed that therapists who emphasize an individual model of treatment—especially those who value work within the transference as the most efficacious route for therapeutic change—are less likely to recommend couple therapy over analysis or individual psychotherapy. It has been my impression that, by virtue of having rigorous training within an individual model of the mind, analysts are taught to listen to their patients' associations as derivatives of the unconscious, often monitoring and assessing those verbalizations as possible manifestations of the transference, the patient's level of ego organization, coherence of the self, psychosexual development, and quality of object relations.

Even when a disturbance in the patient's current relationship structure is presented as the manifest issue, the analyst is apt to listen and then to explore the patient's development by attempting to learn about those early life experiences that might shed light on what is now repeated in the patient's current intimate life. The analyst will then work to demonstrate to the patient how these relationship templates are manifested within the transference, with the goal of working these through until a complete resolution is achieved.

A question frequently remains, however, as to whether a resolution of the transference can actually have such far-reaching implications for problems within the intimate partnership. It is commonly observed that even with a good enough resolution of the transference and with an otherwise helpful analysis, when the patient returns to the original partnership, the difficulties within the couple's relationship will often continue, although the analysand may have established some insights and improved ego strength to tolerate them more effectively. The uniqueness of the couple's intersubjective space, including both partners' contributions to the selfdyad, often has such sustaining power that the problematic relationship is not modified by the analytic work and may even become restored to its original form once the analysis has ended.

Furthermore, without the support that was previously provided by the analyst or therapist, the relationship problems with the partner are sometimes rendered even less tolerable than before, contributing to a resurgence of dissatisfaction and couple conflict. This observation may account for Gurman and Kniskern's (1978) conclusion that the frequency of divorce is significantly higher for those patients with a problematic relationship when treated only in individual therapy and without couple therapy. Without the benefit of the partner's involvement in a conjoint treatment process, which provides the opportunity for mutual therapeutic change through the selfdyad, the problematic relationship is more likely to continue or resume, even when there has been a good enough individual treatment experience. Following the termination of the individual therapy, the patient may now be confronted with the realization that ending the relationship is the only remaining recourse.

It might then be questioned whether the individual therapy was actually a success, when the partner in therapy experienced his relief and liberation as a function of the divorce rather than the treatment itself. Whether a therapist views an eventual divorce or termination of the partnership as a criterion of a successful or unsuccessful therapy may hinge on whether the clinician places essential value on the expression of the autonomous self or on the preservation of the partnership as a criterion of mental health. Couple therapy, with its emphasis on the selfdyad in support of both selves, views both of these as equivalent criteria for therapeutic outcome.

When Transference Becomes a Complication   By now we have established that the most apparent disadvantage of individual therapy compared to couple therapy for problems pertaining to the intimate partnership centers on issues pertaining to the absent partner. A related complication is when the individual treatment introduces the transference between therapist and patient, but in a way that obscures the relationship problem with the partner. All psychotherapists know that the engine driving an effective treatment process is the positive working alliance with the therapist, without which it is unlikely that the patient will improve as a function of therapy. But it is also out of the positive therapeutic alliance that the core relational themes of the therapy *might* eventually yield a recapitulated version of the relational problem with the partner in the form of transference to the therapist. Although there are patients for whom it might be helpful to focus on a transference paradigm that repeats a version of the relational difficulty with the partner, there are also potential side effects that should be considered.

It is important for the therapist to bear in mind that a problem in the selfdyad is fundamentally a transference problem—albeit a transference between the partners in which the mutual projection and introjection process has gone awry. Individual therapy might then mobilize a transference between the therapist and patient that is only remotely or possibly not at all related to the problem with the partner. Opting to work within the transference between therapist and patient now risks bypassing or at least minimizing the more immediate and critical transference that exists between the partners. I am proposing here that the transference impasse between the partners should, at the very least, be given equal weight or sometimes even prevail—rather than focusing exclusively or even predominantly on the transference between the patient and the therapist on the assumption that its resolution will effectively assist with the patient's relationship problem.

Couple Difficulties and the Problem of Triangulation　Couple therapy is intended to assist both individuals in the dyad to address their transference impasse for the purpose of achieving a more balanced solution, hopefully restoring the selfdyad to function in support of both selves. When individual therapy is initiated instead, an additional relational paradigm between therapist and patient is inevitably introduced. This relationship will unavoidably perturb the couple's system as the therapist and patient establish a positive therapeutic alliance, while the other partner remains on the periphery. In establishing the working alliance, a competitive or even an antagonistic relationship between the absent partner and the therapist is sometimes unconsciously created.

What might now possibly emerge are the complications arising out of the vicissitudes of triangulation that Murray Bowen and his family systems colleagues have described (Bowen, 1978; Bowen & Kerr, 1988). The individual therapist might now become a transference object for the partner in therapy—a repository for all that has been desired, while the absent partner becomes further entrenched into the role of the one who denies, withholds, and rejects. This phenomenon represents a splitting of the object in which the therapist has become the good object while the absent partner becomes the bad object. For a period of time this triangulated situation might even stabilize the selfdyad as the couple's conflict is attenuated through the support provided by the therapist. Furthermore, this arrangement might provide an illusion of true intrapsychic growth. It is sometimes later in the therapy, possibly at the time a negative transference comes into ascendancy, when the patient becomes aware of the unattainability or inconstancy of the therapist's benevolence, or at the conclusion of treatment when the patient fully returns to the original selfdyad that a resurgence of conflict then occurs.

The Therapist's Attitude Toward Marriage and Coupling　Although I am not aware of any existing research that addresses the therapist's or analyst's attitudes toward marriage as determining factors in making recommendations to patients regarding one treatment mode over another, I hypothesize that these variables might indeed be influential and even related to the therapist's ability, interest, and willingness to practice one therapy form over another. Furthermore, these factors might be correlated with the value that the therapist places on the expression of the autonomous self versus relationship success as criteria for mental health and for therapeutic outcome. It would be interesting to explore several related dimensions, investigating the extent to which the therapist considers himself to have been successful in achieving and maintaining intimate relationships, whether the therapist has been divorced, his attitude toward relationship success as a criterion for mental health, and even the values he holds concerning family life and divorce.

Furthermore, to address the extent to which the analyst or therapist considers the resolution of the transference to be a key in achieving intrapsychic freedom and cure, as well as whether the patient's future success in the realm of relationship intimacy is considered by the therapist to be an outcome of a favorable transference resolution, would be useful extensions to this line of research. A multivariate research paradigm such as this would shed light on some of these unconscious variables that I hypothesize affect the therapist's decision making, while also assisting to refine those considerations that Gurman and Kniskern (1978), Graller et al. (2001), and Zeitner (2003) have addressed in their writings.

The Therapist's Tolerance of Affect   Although analysts and therapists most assuredly experience their patients' intense affects within the individual treatment setting, especially during erotic and negative transference states, many analysts and therapists are averse to or unwilling to tolerate the constancy of affective intensity that occurs in the practice of couple therapy. This reluctance may sometimes be related to the analyst's or therapist's lack of understanding that couple conflict is fundamentally a transference difficulty, but one that is currently experienced within the selfdyad. Also, because the couple therapist must be constantly monitoring the multiple transferences that exist within couple therapy, including those between the partners as well as those to the therapist himself, there are simply more data to be addressed.

Furthermore, the multiple transference paradigms within couple therapy are frequently replete with aggression, often with mutual blame, arguing, and condemnation flowing freely between the partners. By necessity, the therapist is then required to be considerably more active than in individual therapy, assisting the couple to maintain the introspection that is necessary in sustaining the therapeutic task. During periods of emotional intensity, the goal is always to help the couple to move toward a more constantly maintained depressive position, which through introspection assists them to achieve the tools in more effectively managing their relationship. Many therapists are uncomfortable with this level of activity and prefer listening and intervening within an individual model that is often less affectively intense. Many individual therapists and analysts then welcome the opportunity to refer the patient to a couple therapist when the need for couple therapy or combined treatments becomes apparent.

Summary

In this section I have considered some of the variables that are pertinent to the diagnostic and assessment process of patients and couples presenting with symptoms related to the intimate partnership. I have addressed these from the standpoint of patient and therapist factors, both of which contain potential harbingers of the obstacles encountered by analytically oriented therapists when making decisions pertaining to treatment options. I have discussed how these decisions are influenced by a number of variables, including the resistances, biases, and unconscious conflicts that are held by patients and therapists, as well as the personal preferences and the inevitable differences in training that exist among therapists.

In the following section I address central features of the treatment process. I will not provide a comprehensive overview of psychoanalytic couple therapy. Instead, I will limit myself to a discussion of those principles that are most relevant in working with patients and couples within the framework of the selfdyad that I have been developing throughout this book. I will focus on the therapist's role in working with the couple to establish or to reestablish a meaningful relationship in which the selfdyad supports the selves of both partners, while simultaneously establishing its uniqueness, resilience, and most importantly, its intimacy.

TREATMENT

Establishing a Framework for Treatment

In this section I describe a way of thinking about the treatment process that begins with the first phone contact between one partner and the therapist. Much like individual therapy, there is no sharp demarcation between the assessment-diagnostic phase and the treatment situation. Couple therapy actually begins in the assessment phase with the therapist and the couple working together to establish an understanding of the relationship impasse. In the beginning of the consultation the therapist is formulating questions and other interventions that will help frame a hypothesis about the needs of the self that are not supported by the relationship. When a provisional hypothesis and a contract for meetings have been established, we can say that the work has now moved into the middle or working phase of treatment.

For purposes of our discussion we will assume that, by the time of the first phone contact, the couple has made a mutual decision that conjoint therapy will be pursued. Frequently, the partner who calls to make the appointment is the one who has been more concerned, anxious, and motivated to obtain help with the relationship. Almost always, the call is made at a time of crisis after there has been considerable dissatisfaction and unhappiness within the relationship and when all other efforts to improve the relationship have failed. It is not uncommon for divorce already to have been considered as a possible solution to the problem.

Because I always make my own appointments, I have the opportunity to speak on the telephone with the partner who initiates the consultation. This gives me the distinct advantage of beginning the assessment process on the phone while beginning to establish the therapeutic alliance. Throughout, I have provided several vignettes that have demonstrated how I was able to begin forming impressions about the patient and/or the couple while speaking with one partner on the telephone.

At the time the first appointment is being arranged I routinely ask the caller how the other partner feels about coming in. Although the caller's response might be guarded, superficial, or otherwise defensive, it often provides an initial glimpse into the resistances of the selfdyad, occasionally the crisis precipitating the call, and sometimes even the prognosis. If the partner who calls responds that her husband is eager to come in, but subsequently finds it difficult to find an appointment time that they are both able to make, I infer a resistance in the couple, which almost always has implications for the treatment process that will follow. If the caller proceeds with an extensive elaboration of the partner's issues or responsibility for the presenting problem, creating for me a picture of having been injured by that partner's behavior, I might hypothesize that the partner I am speaking to is attempting to enlist my support by creating a triangle in which I align myself with her or him. Sometimes this forecasts an inclination to project blame and disavow personal responsibility for the problems in the partnership.

The Assessment Phase

When the couple arrives for the first interview there is often a tension between them that fills the room, along with a complicated mixture of dread, hope, pessimism, and, sometimes, great expectations of the therapist. Because the two individuals will often have quite different goals for treatment, I explore their fantasies and expectations for therapy during the first interview, if possible, while the frame and working space for treatment are being established.

I routinely initiate the first interview by directing my greeting and introduction to both individuals, while I try to avoid providing any cues that might encourage one or the other partner to speak first. Whoever speaks first in describing the presenting problem sometimes has implications for the relationship with respect to control, dominance, investment in the relationship, motivation for treatment, psychological mindedness, and a host of other factors. In beginning the first session I identify both individuals by their first names, ask their ages, how long they have been married or partnered, and how many children they have.

If it is a second marriage or blended family, I ask for some of the details pertaining to the new family unit, the shared children, and the old partnerships. For gay and lesbian partners I ask similar questions and then invite a brief discussion about the support they have received for their partnership, demonstrating my attunement to the complications and distinguishing variables of same-sex partnerships. I do not look at the registration sheet for information, and I never take notes during a session. Instead, I rely entirely on my memory, while in my mind I am already constructing a coherent narrative and a guiding hypothesis about the selfdyad and the unconscious structure of the relationship. I later dictate this into my computer for clinical and legal purposes.

In listening to the couple's story I psychologically position myself to establish an understanding of how these two individuals came together to form their intimate partnership, formulating my questions and other interventions to elucidate the dynamics of their selfdyad. Toward this end, I inquire about the nature of their initial attraction to one another, why they continued to see each other after first meeting, and especially what self-needs appeared to be provided by the relationship that had an effect on their remaining together. Importantly, I explore how both of them changed as a function of getting married or establishing their partnership.

In continuing to assess what needs and parts of the self were originally supported by the selfdyad and how the partnership at one time offered the possibility for fulfillment, I closely observe the partners' reactions to one another as I inquire into the pertinent details of their histories, including their families of origin, their relationship with parents and siblings, divorces of parents, and developmental disturbances and traumas—all toward the goal of coming to understand the unconscious pacts and agreements on which their selfdyad was originally founded. It is from this understanding that I formulate a hypothesis about the selfdyad and why and how it has now become dysfunctional. It is on this basis that therapy is initiated.

Much as in individual therapy, I assume that the developmental information that is pertinent in coming to understand the couple will not become fully evident in the initial consultation, but will unfold over time, becoming the subject for the entire treatment process. This is assumed to occur so long as the therapist is thinking and exploring within an analytic-developmental model that includes a consistent tracking of the selfdyad and its variants.

Developing the Therapeutic Alliance

Achieving a neutral and supportive relationship with both partners equally is essential for couple therapy, and yet it is sometimes realistically difficult to maintain. Many couple treatments falter when the therapist loses the necessary equidistance and neutrality between the partners. Because much of the content of sessions centers on the partners' complaints about each other, the therapist can often be pulled into the role of arbiter or interpreter of right versus wrong or reality versus unreality; he is sometimes moved into a position of advising and guiding a partner on how to conduct himself with the other partner. The analytic-exploratory space that is fundamental to psychoanalytic couple therapy is then sometimes vacated, not infrequently because the therapist has formed a complementary identification with one partner and a concordant identification with the other (Racker, 1968).

When the therapist is able consistently to listen to both partners' observations, complaints, and the accompanying affects as reflections of a selfdyad that has failed to support the selves, he is prepared to resist the unconscious pressure to take the side of one partner or the other. With this therapeutic posture, the implicit questions about right and wrong will lose their salience as the therapist is positioned to maintain the necessary neutrality for an effective treatment process. Observing and listening to the ongoing dynamic movement of the selfdyad (including both partners' longings for fulfillment as individuals) and coming to understand how these needs echo thwarted developmental needs and wishes provide a guiding beacon for the therapist conducting therapy along the lines of the proposed model. Assisting the partners to understand how their original selfdyad provided the hope for coming to terms with their developmental longings sets the stage for a potential revision of the partnership as the couple increases its flexibility and space for making changes within the relationship.

After the initiating partner has sufficiently described the problem for which the couple has come to see me, I intervene by asking the other partner to tell his view of the problem. If this partner launches a refutation or quibbles about the first partner's description of the problem, I immediately make an intervention to identify the difficulty in listening without defending oneself. I sometimes add a comment to paraphrase the following idea: Perception is in the eyes of the beholder and if there were no differences in the way they experience their issues, they would not have consulted me in the first place. I then ask the second partner again for his view of the problem. From an ego psychological model, I am actually interpreting a defensive mode of relating while simultaneously setting up a structure and model for future communication within the therapy process and after it has been terminated.

The therapist's style in working with couples should be engaged, friendly, and active, but not effusive or jocular. Occasionally, there are couples who present initially as reflective and introspective and who launch the initial session by easily laying out the details of their situation. But it is more usual for couples to present as openly angry and blaming or as wary and cautious to avoid the intensity of their affects or the affects of the partner. In either case the therapist will ordinarily encounter a fundamental difference from the individual therapy session in which the patient more easily reflects on his self-experience, either spontaneously or with minimal encouragement. Especially in the initial couple session or in the early phase of treatment, the partners will typically be preoccupied with each other's objectionable qualities, problem behaviors, or a partner's dissatisfaction.

With couples who are more overtly angry and blaming, the therapist is often required to be more consistently active to clarify the essential features of their relationship impasse and to address the needs that are not being met in the relationship. With an individual patient, the therapist is able to ask questions, offer clarifications, and even make early interpretations that invite a deepening of the material. In conjoint treatment, however, the therapist must be attuned to the couple's limitations in the flow of information and communication, actively engaging with them to clarify their fundamental problems in relating. Finally, the couple therapist must be attuned to hear the concerns of and reactions to the partner as representing an object relationship script that is replayed, longed for, or dreaded and to be avoided. In this way of working, the therapist is both listening and searching for the developmental antecedents providing the rudiments for the selfdyad.

Addressing Motivation for Treatment

The therapist must consistently monitor the relationship for the inevitable obstacles and resistances that might already exist or later emerge during the treatment process. Because couples often come for the consultation having very different intentions for therapy, it is important for the therapist to observe and listen closely for any contradictions or other clues that might represent interferences in the treatment process. Although I always ask both partners to address their hopes and goals for therapeutic outcome explicitly, it is not unusual for the verbally expressed goals to be quite different from the actual motives for treatment. This is especially common when there are secrets that have been kept from the partner, especially affairs that continue to be both alluring and yet interfering with treatment motivation.

In these situations the partner who has been having the affair may have agreed to therapy less out of a genuine wish to work on the relationship than out of a desire to expiate the guilt or shame for having the affair. Sometimes the treatment situation might be used to confirm the status of a failed relationship so that the partner who has been having the affair or even both partners are able to feel and say that they have taken all imaginable steps to preserve it. Now the blame for the relationship failure can be more comfortably shifted to the therapist or to a failed treatment experience, while guilt, shame, and personal responsibility are attenuated.

Because affairs frequently represent an attempted, albeit abortive, solution to a relationship problem, it is important that the therapist learn about these early in the treatment. But it is also important to recognize that secrets, including affairs, might never openly emerge in the therapy process, sometimes even continuing through the duration of therapy and serving as an insidious resistance that will inevitably spoil the treatment and the potential growth of the couple. If an affair is eventually disclosed or is otherwise discovered during the course of treatment, the therapist must be prepared to deal with what is typically a painful situation for both partners. For the injured partner, the therapist should be prepared to offer additional individual appointments to help deal with the intensity of that partner's pain. Frequently, it is useful to provide additional sessions for the other partner as well to explore the significance of the affair and its implications for the marriage or partnership, as well as that partner's motivation for continuing treatment.

Although there are many motivations for an affair, for our purposes it is important to mention this as a significant obstacle to conducting effective couple therapy that should always be carefully attended to by the therapist. Finally, although it can sometimes be useful to mention early in the treatment process that affairs should be disclosed, I have found that this guidance is rarely followed unless the affair has been previously known to the couple or presents as the reason for consultation.

The Summary Statement, Recommendation, and Setting of the Frame

After one to three sessions, I take a few minutes during the latter part of the hour to summarize briefly my observations and current understanding of the couple's relationship difficulties. This is sometimes a neglected component of the couple consultation because the therapist will frequently assume that the dynamic understanding that he has been acquiring during the assessment phase is equally shared and understood by the couple. No matter how introspective or sophisticated a couple might appear, the anger, blame, and self-righteous indignation that both individuals often harbor mitigate a dynamic understanding of the relationship impasse, regardless of how clear this has become to the therapist during the assessment phase. Because most couples enter the treatment experience with a shared belief that they are misunderstood by the partner, with a primary goal of making oneself heard, while hoping to be vindicated by the therapist, it is unusual in the beginning of therapy for the partners truly to grasp and accept their respective roles in creating their relationship difficulties.

I have found that, at the point at which I have a provisional understanding of both individuals from a developmental standpoint, especially when that information contains implications for the selfdyad, it is useful briefly to summarize my understanding for the couple. I typically address the specific self-needs that both partners originally hoped to have met by the other and how and why I think these needs have been thwarted in the relationship. Because complete histories, with implications for the partners' early development, have not yet emerged, I will also address those areas that I believe we must come to better understand in the course of treatment.

I make it a point to speak in simple and clear terms to address traumas, needs, wishes, and frustrations, and, if possible, to link these to early developmental experiences, making explicit the accompanying hope that the partner would be able to contain these needs and repair pertinent wounds through the relationship. I make it a point to give equal weight and time to both partners' contributions, carefully observing indications of feeling understood by me, feeling misunderstood, or feeling blamed.

Finally, I recommend a schedule of sessions at a minimum frequency of once weekly, emphasizing that the goal of treatment is to deepen an understanding of their relationship dynamics to enable them eventually to better understand themselves and each other in the context of their partnership. I emphasize that this work will provide them increased freedom to make important and necessary changes in their relationship. It is not unusual for couples, even those who are psychologically sophisticated and well motivated for treatment, to harbor misconceptions about what couple therapy entails. If in the course of consultation I sense any misunderstanding of the process—for instance, an expectation that I will simply guide or instruct them on how to improve their relationship—I then take considerable time to educate them about the actual process of couple therapy.

I emphasize the importance of establishing insight into the self and the self of the partner as necessary for change and growth, with a brief excursion into the importance of early development and the unconscious mind. I emphasize the importance of open communication within the therapeutic hour that must include current struggles, observations, and even private musings that both partners might have about developmental precursors affecting their situation. I attempt to be very specific about the structure and process of treatment, including the couple's responsibilities in the process as well as my own.

Once it is clear that the couple wishes to proceed with therapy and we have established a contract to work together, I inform them that during the interval between sessions they will obviously continue to relate and interact with each other. But because they have now introduced me into their lives as an agent of potential help and change, they will inevitably become more observant about their relationship. I frequently add that I cannot predict exactly how this will occur, but that it is important for them to track their interactions between sessions and to bring their observations back into the treatment hour, where we will process and understand them together.

The reader will note that I am taking considerable time to set up a therapeutic frame that emphasizes listening, observation, and introspection, as well as specifying the couple's role and responsibilities in the treatment process. Because the actual content of a session can easily regress into chaos, especially when communicating through the vicissitudes of projective identification, I attempt to establish a tight frame for treatment to assist the couple in moving toward more consistent depressive position functioning, with an enhanced capacity for empathy and concern for each other's needs.

MIDDLE PHASE TREATMENT
The Central Technique

With careful attention to setting the frame, most couple sessions unfold with a brisk and lively interaction that will easily engage the therapist. Although there are some couples who, early in the treatment, spontaneously establish connections between developmental needs, wishes, and traumas and the difficulties in the partnership, this kind of introspection is rare without the active intervention of the therapist. It is more typical for the content of an hour to center on concerns about not being heard and understood, and the injuries that have been inflicted by the partner, as both partners extol dissatisfaction, unhappiness, and a host of other affects. Because of this, the therapist must constantly monitor the various interactions and associations for the opportunity to deepen a dynamic understanding of the wishes, needs, and expectations that are not being met in the relationship, while being prepared to offer an interpretation linking early developmental experiences with current happenings.

Toward this goal, the therapist's listening functions will take different forms at different times while, however, always working toward an understanding of the selfdyad and how it has come to fail to support the partners' needs. With couples whose developmental histories have not yet clearly emerged during the assessment phase, the therapist might be required to inquire actively about family history as it applies to the here-and-now interactions within a session. When and how to intervene to deepen insight into the couple's struggles is an important consideration defining the art and technique of analytically oriented couple therapy. Interactions especially charged with affect that appear disproportionate to the stimulus arising from the partner frequently are indicators for making a more direct inquiry about historical precursors.

At this juncture the therapist might question both partners about family relationships and pertinent history or offer an interpretation if this information is already known. This can be an especially useful technique in ameliorating the anger and blame that interfere with introspection and empathy for the partner. When fortified with a developmental understanding of both individuals, the therapist is then able to hear the echo of an object relationship that is either longed for or one that is to be avoided. *Consistently linking affectively charged wishes and needs expressed toward the partner to the relational scripts that were at one time located in the family of origin works toward reducing the pressure on the partner to fulfill them.*

Similarly, when the therapist observes projective identification to be operating in an interaction, it is useful to address pertinent historical antecedents as a way of assisting the partners to embrace the internal object relational scripts that are affecting the interaction and interfering with effective communication. Projective identification might become apparent to the therapist when observing a partner express a wish, criticism, or observation that, in the process of communicating, actually evokes the very response in the other partner that is dreaded by the first partner. Here the therapist will get a clearer sense of the mutual shaping of interactions in which the partners become entangled in patterns of communication that include both provocation and evocation.

Once again, it is often useful at these junctures for the therapist to work at defusing the intense affect by assisting the partners to reclaim the original object relationship that has been projected and is now found within the other.

The therapist might first point out that a similar version of an early relationship appears to be repeated in the current interaction. This can be tricky because the therapist must be certain to address both partners' contributions to the interaction, avoiding the potential side effect of one partner feeling blamed while the other feels vindicated. The individual projecting the toxic object relational script can experience the therapist's interpretation as a confirmation or agreement that the other partner is *actually* behaving as the original object, rather than behaving *as if*. This can potentially validate that the partner is indeed culpable, fueling the first partner's anger and the couple's despair. To reduce this potential problem, the mutual contribution must be addressed by additionally interpreting the second partner's role in validating the perception, pointing out its distortion and its exaggeration.

The therapist might, for example, comment that the original toxic relationship has endured unconsciously and yet painfully for the first partner, but in a way that now seems to compel him to experience it in the second partner as a way of assuring himself that it can be safely managed and contained. This might be followed by an intervention that addresses the second partner's contribution by pointing out that she correspondingly behaves in a way to confirm its existence, but has misgivings about containing it. This is tantamount to addressing the second partner's valency for the projection. Subsequently, the therapist might address the developmental factors contributing to that partner's valency for the projection, deepening an understanding of the partner's ambivalence around containing it. Again, the technical aspects of this part of the work are consistent with an understanding of the selfdyad as central to the dynamic organization of the couple.

Here I must remind the reader that, to interpret projective identification properly, there must be an emphasis on the couple as a conjoined unit in which the mental contents of both partners are continuously exchanged and felt by each other. Tactfully phrased interventions that address the mutual shaping process occurring in intimate communication will assist in reducing the existing tension and the propensity for using projective identification as a preferred mode of communication. Importantly, for the couple to make substantial and lasting therapeutic gains and for both partners to reclaim their respective toxic objects, the therapist may be required to address these kinds of communications many times during the course of therapy.

A Space for Differentness

As the mutual projection process is continuously addressed, the couple will become more aware of the unconscious desire for the partner to fulfill yearnings stemming from early development and important relationships from the past. To become acquainted with their selfdyad, which at one time provided the hope for needs and wishes to be met by the partner, the therapist must persist in interpreting the projective identification, helping the partners sort out their cycles of interaction. This process paves the way for a gradually increasing space for differentness as both partners become better able to express themselves as individuals less encumbered by each other's contaminating projections and urgent expectations for fulfillment. In this way there is a gradual renegotiation between the selves of both partners and their selfdyad—a selfdyad that has failed in its support of the selves of the partners.

ADDITIONAL TECHNIQUES

The emphasis throughout this book has been on the selfdyad as an interpsychic agency formed through unconscious communication. Understanding and working with the selfdyad provides a fulcrum on which dynamically oriented couple therapy can be conducted. By making repeated interpretations of pertinent developmental antecedents, the therapist assists the couple to come to a better understanding of how and why their selfdyad has failed to remain in support of the selves. The goal of therapy is to restore its essential functions, albeit with possible modifications in its structure. Next, I will address other important considerations for treatment that pertain to technique, all of which are consistent with the model proposed throughout this book.

Equal Time and Space

Although it is common for one partner to take the lead in sessions, sometimes even dominating, it is vital that the therapist monitor the interactions and contributions in the hour to give equal time and space to both partners. When an observation or complaint is made by one partner, the therapist should ordinarily turn to the other partner to invite his reaction and expansions. If a partner holds the floor or persistently interrupts, it is important for the therapist to point this out immediately. This serves to set limits and maintain the structure of the session while setting up a model for effective communication.

Sometimes an educational approach can be taken to instruct the couple on how to listen without interruption while even demonstrating active listening that involves the paraphrasing of each other's positions with empathy at the heart of the communication (Gordon, 1970, 1974; Rogers, 1961). This provides an additional method for increasing the space for both within the relationship. By no means should an instructional-educative approach supplant the exploratory dimension of treatment. Instead, these methods can be most useful when the therapist observes interactions between the partners that easily become entangled in a way that contributes to arguments. Obviously, the therapist must remain comfortably within the depressive position while he provides emotional equanimity in the midst of paranoid-schizoid interactions.

Dimensions of Transference and Countertransference

The construct of the selfdyad is founded on a theoretical structure of transference and countertransference, as well as a theory of projective identification. With intimate partners there occurs a constancy of conscious and unconscious communication that, over time, coalesces into a relatively stable selfdyad formed through repeated projective and introjective cycles, the same interpersonal mechanisms comprising transference and countertransference. In the treatment of couples, the therapist is always monitoring and addressing the couple's transferences and countertransferences to each other, assisting both individuals to understand how their perceptions and expectations of the other are at least partially rooted in developmental experiences.

Additionally, the partners might project relational scripts onto the therapist, creating transferences that prompt countertransference feelings and reactions in the therapist. When observed and understood by the therapist, these internal experiences can be used to better understand the couple's interactions and then usefully interpreted to them. Equally important, the therapist might experience transference feelings toward a partner or toward the couple as a unit. The latter may represent a residual of the therapist's own internal couple, a variant of his parents' relationship, or a past or present partnership. When aware of these projections and their effects on him, the therapist will be empathically attuned to the couple in a way that permits a greater range of potentially useful interventions in working with the couple (Scharff & Scharff, 1991). Here the therapist's knowledge about his psychological interior will permit the necessary neutrality and equidistance to assist his clients toward increased psychological growth and relationship improvement.

When the Therapist Loses His Way

Throughout this writing I have emphasized the multiplicity of factors that must be considered in the actual work of dynamically oriented couple therapy. Many of these factors and principles also apply to individual therapy and psychoanalysis. However, we have also established that in couple therapy there are more existing transferences, so that range of possible transference and countertransference interpretations is more varied and possibly more complicated. For these reasons, the therapist is required to be especially vigilant and flexible about which domain to pursue at any juncture in the treatment, while always questioning what type of intervention might yield the greatest mutative effect.

For example, when in the midst of an angry outburst involving projective identification should the therapist address the manifest anger as a projection of maternal disappointment, using the family of origin as the reference point? Or should he consider the expressed anger at the partner as a transference displacement from the disappointment in the therapist's holding capacity? Because in couple therapy there are more combinations of possible transferences, there is more for the therapist to monitor. A common countertransference reaction in the therapist who feels overwhelmed by the bombardment of stimuli and the uncertainty of how to intervene properly is to take refuge defensively within an individual psychological model of the mind in which, for example, the therapist begins to consider a partner's diagnosis or possibly the need for medication.

A guidepost and potential antidote for the therapist who sometimes finds himself lost on the proverbial sea of uncertainty is to focus on the couple's polarity of closeness and distance (Shoulberg, personal communication, 1981). Here I am invoking both a family systems and an attachment model of human functioning, with the inherent assumption that all couples presenting for treatment, with perhaps as an exception those who are pursuing help to exit their relationship, are attempting to stabilize their relationship by either building or restoring a balance between optimal closeness and optimal distance. When supervising therapists who report sessions in which the emotional tension is especially high and who are experiencing uncertainty or anxiety about how to understand an interaction and how to intervene, I frequently recommend for them to return to a position of listening, while addressing the unconscious longings for closeness or distance. When they are in the midst of intensely negative affect, the partners can then be reminded of their underlying wishes for closeness, regardless of the complexity of dynamics occurring in the moment. Affect is then attenuated and the therapist is able to regain his therapeutic poise and find his way back to his more characteristic way of listening and intervening.

Sexuality: In the Background or Foreground?

Addressing sexuality toward the end of this chapter is by no means a reflection of its importance for the couple or for couple therapy. Sexuality is, in fact, at the very core of the intimate partnership for better and for worse and whether or not it is specifically focused on in the treatment process. To what extent it takes center stage for any one couple is highly variable. For some couples, an optimal sexual functioning may be preserved, even in the face of inexhaustible interpersonal conflict. For these couples, sexual functioning may actually contradict their unhappiness, sometimes preserving enough intimacy to sustain an otherwise fragile relationship. For others, sexual dysfunction or lack of frequency may be an indicator of and even a metaphor for the very difficulties existing in the relationship.

For relationships in which there has been a struggle to maintain a sense of self at the expense of the partnership, the couple's sexual relationship is often adversely affected and sometimes becomes a central feature of the treatment. Frequently, it is the partner whose self is most compromised by the relationship who has pulled away from sexual intimacy. Sometimes, the other partner continues to press for more sexual involvement while simultaneously experiencing anger and frustration about the partner's lack of response.

Once again, there is considerable variability in the extent to which sexuality is central to the couple's relationship dynamics. There are couples who initially present with sexual problems as the focus, including erectile dysfunction, dyspareunia, or disorders of sexual desire, but whose fundamental difficulties are rooted in relationship dynamics around preserving the self versus maintaining a vital selfdyad. These couples might assiduously deny any relationship problems or dissatisfaction of any kind. The therapist's starting point is to assist the partners in broadening their focus of understanding, such that they can come to recognize and work with the relationship issues that underlie their sexual concerns. When these areas of conflict have been revealed and more adequately addressed, the therapist might then be required to bring into the treatment process the repertoire of behavioral strategies that have been developed by clinicians working in the area of sex therapy (Kaplan, 1974; LoPiccolo & LoPiccolo, 1978; Masters & Johnson, 1966).

The Dream in Couple Therapy

Few couples begin the process of treatment with a sustained focus firmly rooted in the depressive position; instead, they are ensconced in anger, hurt, blame, and fault finding. Thus, it is rare for the partners to consider their dreams as relevant to couple therapy. The dream in couple therapy can have great clinical importance. It is usually most helpful when the therapist establishes the usage and importance of dreams early in the treatment process. Alternatively, if the use of dreams is not established early in the treatment, but a dream is spontaneously offered by one of the partners, this can be the point at which the therapist describes and then illustrates their usefulness. I have found this to be yet another way to structure the process of therapy by encouraging introspection and the observation of one's mental processes.

Maintaining an emphasis on projective identification and the selfdyad as organizing constructs for my thinking about couples' difficulties, I inform my couples that, when they report their dreams, I will always invite them both to give their impressions and associations. Talking about dreams in this way implicitly conveys to the partners that unconscious communication between them prevails throughout all aspects of their relationship, even pervading their dreams. The dream then becomes another form of shared space for the couple that, when conjointly analyzed by the partners and the therapist, has important implications for coming to understand the unconscious structure of their partnership, including needs, wishes, disappointments, and developmental antecedents.

CONCLUSION

In concluding this chapter I am fully aware that my exploration of the complex world of psychoanalytic couple therapy is but a mere drop in the proverbial bucket. I have attempted to confine my discussions of technique to *my* understanding of the couple through the lenses of unconscious communication, projective identification, and their critical roles in forming the selfdyad as the intersubjective and private space of the intimate couple. Accordingly, the technique that I have developed for myself and attempt to teach my students centers on the selfdyad as that sector of the couple that I have found to provide the greatest opportunity for making true and lasting changes in the infrastructure of the partnership.

While the range of possible helpful interventions and techniques in the fields of psychotherapy and psychoanalysis is vast, I have attempted to present my ideas in a readable format that has included many case studies to demonstrate the centrality of the couple's unconscious dynamic organization. I have confined my road map for therapeutic change to the concepts most pertinent to the selfdyad as the organizing structure of the intimate couple.

EPILOGUE: THE PERSON
WITHIN THE THERAPIST

In writing this concluding section I fully recognize that I am attempting to address some variables within the fields of psychotherapy that are poorly understood, but might possibly have important implications for psychotherapeutic outcomes for individual, couple, family, and group. Many studies over the years have been undertaken to sort out the complexity of both patient and therapist variables, including personal style, personality features, capacity for insight and concept formation, empathy, and a host of others, as they relate to psychotherapeutic process and outcome (Lambert, 2004).

Unfortunately, to my knowledge, the outcomes of these studies have not been universally applied in selecting individuals who apply for training in our complex professions of mental health and psychotherapy. Rather, it has been assumed that personal therapy or a required analysis for psychoanalytic trainees will serve to resolve those intrapsychic impediments to becoming a competent therapist, while simultaneously enhancing the prognosis of the eventual patient of the therapist in training. I will not attempt a comprehensive discussion or make a polemic of these issues, nor will I review the literature. Instead, I will briefly discuss some of the qualities of the therapist and features of the therapy process that I have found to be important for those who work with couples in psychotherapy.

First, because most couples enter the treatment situation with a mixture of anger, despair, and often hopelessness about the partnership, an accompanying deep sense of failure and a sense of shame can easily be overlooked by the therapist. Importantly, the therapist's ease of relating to both partners while paying careful attention to the underlying shame and the accompanying fear of humiliation is most important in maintaining an effective holding environment. Relating to both partners empathically in a conversational and easygoing manner while maintaining an awareness of both partners' need to be understood is no easy task when in the midst of powerful affects that frequently involve projective identification. As emphasized throughout this book, the couple therapist is required to move flexibly between both partners, while always retaining in mind that there has been and continues to be a mutual shaping process that has formed the selfdyad—the entity that will become the eventual focus of treatment.

Simultaneously, the therapist's ability to stay afloat during affective moments while always listening for the echo of the original hope that at one time was provided by the relationship—a hope for redemption for lost opportunities with early caretakers, but that now ironically is once again thwarted—provides the therapist with a cognitive map of how to listen to a couple while maintaining necessary neutrality. The neutrality and equidistance between the partners, coupled with a well-honed capacity for empathy, a solid theoretical understanding of the mind and relationships, and an ability to inspire hope and self-understanding, must always accompany the therapist's verbal interventions.

Again, what is more important than the therapist's actual words is what he or she unconsciously conveys to the couple. Just as projective identification is at the heart of the unconscious communication with the intimate couple, it functions similarly as the fundamental mode of communication between therapist and patient. Attention paid to these variables will altogether assist the couple therapist in enlightening both partners equally about their inner worlds and their impact on their frustrated longings and expectations for each other.

It is my hope that in this book I have been able to convey my particular way of thinking about and working with couples in a manner that can be integrated with my readers' styles of practice. The chapters you have read contain within them a lifetime of thinking, study, practice, and personal experience. Although there are no substitutes for solid academic training and competent supervision in our very complex field of psychotherapy, life experiences remain our very best teachers and our most important laboratories in which our scientific and theoretical ideas about human relationships can and should always be tested. This is empiricism at its best.

Finally, in my laboratory of life, my most important teacher has been my wife and partner for nearly 40 years. It is in my relationship with her, which includes unconsciously my experience of her within me and me within her, that I have truly come to understand the transformative aspects of the selfdyad. And I believe that I can safely say that it is the same for her. Through her unswerving love, passion, patience, and devotion to me, along with her dedication to our children, my extended family, and now our grandchildren, I have grown as a person, man, parent, psychologist, and psychoanalyst, as well as a couple and family therapist. This has been my most rewarding and enriching laboratory experience, a laboratory of humanity, love, perseverance, and intimacy within which I have been able to try out my ideas, sometimes stumbling, but usually—fortunately—rising to the occasion.

With that, I will close our discussions by offering my sincere gratitude to all my patients, couples, and families for all that I have learned from them and hope to continue learning from them during our times together. And for them and my wife and family, too, I will continue to offer them the best of what I have to give, within the parameters I am able to know and relate to each of them individually. For it is with each of them that I am a different person. This is the essence of intersubjectivity, private space, and the fundamental nature of the selfdyad.

REFERENCES

Ackerman, N. (1958). *The psychodynamics of family life: Diagnosis and treatment of family relationships.* New York, NY: Basic Books.

Ainsworth, M., Blehar, M., Waters, E., & Wall, S. (1978). *Patterns of attachment: A psychological study of the strange situation.* Hillsdale, NJ: Lawrence Erlbaum Associates, Inc.

American Psychiatric Association. (1994). *Diagnostic and statistical manual of mental disorders* (4th ed.). Washington, DC: Author.

Bartels, A., & Zeki, S. (2000). The neural basis of romantic love. *Neuroreport, 11,* 3829–3834.

Bollas, C. (1987). *The shadow of the object: Psychoanalysis of the unthought known.* New York, NY: Columbia University Press.

Bowen, M. (1978). *Family therapy in clinical practice.* New York, NY: Jason Aronson, Inc.

Bowlby, J. (1958). The nature of the child's tie to his mother. *International Journal of Psychoanalysis, 39,* 350–373.

Bowlby, J. (1969). *Attachment, Vol. I: Attachment and loss.* London, England: Hogarth Press.

Bowlby, J. (1980). *Attachment and loss: Vol. 3: Loss, sadness, and depression.* New York, NY: Basic Books.

Bowlby, J. (1982). *Attachment and loss: Vol. 1: Attachment* (2nd ed.). New York, NY: Basic Books. (Original work published in 1969.)

Brooks, J. L., Crowe, C., Mark, L., & Sakai, R. (Producers), and Crowe, C. (Director). (1996). *Jerry Maguire* [Motion picture]. United States: Gracie Films and TriStar Pictures.

Chasseguet-Smirgel, J. (1985). *The ego ideal: A psychoanalytic essay on the malady of the ideal.* New York, NY: W.W. Norton and Company.

Clulow, C. (Ed.). (2001). *Adult attachment and couple psychotherapy: The "secure base" in practice and research.* New York, NY: Brunner–Routledge.

Collins, N. L., Guichard, A. C., Ford, M. B., & Feeney, B. C. (2006). Responding to need in intimate relationships: Normative processes and individual differences. In M. Mikulincer & G. S. Goodman (Eds.), *Dynamics of romantic love: Attachment, caregiving, and sex.* New York, NY: Guilford Press.

Crowell, J., & Treboux, D. (2001). Attachment security in adult partnerships. In C. Clulow (Ed.), *Adult attachment and couple psychotherapy: The "secure base" in practice and research.* New York, NY: Brunner–Routledge.

Dicks, H. (1993). *Marital tensions: Clinical studies toward a psychological theory of interaction.* London, England: Karnac Books. (Original work published in 1967.)

Eagle, M. (1984). *Recent developments in psychoanalysis: A critical evaluation.* New York, NY: McGraw–Hill.

Edwards, J., & Booth, A. (1994). Sexuality, marriage, and well-being: The middle years. In A. Rossi (Ed.), *Sexuality across the life course.* Chicago, IL: University of Chicago Press.

Faimberg, H. (2005). *The telescoping of generations: Listening to the narcissistic links between generations.* London, England: Routledge–Taylor & Francis Group.

Fairbairn, W. R. D. (1944). Endopsychic structure considered in terms of object-relationships. *International Journal of Psychoanalysis, 25,* 70–93.

Fernaine, H. (Producer), & Mendes, S. (Director). (2008). *Revolutionary road* [Motion picture]. United States: Dreamworks.

Fisher, H. (2004). *Why we love: The nature and chemistry of romantic love.* New York, NY: Henry Holt & Company.

Fisher, H., Aron, A., & Brown, L. (2005). Romantic love: An fMRI study of a neural mechanism for mate choice. *Journal of Comparative Neurology, 493,* 58–62.

Fisher, H., Aron, A., & Brown, L. (2006). Romantic love: A mammalian brain system for mate choice. *Philosophical Transactions of the Royal Society, B, 361,* 2173–2186.

Fisher, J., & Crandell, L. (2001). Patterns of relating in the couple. In C. Clulow (Ed.), *Adult attachment and couple psychotherapy: The "secure base" in practice and research.* New York, NY: Brunner–Routledge.

Freud, S. (1898). Sexuality in the etiology of the neuroses. *Standard edition of the complete psychological works of Sigmund Freud* (Vol. 3).

Freud, S. (1905). Three essays on the theory of sexuality. *Standard edition of the complete psychological works of Sigmund Freud* (Vol. 7).

Gordon, T. (1970). *Parent effectiveness training: The tested new way to raise responsible children.* New York, NY: Three Rivers Press.

Gordon, T. (1974). *Teacher effectiveness training: The program proven to help teachers bring out the best in students of all ages.* New York, NY: Three Rivers Press.

Graller, J., Nielsen, A., Garber, B., Davison, L., Gable, L., & Seidenberg, H. (2001). Concurrent therapies: A model for collaboration between psychoanalysts and other therapists. *Journal of the American Psychoanalytic Association, 49,* 587–606.

Gray, J. (1995). *Mars and Venus in the bedroom: A guide to lasting romance and passion.* New York, NY: HarperTorch: Harper Collins Publishers.

Greenberg, J., & Mitchell, S. (1983). *Object relations in psychoanalytic theory.* Cambridge, MA: Harvard University Press.

Gurman, A., & Kniskern, D. (1978). Research on marital and family therapy: Progress, perspective, and prospect. In S. L. Garfield & A. E. Bergin (Eds.), *Handbook of psychotherapy and behavior change* (2nd ed., pp. 817–902). New York, NY: John Wiley & Sons, Inc.

Haley, J. (1980). *Leaving home: The therapy of disturbed young people.* New York, NY: McGraw–Hill.

Hazan, C., Campa, M., & Gur-Yaish, N. (2006). What is adult attachment? In M. Mikulincer & G. S. Goodman (Eds.), *Dynamics of romantic love: Attachment, caregiving, and sex.* New York, NY: Guilford Press.

Jung, C. G. (1968). *Analytical psychology: Its theory and practice.* New York, NY: Random House, Inc.

Kandel, E. (2005). *Psychiatry, psychoanalysis, and the new biology of mind.* Washington, DC: American Psychiatric Publishing, Inc.

Kaplan, H. (1974). *The new sex therapy: Active treatment of sexual dysfunctions.* New York, NY: Brunner–Mazel.

Kernberg, O. (1995). *Love relations: Normality and pathology.* New Haven, CT: Yale University Press.

Kerr, M., & Bowen, M. (1988). *Family evaluation.* Markham, Ontario: Penguin Books.

Kinsey, A. (1948). *Sexual behavior in the human male.* Philadelphia, PA: Saunders.

Kinsey, A. (1953). *Sexual behavior in the human female.* Philadelphia, PA: Saunders.

Klein, M. (1945). The Oedipus complex in the light of early anxieties. In *Love, guilt, and reparation & other works, 1921–1945* (pp. 377–419). London, England: Hogarth Press.

Klein, M. (1952). Some theoretical conclusions regarding the emotional life of the infant. In Money-Kyrle, Joseph, O'Shaughnessy & Segal (Eds.), *Envy and gratitude and other works. 1946–1963* (chap. 6). London: Karnac Books.

Klein, M. (1964). *Contributions to psycho-analysis 1921–1945.* New York, NY: McGraw–Hill.

Kohut, H. (1959). Introspection, empathy, and psychoanalysis. *Journal of the American Psychoanalytic Association, 7*, 459–483.

Kohut, H. (1971). *The analysis of the self.* New York, NY: International Universities Press.

Kohut, H. (1977). *The restoration of the self.* New York, NY: International Universities Press.

Kuhn, T. (1962). *The structure of scientific revolutions.* Chicago, IL: University of Chicago Press.

Lambert, M. (Ed.) (2004). *Bergin and Garfield's handbook of psychotherapy and behavior change.* New York, NY: John Wiley & Sons, Inc. (Original work published in 1971.)

LoPiccolo, J., & LoPiccolo, L. (1978). *Handbook of sex therapy (perspectives in sexuality)*. New York, NY: Plenum.

Main, M., Kaplan, N., & Cassidy, J. (1985). Security in infancy, childhood, and adulthood: A move to the level of representation. In I. Bretherton & E. Waters (Eds.), *Growing points of attachment theory and research (Monographs of the Society for Research in child development* (pp. 66–104). Chicago, IL: University of Chicago Press.

Masters, W., & Johnson, V. (1966). *Human sexual response*. Boston, MA: Little and Brown.

Merriam–Webster's collegiate dictionary (10th ed). (1993). Philippines: Merriam-Webster, Inc.

Mikulincer, M. (2006). Attachment, caregiving, and sex within romantic relationships: A behavioral systems perspective. In M. Mikulincer & G. S. Goodman (Eds.), *Dynamics of romantic love: Attachment, caregiving, and sex*. New York, NY: Guilford Press.

New lexicon Webster's dictionary of the English language. 1989. New York, NY: Lexicon Publications, Inc.

Nyborg, H. (1994). *Hormones, sex, and society: The Science of Physicology (human evolution, behavior, and intelligence)*. Westport, CT: Praeger.

Ogden, T. (1989). *The primitive edge of experience*. Northvale, NJ: Jason Aronson, Inc.

Ogden, T. (1994). *Subjects of analysis*. Northvale, NJ: Jason Aronson, Inc.

Perkel, A. (2001). Psychological mating: The compulsion to compensation. *Psycho-analytic Psychotherapy in South Africa, 9*(1), 46–58.

Perkel, A. (2007). Fusion, diffusion, de-fusion, confusion: Exploring the anatomy of the couple psyche. In M. Ludlam & V. Nyberg (Eds.), *Couple attachments: Theoretical and clinical studies* (pp. 43–62). London, England: Karnac Books.

Pfaus, J., & Scepkowski, M. (2005). The biologic basis for libido. *Current Sexual Health Reports, 2*, 95–100.

Racker, H. (1968). *Transference and countertransference*. New York, NY: International Universities Press.

Riviére, E. P. (1971). *Del psicoanálisis a la psicología social*. Buenos Aires, Argentina: Galerna.

Rogers, C. (1961). *On becoming a person: A therapist's view of psychotherapy*. New York, NY: Houghton Mifflin Co.

Scharff, D. (1998). *The sexual relationship: An object relations view of sex and the family*. Northvale, NJ: Jason Aronson, Inc.

Scharff, D., & Scharff, J. (1991). *Object relations couple therapy*. Northvale, NJ: Jason Aronson, Inc.

Scharff, D., & Scharff, J. (1987). *Object relations family therapy*. Northvale, NJ: Jason Aronson, Inc.

Schore, A. (1994). *Affect regulation and the origin of self: The neurobiology of emotional development*. Hillsdale, NJ: Lawrence Erlbaum Associates, Inc.

Schore, A. (2003). *Affect dysregulation and disorders of the self*. New York, NY: W. W. Norton and Company.

Shaddock, D. (2000). *Contexts and connections: An intersubjective systems approach to couples therapy.* New York, NY: Basic Books.

Shapiro, R. (1979). Family dynamics and object-relations theory: An analytic, group-interpretive approach to family therapy. In S. C. Feinstein & P. L. Giovacchini (Eds.), *Adolescent psychiatry: Developmental and clinical studies.* Chicago, IL: University of Chicago Press.

Siegel, D. (1999). *The developing mind: How relationships and the brain interact to shape who we are.* New York, NY: Guilford Press.

Solms, M., & Turnbull, O. (2002). *The brain and the inner world.* New York, NY: Other Press.

Winnicott, D. (1958). *Through pediatrics to psycho-analysis.* London, England: Hogarth Press, 1977. (Reprinted London, England: Karnac Books, 1991.)

Zeitner, R. (2003). Obstacles for the psychoanalyst in the practice of couple therapy. *Psychoanalytic Psychology, 20*(2), 348–362.

Zinner, J. (1976). The implications of projective identification for marital interaction. In H. Grunebaum & J. Christ (Eds.), *Contemporary marriage: Structure, dynamics, and therapy* (pp. 293–308). Boston, MA: Little and Brown.

INDEX